THE AFRO-ARGENTINES
OF BUENOS AIRES, 1800–1900

THE AFRO-ARGENTINES OF BUENOS AIRES, 1800–1900

George Reid Andrews

THE UNIVERSITY OF WISCONSIN PRESS

Published 1980

The University of Wisconsin Press
114 North Murray Street
Madison, Wisconsin 53715

The University of Wisconsin Press, Ltd.
1 Gower Street
London WC1E 6HA, England

First printing

Printed in the United States of America

For LC CIP information see the colophon

ISBN 0-299-08290-3

A Roye, la luz de mi vida

Contents

Illustrations

Tables and Figures

xi

FIGURES

Acknowledgments

It is impossible to write a book of this sort without contracting innumerable debts to people who helped one at various points along the way. It is a pleasure to acknowledge my gratitude to a number of very special people.

It is the custom in listing acknowledgments to mention one's wife or husband last, often with an awkward disclaimer that this should not be taken to imply that they are in any way least. I have wondered at times why this should be the practice when it is abundantly clear to anyone with experience in these matters that the only person who suffers more than the author during the course of preparing a book is the author's spouse. My wife, Roye A. Werner, endured more rambling discourses on the Afro-Argentines of Buenos Aires, and more gloomy monologues on the difficulties of writing about the Afro-Argentines of Buenos Aires, than would seem humanly possible, and yet somehow always managed to respond with enthusiasm and encouragement. The dedication of this book to her is but a feeble recogition of her role in its creation.

I wish to thank my parents and my parents-in-law, who contributed both morally and materially to the undertaking and completion of this work. Every man should be as fortunate in his family.

A number of historians and fellow researchers proved to be as good friends as they were colleagues. I owe special thanks to Juan Jorge Cabodi, Juan-Carlos Garavaglia, Cesar García-Belsunce, Marta Goldberg, Lyman L. Johnson, Colonel Ulises Muschietti (Ret.), Marysa Navarro, Karla Robinson, Ricardo Rodríguez Molas, Eduardo Saguier, and Luis Soler Cañas for favors too numerous and varied to list here.

I should acknowledge financial support for my research from the

Social Science Research Council, the Fulbright-Hays Doctoral Dissertation Program of the Department of Health, Education and Welfare, and the Graduate School of the University of Wisconsin.

This book was produced as the result of a course of graduate study in Latin American history at the University of Wisconsin. My courses with Philip D. Curtin, the late John L. Phelan, with Thomas Skidmore, and Peter H. Smith formed the foundation on which my later research was based. My adviser, Peter Smith, was especially helpful in criticizing and commenting on earlier drafts of this book. All four men deserve my thanks for a job well done.

Material in Chapter 10 appeared, in somewhat altered form, in the *Journal of Latin American Studies* (1979), and a part of Chapter 7 was previously published in the *Journal of Negro History* (1979).

Translations of foreign-language material are my own.

THE AFRO-ARGENTINES
OF BUENOS AIRES, 1800–1900

BOLIVIA

BRAZIL

P A R A G U A Y

Salta

Paraguay R.

Asunción

Tucumán

R.

Paraná

C H I L E

Paraná R.

Uruguay R.

Córdoba

Santa Fé

URUGUAY

Santiago

Mendoza

Montevideo

A R G E N T I N A

BUENOS AIRES

La Plata

Río de la Plata

P A C I F I C   O C E A N

BUENOS AIRES PROVINCE

A T L A N T I C   O C E A N

N

Scale

0   100   200   300   400   500 Miles

0   200   400   600   800 Kilometers

CARTOGRAPHIC LABORATORY, UNIVERSITY OF WISCONSIN – MADISON

1

The Riddle of the Disappearance

"Negros en Buenos Aires no hay"—there are no blacks in Buenos Aires. So the natives of the city, the *porteños*, tell their visitors, and so it appears. One can roam through the crowded downtown districts for blocks without seeing a single black man or woman. Indeed, a traveler arriving in Buenos Aires after passing through other countries in Latin America cannot help but be struck by the European appearance of the population in this corner of the continent. Though the city's ethnic composition appears to be altering somewhat as the result of a stream of migration from Paraguay, Bolivia, and the Argentine interior, areas in which Indians and mestizos form a larger proportion of the ethnic mix, the capital's population retains a decidedly European tone. One would be forced to concur with his porteño host—there are no blacks in Buenos Aires.

But if he were to remain in Buenos Aires for an extended stay, the traveler or tourist would become gradually aware that this blanket statement is not entirely true, that indeed there are some blacks in Buenos Aires. Though he might see no more than one or two per week in the central areas of the city, he might by chance stumble on the Afro-Argentine neighborhoods in the outlying areas of Barracas, Flores, and Floresta. If he were to spend any time in the Boca, the working-class neighborhood near the port, he could not miss the black people that one frequently sees in the streets there. And if our hypothetical tourist were to visit some of the city's historical museums, he would become aware that even if there were no blacks in Buenos Aires today, there most defi-

3

nitely had been in the past. In the paintings to be found in those museums he would see black people appearing time and again alongside the whites of the city, simultaneous witnesses and creators of the city's colonial and nineteenth-century past.

At that point one would be tempted to ask why there are now so few blacks in Buenos Aires. They were obviously there in the past in sizable numbers—what happened to them, where did they go? Two of the best-known English-language histories of Argentina pose precisely that question. Writing in 1945, Ysabel Rennie described the disappearance of the Afro-Argentines as "one of the most intriguing riddles of Argentine history." Twenty-five years later, James Scobie observed that "the disappearance of the Negro from the Argentine scene has puzzled demographers far more than the vanishing of the Indian."[1] So intriguing is the question that in 1974 the North American magazine *Ebony* sent a staff member to Buenos Aires to gather material for a story on "Argentina: Land of the Vanishing Blacks."[2]

The process of vanishing was a rather abrupt one, not really starting to take effect until the 1850s. The 1778 census of the city showed that black people constituted 30 percent of the population, 7256 out of 24,363.[3] The 1810 census indicated that the percentage of blacks in the city remained constant in the intervening 32 years: in 1810 Afro-Argentines numbered 9615 out of a total population of 32,558.[4] By 1838 the black population had grown to 13,967, though in relative terms it accounted for only a quarter of the city's total.[5] But by 1887 (during the intervening half-century no municipal censuses recorded information on race), the process of disappearance was well advanced. By that year the Afro-Argentines had dropped to a mere 8005 out of a total population of 433,375, less than 2 percent[6] (see Table 5.1, page 66).

Readers seeking an explanation for this decline will find no dearth of material. The body of historical commentary on the Afro-Argentines' disappearance has been more than a century in the making and is correspondingly extensive. It can be synthesized into four basic themes concerning the black population's demise.

Perhaps the most frequently reiterated argument is that the blacks were wiped out in the wars which wracked nineteenth-century Argentina.[7] Drafted in large numbers into the revolutionary armies that battled the Spanish, Afro-Argentine soldiers then fought successively against the Indians, the Brazilians, and the Paraguayans, as well as in the country's interminable civil wars. According to this explanation, by 1869, the end of the Paraguayan War, thousands of Afro-Argentine soldiers had been killed in battle, had died of sickness while campaigning, or had been disabled in service. The resulting lack of males made it virtually impossible for the black population to recoup its battlefield losses.

This explanation is closely associated with the second, that of *mestizaje*, or race mixture.[8] Faced with a shortage of black men, and allegedly wishing to produce lighter-skinned children for purposes of upward social mobility, black women turned to white men as sexual partners. This argument combines the near-elimination of the black males with the heavy post-1850 influx of European immigrant males in a logically appealing explanation for the decline of the Afro-Argentines.

A third argument focuses on the low birth rates and high mortality rates suffered by the Afro-Argentines.[9] Occupying the lowest rungs on the social and economic ladder, the city's blacks were unable to procure decent housing, nutrition, clothing, and medical care for themselves. They therefore succumbed in greater numbers and at earlier ages than the whites. This was supposedly a chronic condition throughout the first half of the nineteenth century and reached its culmination in the yellow fever epidemic of 1871, a catastrophic event in the city's history, and one which is frequently blamed for dealing the coup de grâce to its black population.

A fourth and fairly obvious explanation is the decline of the slave trade. The abolition of the trade in 1813 allegedly marked the end of the large-scale importation of Africans into the country. Lacking new arrivals to make up the losses described in the previous paragraphs, the black community was doomed to gradual extinction.

These explanations, which have been repeated by Argentine historians and foreigners writing on Argentina for the last one hundred years, are logical, coherent, and eminently reasonable. Indeed, there is only one criterion that they fail to meet: little or no effort has been made to prove them. This book began as an attempt to put those explanations to the test and see to what extent they were verifiable using the primary documentation available in Argentina's archives and libraries. As originally conceived, this study was to cover the demographic history of Argentina's entire black population, but time and practicality argued for confining the research to a more limited area. A number of factors made Buenos Aires the logical site. First, the city's importance as a slave-trade center for southern South America and consequently its large black population were obvious reasons for choosing the capital. Doubtless because of the concentration of black population there, the bulk of the secondary literature on the Afro-Argentines deals specifically with the blacks of Buenos Aires. Second, the capital offered a body of sources not readily available in the interior. Several reasonably good censuses of the city survive for the 1800–1860 period, as well as annual demographic and statistical reports issued by the provincial government between 1822 and 1825 and between 1854 and 1880. Also, military records essential to such a study were located in the capital and were especially complete for material concerning recruitment and disposition of troops from Buenos Aires city and province. Indeed, the concentration of libraries and archives in the capital meant that access to virtually all secondary and primary material on the Afro-Argentines would be easiest in Buenos Aires.

As this study proceeded, it became clear that the traditional explanations have serious shortcomings. Though true in part, they are true *only* in part, and they distort the history of the Afro-Argentines in surprising and unexpected ways. Demographic distortions in turn form part of a larger phenomenon, that being the obscuring, be it intentional or unintentional, of the role of the Afro-Argentines in their nation's history. As the North American historian Leslie Rout discovered while conducting research on the country's black population, one can read the major histories of Argentina and catch only the most fleeting glimpses of its black men and women.[10] Much is made of their role as common soldiers, but there is only passing mention of those black men who rose to be officers commanding battalions and regiments. Little is said about the Afro-Argentines' mutual aid societies, which predated those of the immigrants. Nothing is said about the black writers, artists, intellectuals, and journalists who blossomed in the city in the nineteenth century. In short, a reader relying solely on those histories for his understanding of Afro-Argentine history would come away with a picture of failure and despair, of a people dying and leaving no achievements or accomplishments as their memorial.

Clearly these basic inaccuracies had to be corrected before the question of the disappearance could be resolved. Thus what began as a study of a purely demographic phenomenon, the decline of the Afro-Argentine population, grew into an attempt to reconstruct the true story of the Afro-Argentine past in the areas of social, cultural, and military history. It is also an attempt to explain what motivated the Argentines to deny black people their rightful place in the record of the country's past.

The historical case of the Afro-Argentines might be of little more than passing interest were it not that similar disappearances of black people from the pages of their countries' histories have occurred in virtually every Spanish American republic. Writing in 1970, Magnus Morner observed that "as far as Spanish America is concerned, historians seem to lose all interest in the Negro as soon as abolition is accomplished. In any case, he disappears almost completely from historical literature."[11] In his book *The African Experience in Spanish America*, Leslie Rout returns to this theme time and again. He finds that in Chile there is "an almost total disinterest of national researchers in the Afro-Chilean since emancipation." In Venezuela, "national historians and sociologists who deal with racial issues have displayed a remarkable propensity to limit the focus of their investigations to the pre-1854 years. In fact, no comprehensive study of postabolition racial conditions and policies seems to have been published." In Colombia, "not one of these scholars [writing on Afro-Colombian history] takes his investigation past the year 1852." In conclusion, Rout finds that while several Spanish American nations have rehabilitated the Indian as a mythic symbol of resistance against colonial and neocolonial aggression, "there is no desire to add another group to this category, or to delve into the issue of African cultural contributions."[12]

The case of the Afro–Argentines is therefore representative of a pattern that affects Afro–Spanish Americans as a whole—an almost exclusive focus on slavery and the colonial period is readily apparent from a survey of recent publications on black history in Spanish America.[13] The lack of studies on the postabolition period has frequently been ascribed to problems of documentation. A number of Latin American countries discontinued the use of racial labels in censuses and other documents following independence. As a result, researchers working in national-period archives find it difficult to identify individuals or groups as Afro–Latin American. Indeed, a noted Mexican scholar has argued that the disappearance of racial descriptions from Mexican documents indicates a process of integration by which Afro-Mexicans were absorbed into the larger population under conditions of relative equality with other racial groups.[14]

Whatever the reasons behind it, this failure to examine the history of Afro–Spanish Americans since abolition has formed an enormous obstacle to our efforts to understand present-day patterns of race relations in Latin America, how they vary within the region, and how they compare to those found in other multiracial societies. As Magnus Morner has argued on more than one occasion: "It is my belief that post-Abolition conditions have been more crucial in molding the existing patterns of race relations in the Americas than slavery in its various forms. . . . post abolition problems, at the present time, appear to me as the most urgent research task for historians interested in the problems of socioracial inequality."[15] Certain historical processes were set in motion by the decision to employ Africans as impressed laborers in the American colonies. Those processes did not end or reach a resolution when the masters freed their slaves. Rather, they entered a new and different phase which was at once the heritage of the slave regime and its autonomous creation. An understanding of the slave societies is essential to an understanding of current problems of race in the hemisphere, but equally important, if not more so, is an understanding of the historical evolution of race relations since the demise of slavery.

Thus, although it deals with slavery and the slave trade as they manifested themselves in Buenos Aires, this study concentrates most of its energies on the national period. In so doing it suggests that the difficulties of conducting research on Afro–Latin Americans since abolition have been somewhat exaggerated and that in fact there is a rich variety of sources and approaches available to the historian interested in investigating this topic.

It also seeks to contribute to a fuller understanding of race relations throughout the Americas. Of necessity the book examines a series of questions relevant not just to Buenos Aires but to the rest of the hemisphere as well, such as postabolition demographic trends, avenues of upward mobility for black people, their position in the class-based societies that formed in certain South and North American cities toward the end of the nineteenth century, the mechanisms for community mobilization and organization, and so on. I have attempted to draw frequent comparisons between the historical experience of Buenos Aires and those of other North and South American countries; several sections, such as the analysis in Chapter 5 of the questionable accuracy of the city's nineteenth-century censuses, or the discussion in Chapter 6 of Argentine racial ideology, benefited greatly from the results of previous research conducted by scholars working in Brazil, the United States, and elsewhere. Chapter 11 attempts to pull together some of the major threads of the book and to view the Afro-Argentines in explicitly comparative perspective. It is my hope, then, that this volume will illuminate not only the sadly neglected history of the Afro-Argentines, but will also shed some light on the past and present of all Afro-Americans, both North and South.

Before turning to the Afro-Argentines, some clarifications of terminology are in order. "Black" in the United States has come to mean any person with visible African ancestry, regardless of whether that ancestry is pure or mixed with other races. The word will be used in that sense throughout this work. Students of Latin America are aware that Spanish Americans and Brazilians make a distinction that is not often observed in the United States, namely between people of pure African descent and people of mixed racial ancestry. The Argentine words used to label these two groups will be used to distinguish between them. Thus a person of pure African descent will be called a *moreno*; a person of mixed descent, regardless of whether the mixture is with Europeans,

Indians, or both, will be called a *pardo* or, in the English usage, a mulatto. These two words came into use throughout Spanish America during the late colonial period to replace the harsher *negro* and *mulato*.[16] "Afro-Argentine" will be used interchangeably with "black," though occasionally a distinction will be made between foreign-born black people (e.g., Africans or Brazilians) and native-born Argentine blacks. In those instances the more narrow use of the word should be clear.

A glossary of Spanish terms appears in the reference material at the back of the book. Spanish terms are italicized only at their first occurrence in the text.

2

The Setting

The history of the Afro-Argentines cannot be explained and comprehended in isolation from the history of the city and province of Buenos Aires. The lives of individuals and groups do not unfold within a vacuum. People live within their environments, and the boundaries of their lives are defined by those environments. In seeking to explain the historical experience of the Afro-Argentines, and how and why that experience was similar to or different from those of other peoples in other times and places, it is essential to have a basic understanding of the setting in which the black people of Buenos Aires lived and worked, fought and died.[1]

Buenos Aires is the name of the largest and wealthiest of Argentina's twenty-two provinces. Bounded on the east by the Atlantic Ocean and on the north by the huge freshwater bay known as the Río de la Plata, it occupies more than seven hundred miles of coastline and extends at its widest point approximately four hundred miles inland. Its total land area is 118,800 square miles, roughly the same size as Belgium, the Netherlands, and West Germany combined. The province's predominant physical characteristic is the world-renowned *pampa*, the flat grassy plain which forms a tremendous expanse of some of the richest agricultural soil in the world.

Buenos Aires is also the name of Argentina's capital and largest city. Although located within Buenos Aires province, since 1880 Buenos Aires city has functioned as a separate and autonomous administrative unit, the nation's Federal District. The current population of Greater Buenos Aires (the Federal District and its suburbs) exceeds eight million, representing nearly a third of the total population of the country.

The city was initially founded in 1536, abandoned five years later, and then permanently reestablished in 1580. Its settlers believed that its location on the shores of the Río de la Plata and at the mouths of the Uruguay and Paraná rivers would make the city southern South America's major Atlantic port. Unfortunately, the flatness of the province's terrain is particularly unrelieved around Buenos Aires city, and the settlers soon discovered that the bay's bottom is essentially a continuation of the pampa. Since it therefore drops off only very gradually, anchorages close to the city were impossibly shallow until port works were completed in the 1890s. Visiting ships were forced to anchor a mile or two out in the bay, and goods and passengers were then transported to the docks in horse-drawn carts with enormous wooden wheels.

Spanish colonial policy further inhibited the city's development. The Crown sought to maintain strict control over trade with its colonies, and one way that it did so was to permit only four of its American ports to engage in European commerce. Despite Buenos Aires's advantageous location, it was not chosen to be one of those fortunate cities. Nor did it enjoy much political prestige. It formed one of the most peripheral regions of the Viceroyalty of Peru, the capital of which was Lima, several months' journey from Buenos Aires. As a result, the city was condemned to the status of imperial backwater until almost the end of the colonial period, which lasted from about 1500 to 1810.

Like most Spanish American ports, however, Buenos Aires contrived to participate in the trade with Europe, Africa, and the rest of the Americas through both legal and illegal means. The city's merchants and administrators prevailed on the Crown to grant a number of special permits for the port to receive a limited amount of trade during the 1600s and 1700s. More important in terms of volume and value was the contraband traffic in all manner of merchandise. Royal attempts to control it proved useless, mainly because it was so profitable that it generated handsome bribes for the local law enforcement officials. Illegal goods smuggled through Buenos Aires were marketed throughout Argentina, Paraguay, Chile, and Bolivia.

Changing governmental philosophy, coupled with the realization that Spain could not hope to control the booming contraband trade, prompted the Crown to declare the colonies open to free trade in 1778. Though this was limited free trade, confined to ships flying the Spanish flag, it was a boon to Buenos Aires, which took on increased commercial importance while it continued to conduct illicit dealings with foreign merchants, chiefly Portuguese and English. Equally propitious for the city's development was the creation in 1776 of the Viceroyalty of la

Plata, comprising the territory which now forms the nations of Argentina, Bolivia, Paraguay, and Uruguay. Alarmed by Portuguese and British military and economic incursions into the region, the Crown made Buenos Aires the capital of this new administrative unit in hopes of shoring up the defense of an unprotected flank. Those hopes were not completely realized, but Spain's policies did have the effect of rousing Buenos Aires out of the enforced quietude of two centuries. Commerce boomed, and the population grew by 50 percent between 1778 and 1810 as immigrants were drawn to the city by its new economic and administrative importance. Europeans and Africans arrived in growing numbers, the Europeans voluntarily and the Africans, of course, against their will.

The collapse of the Spanish government caused by Napoleon's invasion of Spain in 1808 found a vigorous merchant oligarchy ready and willing to fill the power vacuum in Buenos Aires. On May 25, 1810, the town council officially assumed the authority previously exercised by the viceroy, and six years later the Congress of the United Provinces of the Río de la Plata (supposedly representing the entire viceroyalty but in fact boycotted by Bolivia, Paraguay, Uruguay, and several Argentine provinces which had no desire to fall under porteño domination) declared the region independent of Spanish rule.

The revolution initiated in Buenos Aires in 1810 was not finally won until 1825. Fighting occurred across the river in Uruguay, and Spanish troops based in Bolivia repeatedly invaded northwestern Argentina, but Buenos Aires itself was spared the most direct effects of war. The city entered the national period more or less unscathed, though with its population depleted by the drafting of large numbers of men to fight the Spanish.

The beginning of the national period found a seriously divided Argentina. The country was really two countries, or, according to the thinking of some of the provincial governors, many little countries, each province forming a separate entity. The basis of the conflict among the provinces was Buenos Aires's steadily strengthening economic position. Situated on the Atlantic coast and possessing the country's only ocean port, Buenos Aires served as the shipping point for Argentine exports and the receiving point for imports of immigrants, merchandise, capital, and ideas. One of the driving forces behind the city's quest for independence had been its desire for free trade unhampered by colonial controls. Such trade was all very well for Buenos Aires province, whose ranchers quickly adjusted to producing cattle and sheep for the export trade, but it was disastrous for the economies of the interior.

These provinces had been colonized not from the sea, like Buenos Aires, but rather by settlers traveling overland from Chile and Bolivia. Enormous distances separated them from the coast; at the same time the Andes made communication with Bolivia and Chile difficult. These isolated areas had developed their own cottage industries to keep themselves supplied with clothing, furniture, construction materials, and so on. These goods were sufficient to satisfy local demand during the colonial period, but they could not compete against the cheaper and higher quality European manufactures that entered the country after the colonial restrictions were removed. For a time the expense of shipping goods inland by mule or wagon gave the interior some protection, and its producers were able to retain their local markets. But they soon lost their outlets in Buenos Aires and the littoral provinces, those located along the Uruguay and Paraná rivers and which therefore have navigable outlets to the sea. In the second half of the nineteenth century, when expanding railroads provided cheap transport to and from the interior, these local producers collapsed completely. Imported British and German cloth replaced domestic linen and woolens, Brazilian sugar replaced Tucumán sugar, and French wines replaced the wines of Mendoza.

The growth of the Argentine-European trade wrought further changes in the nation's economy. During the colonial period the flow of trade had followed an extended route stretching from Europe to Bolivia. The wealth of the Bolivian silver mines attracted imports through Buenos Aires, and though the capital reaped its profit from this commerce, the trade also served to enrich the interior provinces of Córdoba, Tucumán, Salta, and other way stations on the route. The decline of the silver mines, the revolution's disruption of trade with Spanish-controlled Bolivia, the removal of colonial controls on imports, and a growing willingness on the part of European merchants to accept hides and salted meat in exchange for manufactures resulted in the marketing by Buenos Aires of its own export goods in place of Bolivian silver. This direct trade between the capital and Europe rendered the interior provinces completely dispensable and consigned them to a stagnation from which, to a large extent, they have still not emerged.

The resulting conflict between Buenos Aires together with its hinterland (allied at times with the littoral provinces of Santa Fé, Entre Ríos, and Corrientes, whose river ports and fertile grazing lands made their economic interests similar to those of Buenos Aires) versus the interior forms the central political issue of nineteenth-century Argentine history. Vestiges of it linger in the life of the country to the present, though Buenos Aires is generally conceded to have won. The country divided itself into what appeared to be two factions, but which were actually more than that. Those who supported a strong central government were known as unitarians (*unitarios*). In reality they were promoting Buenos Aires's hegemony over the rest of the country, since such a government would almost inevitably have to reside in Buenos Aires and exercise authority from there. Unitarians also tended to support free trade, liberal economic principles, and a republican form of government. They were strongly influenced by the political thought of the English and French Enlightenment and to a certain extent by the political example of the United States. The federalists (*federales*), on the other hand, favored a looser system of confederation in which a national government would handle foreign relations while the individual provinces retained almost complete autonomy over their internal affairs. Federalism as a movement was supported by the *caudillos*, the personalist military strongmen who ruled the interior provinces into the second half of the century. It possessed almost as many schools of thought as there were caudillos; just as it proposed a loose aggregation of independent provinces in a weak confederation, as a political movement it was an uncohesive movement in which the major leaders sought to retain almost complete independence and freedom of action. Opposition to the growing power of Buenos Aires was one of its few unifying themes.

The struggle between Buenos Aires and the interior was joined during the very first years of independence. In 1816, delegates from the various provinces had met in Tucumán to declare Argentine independence. Shortly thereafter, the Congress and the Supreme Director of the United Provinces of the Río de la Plata moved to Buenos Aires. Falling under unitarian control, the Congress promulgated the centralist Constitution of 1819, which was offered to the United Provinces for approval. The federalists rejected the document and invaded Buenos Aires the following year. They easily defeated the demoralized porteños, initiating a year of acute political instability in the capital. Eventually order was restored, and by 1826 the Congress had recovered sufficiently to propose another centralist constitution and to elect as president the unitarian Bernardino Rivadavia. The federalist provinces threatened to invade Buenos Aires again if it attempted to impose this constitution on the rest of the country, so the project was abandoned and Rivadavia resigned from office.

Despite its defeats, Buenos Aires was quietly laying the economic foundation for its eventual victory over the rest of the country. Trade with Europe continued to expand, as did the wealth of the province's agricultural establishments. By the 1820s Indians still controlled the southern two-thirds of what is now Buenos Aires province, but there was no shortage of land on which to raise millions of cattle for the export trade. *Saladeros*, the processing plants in which cattle were killed and skinned and their meat salted, sprang up around the city and worked full time preparing meat and hides for export. Ranchers also raised sheep for wool and meat, but the primary exports were beef and hides. In the wake of this expanding trade the city experienced important political and economic change. Whereas urban merchants had been the unquestioned elite of the city in the late colonial period, they were now joined and competed against by the *estancieros*, the ranchers who were becoming increasingly influential actors in provincial politics. The dominance of the estancieros was confirmed by the provincial legislature's election in 1829 of Governor Juan Manuel de Rosas, who took power in response to the continuing political instability reigning in the province. He ended that instability, but at great cost. His administrations, which lasted from 1829 to 1832 and from 1835 to 1852, were responsible for the death, bankruptcy, and flight into exile of thousands of porteños. Nominally a federalist, Rosas borrowed heavily from the unitarians in constructing his policies. For instance, the issue of the national customs house at Buenos Aires had long been a sensitive one in Argentine politics. The unitarians favored the retention of all customs proceeds by Buenos Aires province, while the federalists argued that the money belonged to the entire nation and should be divided equally among the provinces. Rosas not only continued the unitarian practice of retaining all customs duties for the province, but also blockaded the entrance to the Paraná and Uruguay rivers and demanded tolls of any ships enroute to the upriver littoral ports.

Rosas spent thousands of dollars and lives in military campaigns against the provinces of the interior and against Montevideo, the competing trade entrepôt on the Uruguayan side of the Río de la Plata. These military and political aggressions eventually resulted in his defeat and subsequent banishment by an allied army commanded by the federalist Governor Urquiza of Entre Ríos province. But the dictator's rule had aroused even more opposition among the unitarians of Buenos Aires province than it had among the federalists of the interior. When repression made anti-Rosas political activity impossible in Buenos Aires, thousands of porteños migrated to Uruguay to serve with the besieged forces there. So bitter was the hostility between the dictator and his enemies that, after his fall, his unitarian successors transformed his memory into an almost mythic presence that formed the axis around which Argentina's nineteenth-century politics revolved. His name was regularly trotted out and ritually abused every Independence Day, and unpopular political programs were denounced as Rosista plots. Rosas became the political anti-Christ of unitarian-dominated Buenos Aires, the symbolic representative of all the forces and ideas that were anathema to the liberals of the province.[2]

The unitarians were guilty of considerable falsification and exaggeration in their portrayal of Governor Rosas and his misdeeds, but this was because the dictator was in fact the exponent and promoter of many ideas diametrically opposed to their own. For instance, while the unitarians looked to Europe for capital, immigrants, and ideas on how best to develop their country, Rosas presented himself as the champion of Argentine nationalism. He abandoned earlier unitarian efforts to attract European colonists to the country, deliberately defaulted on British loans to the provincial government, and successfully fought off French and British efforts to blockade the port of Buenos Aires.

Even more threatening to the unitarians, however, was Rosas's adept use of the urban and rural non-elites as a base of political support. Though Rosas initially served as a spokesman for the estancieros, he rendered his political position almost impregnable by also cultivating and winning the support of the province's workers. In so doing he became the first in a succession of Argentine populist leaders who have always horrified the unitarians and their political descendants. As previously mentioned, the unitarians were staunchly republican in their political principles; they most assuredly were not democrats. While they believed in free and regular elections, they wanted suffrage closely restricted by stiff property requirements so that only men of the better sort would be permitted to vote and hold office. Rosas observed these rules the first time he won office, in 1829. At that time he was voted into office by a legislature desperate to end the province's chronic political turmoil, and he took office entirely legally. But during this first term he recognized the political necessity of forming a broad base of political support in order to remain in power. Already enjoying the backing of the cattlemen, he set to work capitalizing on the multiple discontents of the workers of the capital and the countryside. The attention he lavished on those sectors was amply repaid in 1833 by the popularly supported coup that overthrew Governor Balcarce and paved the way for Rosas's return to power eighteen months later.

By enlisting the common people as part of his political apparatus, Rosas violated two basic tenets of the unitarian creed. First, he bypassed the normal electoral process and thus seriously undermined the legitimacy of the republican institutions that the porteño liberals were seeking to impose on the province and eventually, it was hoped, on the rest of the country. Second, Rosas committed the unpardonable sin of not only admitting but actively encouraging the masses to become par-

ticipants in Buenos Aires's political system. This participation was of a limited and controlled sort, carefully overseen by a skilled political manipulator who had no intention of allowing his supporters to get out of control, but it was nonetheless participation, and therefore a radical departure from the colonial and early independence periods, during which the non-elites had had no voice in the political, economic, and social decisions that determined how life was lived in the province of Buenos Aires.

Describing the social composition of any Spanish American city during the late colonial and early national periods is an imposing undertaking, due mainly to the complex calculus of race and ancestry, ascribed social status, institutional affiliation, and economic position that determined one's place in the social hierarchy.[3] Historians seeking to simplify the complexities of colonial social structure have described an essentially dichotomous arrangement in which a small, closely circumscribed elite ruled over the great mass of non-elites. This elite, known in Buenos Aires as the *gente decente*, was readily recognizable in any Spanish American society. Members of elite families shared a set of attributes which clearly differentiated them from their social inferiors. They were almost universally of white racial ancestry, or commonly accepted as such. The town council and other official and semi-official bodies were composed entirely of males from those families. Ties of kinship and friendship (often cemented by the relationship of god-parentage) bound the gente decente together—intermarriage among them was commonplace. Economic ties complemented social ties, members of the elite showing a marked tendency to conduct business among themselves rather than with outsiders. In Buenos Aires, as in many other colonial cities, their wealth was based mainly on commerce, though by the end of the colonial period more large landowners and *saladeristas* (owners of meat-processing plants) were pressing for admission into the society's ruling stratum.[4]

A dichotomous description of Buenos Aires's social structure makes clear the sharp distinction between the gente decente and the non-elites, the *gente del pueblo*, a distinction which was very much a part of the porteño social reality. It has the unfortunate effect, however, of obscuring the variety of strata and groups to be found among the non-elites. Indeed, one of the most striking contrasts between the elite and the non-elite populations of Buenos Aires city is the discrepancy between the respective levels of cohesiveness among the two groups. The internal relationships that bound together the gente decente produced a social class with a high degree of solidarity and self-consciousness, well organized and highly effective in defending its economic, social, and political interests. The gente del pueblo, on the other hand, consisted of a fragmented, divided mass of individuals separated into competing social groups by several determinants. One of the most important was race. While the gente decente prided itself on its racial homogeneity, the non-elites were divided into a bewildering variety of racial estates, codified by Spanish colonial legislation and arranged in a carefully established hierarchy. Whites cherished their racial status as their most precious and inalienable asset, an inheritance which entitled them to unquestioned legal superiority over nonwhites. Indians lived under special paternalistic legislation which in some cases made them superior to black people, in other cases, inferior. Free blacks had escaped the constraints of slavery to occupy an intermediate position halfway between the slaves and the whites. Racially mixed mulattoes and mestizos strove for the privileges accorded white people, sometimes attaining them, sometimes being rebuffed. At the bottom of the scale, the slave population endured a social and legal status subordinate to those of all other estates.

Birthplace was another divisive force. European-born whites claimed superiority over American-born whites. Native-born Afro-Argentines had little in common with slaves newly arrived from Africa.

There was also substantial economic variation among the non-elites. Many eked out a bare living through occasional day labor at unskilled jobs, punctuated by periods of unemployment or underemployment. Others worked on a more regular basis and achieved a more secure economic base. The upper levels of the gente del pueblo, in purely economic terms, were populated by the artisans, shopkeepers, innkeepers, and retailers who earned substantially more than the unskilled or semiskilled laborers. These groups viewed themselves as higher in status than the rest of the gente del pueblo, and phenomena such as the artisans' efforts to establish craft guilds in the period from 1780 to 1820 are indicative of their desire to set themselves apart from the masses. The complexity of the divisions within the gente del pueblo becomes abundantly apparent, however, in the history of the guilds, for these abortive attempts to mobilize the non-elites failed due to ethnic and racial conflict between the European and creole (native-born Argentine) artisans and between the whites and the nonwhites.[5]

Lacking the cohesion and corporate self-consciousness that characterized the elite, the urban and rural workers formed a passive, inarticulate mass almost completely vulnerable to the controls exercised over them by their superiors. Part of the genius of Governor Rosas was that he was able to transform that mass into a potent political instrument that he could then use on his own behalf. Under Rosas the non-elites became, for the first time in the history of the province, a force to be reckoned with. According to the unitarian vision, Governor Rosas was the porteño counterpart of the barbarous, violent caudillos of the interior, who used loyal bands of *gaucho* (cowboy) retainers to seize and hold power.

Following Rosas's fall the unitarians assumed control of Buenos Aires province while the federalists retained the rest of the country. As a result of this division Buenos Aires refused to join the Argentine Confederation, formed by the other provinces in 1853. The port and its hinterland remained aloof, waxing ever more prosperous on its gradually expanding export trade and its control of the import trade. The Confederation soon found that Argentina simply could not survive as a viable nation without the participation of its largest province. After several pitched battles and prolonged negotiations, Buenos Aires consented to join the rest of the provinces. In 1862 the porteño Bartolomé Mitre was elected president of the Argentine Republic and the capital of the nation was moved from Entre Ríos province to Buenos Aires city, where it has remained ever since.

The unification of the country at last permitted the unitarians to begin the task of restructuring Argentina along the lines dictated by their political, economic, and social philosophies. This remarkable experiment in national planning was initiated by a group of leaders who became known as the Generation of 1880, and, at least in the short run, the experiment was extraordinarily successful. The unitarian program was based on a conscious decision to integrate Argentina as fully as possible into the world economy by exploiting the country's fabulous agricultural resources. Several technological advancements made the second half of the century a particularly fortuitous time for taking such a step. The introduction of wire fencing and new breeds of beef cattle in the 1840s and 1850s had resulted in increasing rationalization of Argentine beef production, but the processing of the meat continued to present obstacles. Salted and dried beef did not appeal greatly to European consumers, so exported Argentine meat went mainly to feed slaves in Brazil and the Caribbean. The breakthrough of refrigeration in the 1880s enabled Argentina to send chilled beef and mutton to Europe in a much more palatable state. At the same time, the extension of British-owned railroads deep into the pampas opened new areas for agricultural exploitation, as did the anti-Indian campaigns of the 1870s. Between 1872 and 1895 the amount of cultivated land on the pampas increased by fifteen times; the value of exports quintupled.[6] North American meat and cereal exporters viewed the Argentine boom with trepidation.

The rapid growth of the export economy after 1870 wrought profound changes in the capital. The Buenos Aires of that year differed only slightly from the city that had proclaimed its independence from Spain in 1810. Although larger, having grown from 40,000 to 187,000, in many ways it was still "the big village" that its inhabitants affectionately called it. The downtown area was still small, most of the city's streets were unpaved and poorly drained, the buildings were one- or two-story constructions in the colonial style, and the traditional social relationships between the gente decente and the gente del pueblo survived essentially unchanged from the colonial period. Between 1880 and 1914 the Buenos Aires of old gradually dissolved, to be replaced by one of the world's great metropolitan centers. Income from the export boom poured into the capital, and there it stayed. While the provinces of the interior sank further and further behind in economic competition, the national government invested enormous sums in port development in the capital and in La Plata, the provincial capital thirty miles down the coast. Large portions of Buenos Aires were demolished and rebuilt in the styles of Paris and London. The great international banks and investment houses opened branches in Argentina to accommodate the inflow and outflow of capital. Prices of agricultural land rose dramatically, making millionaires of the province's ranchers and catapulting them into a position of clear-cut superiority over the merchants against whom they had so long competed. The fabulously wealthy cattle barons built sumptuous mansions in Buenos Aires and toured Europe regularly.

And, of course, the immigrants came. One of the unitarians' fondest dreams had been to replace the vagrant, lazy, racially mixed Argentine masses (these loaded terms are used to illustrate the unitarian vision of Argentine social reality) with hard-working, educated Europeans. This had been part of the unitarian program ever since the declaration of independence, but not until the 1870s and 1880s did policy makers possess the power and resources actively to pursue such a goal. As in the case of the export boom, the results of their programs exceeded their wildest expectations. Between 1869 and 1895 the country's population more than doubled in size, from 1.8 million to 4.0 million; by 1914 it had almost doubled again, to 7.9 million. The growth of the capital was even more spectacular: from 187,000 in 1869 to 650,000 in 1895 to 1.5 million in 1914. By 1914, 30 percent of the Argentine population was foreign-born, a proportion greater than that of the United States. Though those immigrants and their descendants eventually distributed themselves more or less evenly around the country, during the nineteenth century they were heavily concentrated in the city of Buenos Aires. In 1869 almost half the foreigners in the entire country lived in greater Buenos Aires, at a time when the capital accounted for only 12.9 percent of the national population. In 1895, 38.6 percent of Argentina's immigrants lived in the capital.[7]

Despite this dramatic influx of immigrants, the city's social structure proved more resistant to change than its physical structure. The concept of the gente decente, embracing probably not more than 5 percent of the city's population, remained very much in force.[8] Politics throughout the 1860–1916 period were conducted by parties controlled by the traditional oligarchy, leading historians to dub this period in Argentine history the Conservative Republic. The bulk of the population remained effectively barred from direct political participation. This was the direct result of the checks introduced into the political system by an elite who had no intention of allowing another Rosas to capitalize on lower-class discontent and come to power.

Nevertheless, changes were in the making. Perhaps most important, the non-elites were becoming increasingly divided into incipient middle and lower classes. Skilled craftsmen, white collar workers, owners of small stores and businesses—these men and their families viewed themselves as being on a significantly higher social plane than the day laborers, port and construction workers, domestic servants, and indigents who consituted the bulk of the non-elite population. Those who could afford to do so sought to establish their families in the genteel and respectable conditions that would set them apart from their poorer compatriots. Education for one's children, an essential prerequisite for high social status, was a priority item for upwardly mobile families. In dress and behavior, the nascent middle class modeled itself closely on the elite, whom the more optimistic among them aspired someday to join.

Mobility from the gente del pueblo into the gente decente remained rare, but not as rare as it had been earlier. The leap from middle class to upper class was not as long as from the working masses into the elite, particularly when it was spread over two or three generations. Though a successful Italian entrepreneur might find himself ineligible for membership in the Jockey Club, his son would probably be able to enter with relative ease, providing that the family wealth had remained intact.

Much more common than movement from the middle class to the elite was movement between the lower and middle classes. Though rigorous studies of social mobility in nineteenth-century Buenos Aires remain to be done, it appears that immigrant groups experienced considerable upward and downward mobility over several generations. Transitions among the various levels of the gente del pueblo produced a turbulent social structure in which hopes of further upward progress sometimes blinded members of the middle strata to the possibilities of class organization.

Still, by the end of the century class-based associations and organizations had become increasingly active and important in porteño social and political life. By the 1850s immigrant and native-born workers were founding mutual aid societies based on the model of the anarchist societies in Europe. By 1880 several small unions had been formed and the first recorded strike in Argentina had occurred when printers' demands for higher wages and shorter hours were not met. Strikes became widespread during the recession of the 1890s, and a crippling general strike in 1902 prompted the government to declare a state of siege in Buenos Aires and several other provinces. The founding of the Socialist Party in 1896 and the Argentine Workers' Federation in 1901 marked the increasing organization and centralization of the workers' movement. Meanwhile the middle class, squeezed by the inflation and recessions of the 1890s and frustrated in its hopes for a more active role in the country's political life, banded together to form the Radical Party, dedicated to overthrowing the oligarchy's control of the government. Congress's enactment of universal male suffrage and the secret ballot in 1912 signaled the end of the oligarchy's control of elections. Four years later the Radical candidate Hipólito Yrigoyen won the presidency over the strident opposition of the porteño elite, who saw in him another Rosas-style demagogue.

By 1900, therefore, the city of Buenos Aires was well on the way to developing the sort of class structure associated with modern, urbanized, industrialized societies. Aspects of an earlier, more traditional society continued to survive in the life of the capital, but in comparison to the provinces of the interior, and indeed to most of Latin America, Buenos Aires was growing and evolving at a dizzying pace. The interior, by contrast, had changed relatively little over one hundred years. The caudillos had been defeated and all the provinces acknowledged Buenos Aires as the country's leader, but they were still ruled by traditional, conservative elites who brooked no change in local customs and usages and who faced few demands for such change. More and more the capital was distinct from the rest of the country, bearing a stronger resemblance to Paris or New York than to Córdoba or Tucumán. The backwater of the colonial period had outstripped its competitors; Buenos Aires entered the twentieth century as the premier city not only of Argentina, but of all South America.

3

Slavery and the Slave Trade

THE TRADE IN BUENOS AIRES

The first royal permit to import slaves into the Río de la Plata region was granted in 1534, two years before the first founding of Buenos Aires.[1] As of 1595, however, only 233 Africans had been imported into the city, a figure inadequate to meet the local demand for slave laborers.[2] Responding to the colonists' repeated requests for additional slaves, in that year the Crown granted an *asiento*, a royal concession, to the Portuguese slaver Pedro Gomes Reynel to bring 600 slaves into Buenos Aires annually for a nine-year period. Gomes Reynel proved unequal to the task, providing only 2252 slaves to the labor-hungry townspeople. But there were plenty of men eager to try where he had failed, and a new asiento was awarded to another Portuguese merchant in 1602.[3]

The system of granting asientos to selected individuals was part of Spain's mercantilist policy of maintaining tight control over all economic activity in the New World, especially commerce. The Crown issued a series of these permits during the seventeenth century, but its efforts to supervise and limit the slave trade failed spectacularly. Contraband in all types of merchandise was rampant in the Río de la Plata during the colonial period, and the slave trade was no exception. The involvement of royal officials in the contraband slave traffic was a frequent scandal: the first reported instance of illegal slaving in Argentina involved the Bishop of Tucumán, who in 1585 was caught importing Africans from Brazil without a permit.[4] Though the bishop's slaves were confiscated, he continued his smuggling operation until

1602, when the king intervened directly to accuse him of bribing the top port officials of Buenos Aires.[5]

Other irregularities occurred that could only have taken place with the connivance of the authorities. A common practice was for slavers to enter the port of Buenos Aires claiming that their ship had been damaged at sea and required repairs before going on. While the repairs were being made, the cargo of slaves would be unloaded, usually under cover of night, marched out of the city, and then brought back into town as *negros descaminados*, "blacks who have lost their way." Such slaves could then be sold in a sort of semilegal way, despite the fact that they had no import licenses or documents of entry. This surreptitious disembarking of a shipload of people and their marching out of the city could only have been carried out with official cooperation. Such cooperation was readily forthcoming: even during the administration from 1598 to 1609 of Governor Hernando Arías, a firm opponent of contraband, over 1100 Africans were sold as descaminados. This period, moreover, covered several years in which no permission existed for anyone to import slaves.[6]

The existence of this contraband trade makes it difficult to determine exactly how many slaves entered Buenos Aires during the colonial period. A few statistics suggest that the volume of the legal trade scarcely compared to the illegal. Of 12,778 slaves recorded as entering Buenos Aires from Brazil between 1606 and 1625, only 288 did so under royal permit. Full 11,262 were slaves confiscated from contrabandists and sold by the city, and 1228 more appear on the manifests of ships that were allowed to unload slaves without a permit.[7] Another source reports that between 1606 and 1625 8932 slaves were confiscated from smugglers and sold by the royal authorities.[8] And these are only the slaves that were apprehended; how many more entered the city undetected, leaving no trace in the royal records? We can only guess. Certain it is, though, that the 22,892 Africans registered as arriving at the port between 1595 and 1680 form only a fraction of the true number.[9]

Buenos Aires itself had no need of the large quantity of slaves brought into the city during the seventeenth century. A small town with an economy based on trade and some agriculture, it did not require the tremendous infusions of slave labor essential to the labor-intensive plantation economies of Brazil and the Caribbean. But the city also served as the receiving port for an enormous hinterland, including all of central and northern Argentina, Paraguay, Chile, and Alto Perú, now known as Bolivia.[10] Most of the Africans who arrived in Buenos Aires therefore stayed for only a short period before proceeding inland to their final destination. The outflow of slaves leaving the city was large and constant, at times even exceeding the inflow: in 1616 Governor Hernandarias informed the Crown that between 1612 and 1615 official records showed 3463 Africans arriving at the port and 4515 leaving for the interior, an excess of over a thousand.[11] Of the 9970 slaves brought to Buenos Aires by the British South Sea Company between 1715 and 1752, over three-quarters were sent inland.[12]

During the eighteenth century the Crown sought to stimulate and regularize the slave trade by granting asientos to companies rather than to individuals. The first permit of this type was granted in 1696 to the Portuguese Cacheu Company, also known as the Guinea Company. Dismayed by the inefficiency and corruption of the Portuguese operation, Spain revoked this permit in 1701 and transferred it to the French Guinea Company, which proved to be just as indifferent to Spanish rules and regulations as the Portuguese company. When evidence of the French flouting of customs laws could no longer be ignored, the Crown decided to make a last try with the British South Sea Company, which held the asiento on and off from 1715 until 1750. The British were just as disappointing as the Portuguese and the French, and the company's operations in the Río de la Plata were greatly complicated when Spain and Great Britain went to war twice during this period.

Though the French and British companies brought some 14,000 slaves to Buenos Aires between 1700 and 1750, Spain concluded that the disadvantages of allowing foreign companies to operate openly in the region greatly outweighed the value of the slaves introduced. Royal officials continued to display an alarming willingness to take bribes from contrabandists: in 1716 the governor of Buenos Aires agreed to allow representatives of the South Sea Company to sell slaves and manufactures (the latter illegal) free of duty in exchange for a 25 percent share of the profits.[13] In 1750 there was a return to the system of granting asientos to individuals, but in 1778 Spain finally recognized the failure of this exclusionary policy and opened the colonies to limited free trade, allowing Spanish ships to call without hindrance at Spanish American ports. This new freedom stimulated commerce somewhat, but the slave trade entered a boom phase after 1789 and 1791, when commercial regulations were further liberalized to open colonial ports to foreign traders. Of 124 slavers that docked at Buenos Aires between 1740 and 1806, 109 did so after 1790.[14] The post-1790 trade continued to be dominated by Portuguese and Spanish vessels, though ships flying the United States flag formed an increasingly important minority in the Río de la Plata traffic.[15]

A description of the mechanics of the slave trade can easily obscure the matter which most concerns us: the experience of the Africans and Afro-

Argentines who formed the black population of Buenos Aires. The agony of the first step in the experience, that of being captured in Africa and transported to the New World, can only inadequately be conveyed in words. A ship's doctor on a Buenos Aires–bound British slaver in the 1740s described the conditions under which Africans migrated to Argentina:

For more than seventy days, I had to get up every morning at 4:00 and go down to where the slaves were, to see who had died and to care for the dying. I would dress at 7:00 and minister to more than one hundred of the sick and injured. At 10:00, I would attend to the whites of the crew and then attend to both whites and blacks again at 4:00 in the afternoon. At 6:00, we would take the slaves to the rest area after checking their clothing, a precaution taken for fear of their having hidden arms, knives, nails, etc. At 8:00 in the evening we would administer the medicine indicated for that hour and then, at midnight, we would give the sick ones a small dose of water. Their illnesses required special vigilance to prevent their drinking too much water. The preparation and composition of their remedies took up a great deal of our free time. It could be said, in all truth, that John Abbott, the first surgeon, and myself, were the slaves of the slaves. No galley slave ever worked as hard, rowing, as we did, faced with the pain of knowing that our work was obviously in vain. The dropsy was a fatal disease. Of 455 slaves, including men and women, we buried more than half. The dropsy struck individuals not accustomed to being enclosed, due to the lack of exercise and the reduced diet of beans, rice, etc. The illness caused by these conditions would have been hard enough to cure on land, and at sea it proved incurable, its seriousness aggravated by the presence of scurvy.[16]

Another factor contributing to mortality in the Middle Passage, the journey across the Atlantic from Africa to the New World, was the condition in which slaves boarded the ships in Africa. In a case in 1804 in which a board of physicians in Buenos Aires was asked to rule on whether a shipload of diseased Africans should be allowed to disembark, one of the doctors who had lived in Mozambique recalled the manner in which the slaves arrived from the interior: "The blacks arrive at the coast with all the symptoms of illness. Kept in chains for many months, drinking little, eating roots, wild fruits, and small lizards, weakened by the heat and the fatigue of their marches, exposed to all kinds of bad weather, they arrive at Mozambique almost exhausted."[17]

He added that their resistance to disease was often further weakened by their refusal to eat and regain their strength in the port town, since many of them were convinced that the whites wanted to fatten them up prior to eating them. Another of the doctors summed up briefly the trauma suffered by all blacks brought to the New World. "Raised free," he observed, "they are then conquered by their fellows and taken as

Table 3.1. Birthplaces of Africans Resident in Buenos Aires City, c. 1750–1830, Tabulated from Three Different Sources

	Slave imports, 1742–1806	African enlistees, 1810–20	Africans listed in sample of municipal census, 1827
West Africa	3,979	44	127
Congo and Angola	2,742	—	—
Congo	—	25	41
Angola	—	40	25
South Africa	114	0	0
East Africa	4,708	21	10
Unspecified or unknown African location	1,529	19	51
Total	13,072	149	254

Sources: Column 1: Elena F. Scheuss de Studer, *La trata de negros en el Río de la Plata durante el siglo XVIII* (Buenos Aires, 1958), pp. 324–25; *Column 2:* Archivo General de la Nación, 3 59-1-1, 59-1-6, 59-2-1, 59-2-4, 59-2-7; *Column 3:* Archivo General de la Nación, 10 23-5-5, 23-5-6.

prisoners to the seaports, experiencing along the way thirst, hunger, imprisonment, bad treatment and everything that is capable of wounding the human heart, such as leaving their friends, their country, their freedom, and being deprived of all the things that gave them happiness."[18]

From what areas of Africa did the blacks of Buenos Aires come? Table 3.1 is a compilation of data from several sources that can be used to determine the origins of the city's Africans. The first column is a count of the slaves imported into Buenos Aires directly from Africa during the second half of the seventeenth century. The table omits an additional 12,473 slaves who entered the city from Brazil and whose exact African origins are unknown. The second column is a count of the birthplaces listed by 149 Africans drafted into the Argentine army during the independence wars. Their enlistment records were found in five volumes of military documents from the period. The third column is a count of the birthplaces listed by 254 Africans contained in a sample of the black population taken from the municipal census of 1827, discussed at length in Chapter 5.

Historians of the Río de la Plata have traditionally pointed to Angola, the Congo, and Mozambique as the sources of the region's slaves. It is clear that they have underestimated the importance of West Africa. Of slaves imported between 1742 and 1806, West Africans made up a third of those Africans of known origin. West Africans also formed one-third of the sample of Africans drafted into Buenos Aires's regiments during the independence period, and they constituted almost two-thirds of Africans of known birthplace documented in the 1827 census. This last figure may be somewhat inflated due to the porteño tendency to use Guinea as a synonym for Africa. Thus Africans, regardless of their birthplaces, were often referred to in Buenos Aires as *negros de Guinea*. Still, it is significant that the name of a region of West Africa should have been used in this way—apparently the whites of Buenos Aires had had considerable contact with West African slaves.

Although there was some direct trade between Buenos Aires and West Africa, it seems that most of the West Africans resident in Buenos Aires arrived there by way of Brazil. The Brazilian port of Bahia received millions of West Africans during the colonial period, many of whom were then sent on to Rio de Janeiro; from there they found their way to Uruguay and Buenos Aires.[19]

Slave ships arriving in the Río de la Plata after 1791 were required to dock first at the Uruguayan port of Montevideo for a sanitation inspection. There some of the Africans disembarked, but the majority continued on to Buenos Aires, a couple of days' sail away. They were then taken off the ships and sent to the slave market, there to be lodged until sold or sent inland. Their first vision of Buenos Aires could not have been a reassuring one. During the course of the eighteenth century the city had three slave markets, and the major element held in common by all three seems to have been their utter squalor. The first, belonging to the French Guinea Company, was situated on the riverbank slightly south of town, in what is now the Parque Lezama. The second, belonging to the British, was located north of town in the Retiro area. This market was abandoned when the British asiento ended, and by 1800 it was in ruins.[20] In 1791 the government established a new market in the royal customs area—the various merchants paid fees for the right to keep their slaves there.

The town council fought a running battle throughout the 1700s to keep the slave market away from the center of town, and especially away from neighborhoods in which the more well-to-do families lived. When the first market was opened by the French, the council stipulated that it be located at least a quarter league away from the town. Such requirements continued to be imposed on the slavers by the council, and the controversy came to a head in the late colonial period as the city and the slave trade both expanded. In 1787 the royal intendant proposed to construct a new slave market on the site of the old British one, an area which had previously been suburban but which was now part of the city.

The town council was irate, and its description of the market then existing suggests how miserable conditions there were. The council brought up several objections to the intendant's proposal, one being that the slave market would lower property values ("if a market of this nature is established in that area, nobody will want to buy the surrounding land because of the bad quality of the neighborhood"), the other that the market posed a serious threat to public health: "diseased blacks, full of lice, skin diseases, and scurvy, and exuding from their body a foul and pestilential odor, can infect the whole city, especially when that site dominates the city and lies to the north of it, the direction of the prevailing winds."[21] Although the new slave market was not built in the Retiro area, neither was it built where the council wanted it; it was constructed in the royal customs compound, near the docks.

The city's oligarchy continued to try to push the market out of town. In 1799 the Consulado of Buenos Aires, a semiofficial Chamber of Commerce composed of the city's leading merchants, proposed that a new market be constructed some fifteen miles down the coast.[22] In 1803 the council protested an especially barbarous practice of the slavers, that of simply turning unsold slaves out into the streets of the city unclothed, speaking no Spanish, and with absolutely no means of support. Most of these abruptly freed slaves were in no condition to fend for themselves, as evidenced by the fact that they had attracted no buyers in a labor-hungry society, and almost all of them died in the streets shortly after being "freed." The viceroy corroborated the council's complaints and forwarded them to the king, though he seems to have been more offended by the Africans' nakedness than by their desperate situation.[23] Again in 1809, just one year before the revolution, the council raised yet another petition to get the market out of town.[24]

SLAVERY IN THE CITY'S ECONOMY

While few porteños cared to face the cargoes of human misery that passed through the slave market, fewer still would have denied the importance of those cargoes in sustaining the city's economy. Colonial Buenos Aires presents the spectacle of a society utterly dependent on its slave laborers. When in 1787 the town council protested the intendant's plan of constructing a new slave market in the Retiro, the intendant reproved its members for their shortsightedness and conjured up the gloomy prospect of a city and its hinterland deprived of slaves to man their units of production. The large ranches, the *haciendas*, would go barren and uncultivated, both for lack of men to farm them and for lack

Young servant boy with his mistresses, one of whom is drinking *mate*, the Argentine herb tea. This lithograph by the Swiss printmaker César Hipólito Bacle was made around 1830, which means that the boy is almost certainly a liberto (see Chapter 4).

of the necessary tools and equipment made and repaired by the artisan slaves. The intendant warned that the projected factories for processing meat to send abroad, factories on which construction had recently begun, depended almost entirely on abundant slave labor, both for the construction and then for the subsequent operation of the installations once they were completed. Sabotaging this project by depriving the city of slaves would be sabotaging the elite's own economic future.[25]

Although the council continued its opposition to the proposed market, its members never denied the intendant's description of the city's dependence on its slaves. It is fair to say that if every slave worker in the Buenos Aires of 1800 were suddenly to have vanished, economic activity would have come to a standstill in a matter of hours. Slaves dominated or formed a major part of the work force in any number of occupations. They were probably most visible in the field of domestic service. As in other Spanish American colonial cities, no family that aspired to high social status in Buenos Aires could do without its retinue of black servants.[26] In slave sale documents as well as in newspaper ads, the skills most frequently attributed to the slaves being sold are housekeeping skills: cooking, laundering, ironing, sewing, and otherwise "able to do all manner of housework." Foreign visitors to Buenos Aires occasionally charged that these domestic skills were a strictly secondary consideration, the servants having been purchased primarily for ostentation. Anthony King, a North American who arrived in Buenos Aires in 1817 and spent twenty-four years in Argentina, recalled how no respectable Argentine woman would think of going to mass without a black maidservant to carry her rug and attend to her during the services.[27] Several paintings of early nineteenth-century Buenos Aires show precisely that scene; Léon Pallière's series of paintings entitled *Interior of a Temple* are especially vivid representations of Buenos Aires matrons accompanied by their female retainers.[28]

The colony's intellectuals tended to concur with foreign observers that the number of slaves employed in domestic service was far out of proportion to the city's needs. Buenos Aires's first newspaper, the *Telégrafo Mercantil*, ran an editorial in 1802 attacking the practice of maintaining large staffs of domestic slaves. Its opposition was based on two grounds: first, that having so many slaves of all ages and sexes living together in close quarters was an open invitation to lasciviousness and vice; second, that the labor wasted in domestic service could be used more productively in occupations such as agriculture or the trades. The editors proposed that no family be allowed to employ more than one married slave couple as servants.[29]

Though it is probably true that the servant staffs of the elite porteño families were wasteful and out of proportion to the immediate economic needs of the household, the importance of the economic function filled by domestic slaves should not be passed over lightly. Keeping house in colonial Buenos Aires was a very far cry indeed from keeping house in a modern Western city, and families wanting to maintain themselves in any degree of physical comfort and cleanliness would have been hard pressed to do so without aid from servants. Lina Beck-Bernard, an Alsatian woman who lived in Argentina from 1857 to 1862, recalled the drastic decline in the quantity and quality of domestic servants in the years following abolition.[30] Newspaper editorials appearing in the Buenos Aires press during the 1830s and 1850s commented on the critical shortage of workers willing to enter service and proposed the forcible impressment of free black people to remedy the situation (see Chapter 4). The number of slaves in domestic service may have been larger than was absolutely necessary, but when that number was reduced and eventually eliminated, the city found itself hard pressed to continue functioning in the manner to which it had become accustomed.

But from the owner's point of view, domestic slaves had one serious shortcoming: they produced little or no cash income. True, they saved expenditures of energy and money that would otherwise have been necessary to get the household's work done, but they generated no visible, tangible income. Owners interested in obtaining a return on their investment were better served by having artisan slaves, who became extremely numerous in the city during the colonial period. By the 1770s the majority of the city's craftsmen were nonwhite—mainly blacks, with some mestizos and Indians.[31]

When Buenos Aires was made the capital of the viceroyalty and opened to free trade, European artisans were drawn there by its increased economic importance and activity. Once arrived, however, they were dismayed to find the mechanical arts dominated by nonwhite practitioners and therefore accorded correspondingly low social status. The Europeans responded by seeking to bar people of African and Indian descent from the trades, or at the very least to reduce their numbers. For instance, Europeans in the shoemakers guild tried to prohibit slaves from attaining master rank (the highest level in the artisan hierarchy, followed by journeyman and apprentice) and also sought to prevent Africans and Afro-Argentines from voting in guild elections or holding guild office.[32]

The 1788 census of artisans in the city shows that the Europeans succeeded in imposing a discriminatory racial structure on the trades. Black men were significantly underrepresented at the master level and over-represented at the journeyman and apprentice levels. Also, Africans and Afro-Argentines were concentrated in the least lucrative professions, shoemaking and tailoring. Although some did make it into the more rewarding fields of carpentry and of being a *barbero*, a barber-surgeon, black men tended to be consigned to the lowest levels of the least remunerative crafts. The best jobs were reserved for Europeans, while creole whites occupied an intermediate position.[33]

But the Europeans' efforts to eject the Afro-Argentines completely from the trades had little success. Participation in the manual crafts remained so closely associated with African descent that between 1800 and 1805 elite social figures in both Buenos Aires and Montevideo urged the royal government to restrict even further the number of blacks allowed into the trades, since "the whites prefer poverty and idleness to going to work beside blacks and mulattoes."[34] An Englishman in the city in 1807 noted that, "superior and unsuited to mechanical trades, as much by pride as by laziness, the Spaniards and creole whites leave such occupations to their darker countrymen, who work hard at such jobs" as shoemaking, tailoring, and carpentry, among those he named.[35] Another Englishman remarked in the 1820s that "the mechanical arts are confined to such as are absolutely indispensable; and these are practiced by poor Spaniards from Europe or by people of color."[36] Newspaper ads of the 1820s repeatedly offered to buy and sell slave artisans, the most frequently mentioned professions being those of shoemaker, mason, tailor, and blacksmith.[37]

Efforts to eliminate black participation from the trades proved fruitless primarily because it was in the interest of too many people to continue such participation. Students of slavery in the Americas have described a phenomenon known in the United States as "hiring out," in which masters rented their slaves to other people who needed their services, thus receiving a direct cash income from the slave's labor.[38] Such an enterprise could be quite lucrative, especially if the slave was a skilled laborer who could command high wages. Hiring out occurred much more frequently in urban areas than in rural ones, and was very widespread in Buenos Aires. One visitor to the city in 1794, and another in 1806, recorded very similar impressions of the phenomenon, concurring in saying that the renting out of slaves was so common that it had had the effect of dissuading whites from becoming artisans since the work was dominated by blacks and therefore of very low status. The 1806 visitor described the system:

> The desire not to work and to put to use a small amount of capital, has suggested the idea of using it to buy slaves and train them for the crafts, so that their work will recoup somewhat more than the interest on the amount invested in such

speculation; by this means all the workshops have been filled to the brim [with slaves] by these mercenary people, and consequently the respectable desires of the poor residents to train their sons in that kind of trade have diminished.[39]

The profitability of this kind of investment meant that the efforts of the European artisans to close the crafts to the *castas* (people of mixed racial ancestry) were doomed to failure. The authorities recognized the folly of attempting to overturn an economic system from which a large portion of the city's white population benefited. Indeed, it was a system which provided the sole source of income to many people, particularly unmarried women, whose own employment opportunities were limited. Ownership of a skilled slave could provide them with the wherewithal to become self-supporting, in a curious use of the word.[40]

The potential abuses of hiring out were several. A *Telégrafo Mercantil* editorial of 1802 attacked the numerous slaveowners who supported themselves on the earnings of their slaves. The paper reported that many owners did not even bother to train the newly arrived Africans in a trade, but rather sent them directly into the streets to beg. Many owners demanded wages that the Africans simply were not capable of earning and then left their slaves to fend for themselves.[41]

The *Telégrafo Mercantil* also singled out another problem area, one which frequently worked to the slaves' advantage. The paper charged that the hiring-out system gave the slaves entirely too much freedom, since as long as they supplied their owners with the required wages, the masters cared little how or where they spent their time. A similar point had been made in a 1790 court case in which a young slave had been charged with rape. The court noted that the slave was one of those who wandered freely about the city, and who "as long as they supply a modest monthly fee to their owners, know no other control."[42] Though the defense established that the slave had never raped anyone, he was sentenced to two hundred lashes and six years in prison, perhaps to serve as an example to other slaves not to abuse the relative freedom that the hiring-out system afforded. In 1822 the government took further action to prevent slaves from posing as free in parts of the city where they were not known. Thenceforth slaves were required to carry at all times registration papers which would include the names of their owners.[43]

The freedom that a slave could win in the streets, away from his master's control, was one important advantage of the hiring-out system. An even greater one was the possibility that this street freedom, which was only partial and could be terminated at the master's whim, might someday be converted into complete and permanent freedom. Royal and municipal legislation limited the sums that slaves were required to turn over to their owners; anything that they made above that was theirs to keep and spend as they pleased. Spanish law also stipulated that slaves were entitled to retain whatever money they earned on their own time, which included Sundays, religious holidays, and the hours they had to themselves after they had satisfied their masters' labor demands. Many slaves used this free time to make and sell articles on the street. No memoir of life in early nineteenth-century Buenos Aires fails to mention the black street vendors and the rhymes and jingles with which they

A pastry vendor. He is using the feather duster to keep dust and dirt off his wares. Lithograph by César Hipólito Bacle, c. 1830.

hawked their wares.[44] Black vendors monopolized the market in all
sorts of produce, including pastries and *empanadas* (meat pies), prepared
olives, brooms and dusters, candles, and dairy products. Whether they
were unskilled slaves thrown into the street and ordered by their owners
to produce a daily wage, or domestic servants working in their spare
time to earn money of their own, the black men and women in Buenos
Aires demonstrated an obvious entrepreneurial capacity in their small

Washerwoman on her way to work. Lithograph by César Hipólito Bacle, c. 1830.

businesses, a capacity whose full realization was prevented by their legal and economic limitations.

Other slave and free women earned money by taking in laundry. The black washerwomen were as much a part of the urban scene as the black street vendors. They could always be found washing and drying clothes along the riverbank, and the *niños de bien*, the sons of the city's elite families, used to delight in taunting these women and tracking mud on their freshly washed clothes. Constrained by their social and legal status from retaliating against their tormentors, the washerwomen were limited to hurling furious insults at the young dandies, which apparently was a perennial source of high amusement to the townspeople.[45] Needless to say, working year round on the wet and marshy riverbank was not a healthy way to make a living, and at least one contemporary observer pointed to the washerwomen's practice of taking their children to work with them as a major cause of high infant mortality among the Afro-Argentines.[46]

Black people also dominated a variety of other occupations. Almost all of the city's pest exterminators were black, and according to contemporary accounts they rarely lacked employment.[47] Until the city began to establish a system of water mains in the 1870s, water was sold door-to-door from huge carts; many of these *aguateros* were slave and free blacks.[48] Black men worked as *changadores*, carriers of loads around the city. They found most of their employment at the docks, unloading luggage and freight and carrying it to its destination.[49] Some black men and women took advantage of the consumption patterns forced on the Afro-Argentine community by its poverty to become *achuradoras*, those who worked at the slaughterhouse salvaging tripe, lung, organs, and diseased meat from slaughtered animals. The achuradoras then sold this cast-off meat to blacks and poor whites who could not afford anything better.[50] The Afro-Argentines thus gave Argentina one of its favorite dishes, *chinchulines*, braided and grilled intestines, the same dish known as chitlins in the United States.

Slaves also participated in two other vocational areas, which tend to be passed over in traditional treatments of the Afro-Argentines. The first is that of manufacturing. Bakeries, the first enterprises in the region to employ techniques of mass production, made heavy use of slaves.[51] By 1805 the largest bakery in Montevideo employed forty slaves, while the 1810 census of Buenos Aires shows at least eight bakeries employing fifteen slaves or more, often in conjunction with free workers.[52] The 1810 census also shows several *fábricas* (literally, factories) which produced furniture and other items and which employed from five to fifteen slaves. Not factories in the twentieth-century sense, nor even in the nineteenth-century British sense (they were actually more like large workshops), the fábricas represented the cottage-industry phase of industrialization, the first steps toward rationalized production of manufactured goods in the colony. The government indicated the importance of these establishments in 1813, when it drafted slaves to fight the Spanish. While owners of domestic slaves were required to contribute one-third of their adult males to the state, owners of bakeries and fábricas were required to contribute only one-fifth.[53]

Even after the independence wars had reduced the male slave population, slaves continued to form a significant percentage of industrial workers in the city. The census of 1827 shows at least four bakeries and three fábricas employing between ten and twenty slaves, and a secondary source mentions a comb factory functioning in the early national period that employed 106 slaves.[54] In June of 1824 a hat-manufacturing establishment manned by sixteen slaves was advertised for sale in one Buenos Aires paper; the following month the same paper advertised the sale of a tallow factory with an unspecified number of slaves.[55] Though industrial slave labor was dealt a blow by the independence wars, it was by no means eliminated.

The second vocational area in which slaves participated heavily was agriculture. Newspaper ads offering to buy and sell slaves skilled in horsemanship and in work on the *estancias*, the large cattle ranches, appeared frequently in the city's newspapers. One eighteenth-century traveler in the province reported that "all these *haciendas* are full of gauchos who receive no pay, because instead of employing *peones*, the rich *hacendados* keep only foremen and slaves."[56] Account books of many of the estancias mention slave laborers, and one semilegendary establishment on the Indian frontier in the far south of the province was manned entirely by slaves, including the foremen.[57] Black foremen appear frequently in records of the period, and even slave foremen were not rare.[58]

Buenos Aires's agriculture had little in common with the tropical agriculture of the Caribbean, Brazil, or the southern United States. The cattle and wheat produced in the province were much less labor-intensive than such crops as sugar or cotton, so no Buenos Aires slave had to work on the field gangs usually associated with agricultural slavery. If anything, agricultural slaves in the countryside enjoyed freedoms that the city slaves never experienced. Rural slaves were by definition horsemen who moved relatively freely across the uninhabited and unpoliced pampa. Since Argentine agricultural labor was in no way as socially demeaning as the field labor of the Caribbean or Brazil, free blacks, mestizos, and whites worked as salaried peons side-by-side with the slaves, and the distinctions between slaves and freemen wore down some-what in the process.[59] Several historians focus on agricultural work and becoming a gaucho as among the most liberating experiences an Argentine slave could have. Certainly being a horseman on the pampa, where food was to be had for the taking, must have been one of the freest and most unrestricted ways of living imaginable.[60]

The colonial authorities were well aware of the ambiguous nature of slavery in the countryside and enacted special legislation against the *negros alzados*, "risen blacks" who fled on horseback to join the roaming bands of gaucho desperadoes. Owners who failed to report the flight of a gaucho slave within three days of its occurrence were fined twenty pesos in gold, a very steep sum, especially in the countryside. Any escaped slave who spent more than six months with such a gang was supposed to be automatically executed if recaptured, though some were deported to penal colonies instead.[61] These penalties were much stiffer than those applied to runaway slaves in the city, and reflected the authorities' fear of a large and uncontrollable runaway population in the interior.

One can only conclude by agreeing with the intendant's description of the dependence of Buenos Aires on slave labor. That dependence was profound, in the sense that slave labor formed the foundation of the vocational pyramid of the city, the very bottom layer. The foregoing survey of work performed by the Afro-Argentines reveals the discriminatory process of job selection that went on in the Buenos Aires of 1780–1850. The least desirable, most degrading, unhealthiest, and worst-paying jobs were reserved for the Afro-Argentines. Blacks were allowed to participate in the mechanical trades only because of the shortage of whites willing to enter the trades, the reliance of many slaveowners on the earnings of their slaves, and the traditionally low social status of manual labor in Spanish and Spanish-American society.[62] As blacks continued to be channeled into the most undesirable occupations, the low occupational status and low racial status accorded the Afro-Argentines reinforced each other in a circle that became impossible to break. One consequence of this process was that the occupational structure of free Afro-Argentines tended to replicate that of slaves. When a washerwoman won her freedom, it was rare indeed for her to rise in the occupational scale. Even when legally free, Afro-Argentines remained subject to the strictures of a society that reserved the best jobs for whites.

Samples taken from the 1810 and 1827 municipal censuses provide evidence in support of this observation. (See Appendix B for a discussion of these samples and the manner in which they were taken.) Unfortunately, the conclusiveness of this evidence is open to question due to the frequent failure of the census takers to record the occupations of individuals being canvassed. In the 1810 sample, 76.7 percent of the whites had no listed occupation, compared to 80.6 percent of the free blacks and 98.2 percent of the slaves. In the 1827 sample, 71.9 percent of the whites

Table 3.2. Occupational Distribution of a Sample of the 1810
Municipal Census of Buenos Aires[a]

	Whites	Free blacks	Slaves	Total
Occupational category				
Property owners	2	0	0	2
Professionals	38	1	0	39
Commerce	64	0	0	64
Small farmers	8	1	1	10
Artisans	40	22	6	68
Semiskilled	43	6	4	53
Unskilled	16	6	1	23
Inactive	9	0	0	9
Total	220	36	12	268
No occupation listed	724	150	644	1,518

Source: Author's sample of the 1810 municipal census of Buenos Aires, discussed in Appendix B. Census manuscript located in Archivo General de la Nación, 9 10-7-1.

[a] For an explanation of the occupational categories, see Appendix A.

Table 3.3. Occupational Distribution of a Sample of the 1827
Municipal Census of Buenos Aires[a]

	Whites	Free blacks	Slaves	Total
Occupational category				
Property owners	8	0	0	8
Professionals	30	2	0	32
Commerce	125	2	1	128
Small farmers	15	1	4	20
Artisans	92	34	14	140
Semiskilled	49	17	10	76
Unskilled	26	33	12	71
Inactive	8	3	0	11
Total	353	92	41	486
No occupation listed	903	521	312	1,736

Source: Author's sample of the 1827 municipal census of Buenos Aires, discussed in Appendix B. Census manuscript located in Archivo General de la Nación, 10 23-5-5, 23-5-6.

[a] For an explanation of the occupational categories, see Appendix A.

had no listed occupation, compared to 85.0 percent of the free blacks and 86.4 percent of the slaves. Many of the individuals with no reported occupation were children and women, who tended not to have formal occupations even though they might have been working full-time at various tasks. Other uncategorized persons were probably domestic servants, a large occupational group in the city and one which is suspiciously underrepresented in both censuses.

Despite the shortcomings of the data, a comparison of the occupational distributions of the white and black groups in the samples strongly suggests the equally disadvantaged position of free and slave blacks. Table 3.2 shows that in 1810 the three categories of manual laborers (artisans, semiskilled, and unskilled labor) accounted for 94.5 percent of all free blacks who listed occupations and 91.7 percent of slaves who listed occupations. Those three categories accounted for only 45.0 percent of white workers. The reader is cautioned that in the case of the Afro-Argentines these percentages are based on very small absolute numbers. Still, the tendency is clear: 47.3 percent of the whites were in the top three occupational categories; only one free black person was, and not a single slave.

Things had not improved greatly for the Afro-Argentines by 1827. Table 3.3 shows that the three largest categories for free blacks and slaves alike remained those associated with manual labor: artisans, unskilled laborers, and semiskilled laborers, in that order. Of free black workers, 91.3 percent fell into those three categories, as did 87.8 percent of slaves. Only 47.7 percent of the whites did so. All three of these percentages are very close to those recorded in 1810. Among whites, the most heavily represented vocational categories were commerce, artisans, and semiskilled workers. Unskilled labor, the second largest category among the blacks, was fifth among the whites. The predominance of whites in the highest categories in the 1810 sample repeated itself in 1827; indeed, commerce was the single largest category for the whites.

In short, it was a rare black man who could expect to rise above the level of a moderately successful artisan, just as it was a rare black woman who could anticipate more from life than a comfortable position as a trusted housekeeper. Though occasional Afro-Argentines might break through and experience considerable upward mobility after being freed, most black people failed to breach the barriers that kept the community on the lowest level of the social and vocational pyramid throughout the early national period. The most important progress made by the mass of Afro-Argentines in the first four decades after independence would be the slow and grudging transition from legal slavery to legal freedom. Chapter 4 chronicles that transition.

4

The Transition from Slavery to Freedom, of a Sort

CONDITIONS OF FREEDOM IN THE COLONIAL PERIOD

Spanish law and customs tempered the harshness of slavery by granting slaves a number of rights, the most important of which was the opportunity to win their freedom. The *Siete partidas*, the thirteenth-century codification of Spanish law by King Alfonso the Wise, listed a variety of ways for slaves to escape from bondage. To cite just a few, if a master made a slave the tutor of his children, the slave was entitled to freedom. If a slave married a free person with the master's knowledge and consent, the slave was free. If a slave was made an heir of the master in the master's will, the slave was free. Any slave forced into prostitution by her master was entitled to freedom.[1]

Such legal niceties were seldom observed in the New World, however, and few slaves won liberty by exploiting these little-known statutes. Broadly put, slaves in the colonial period either bought their freedom with cash or service, or they received it as an outright gift from their owner. Research on manumissions, the freeing of individual slaves, in colonial Peru and Mexico has demonstrated that more slaves bought their freedom than received it as a gift from their master,[2] and the same was true in Buenos Aires. A study of manumissions in the city between 1776 and 1810 showed that fewer than a third of slaves freed during that period were granted their freedom outright: 59.8 percent of manumissions involved cash payment, and an additional 10.9 percent required the freed person to meet various conditions (usually promises of future service) set by the former master.[3]

Another mechanism by which Spanish American slaves could win their freedom was by heroic service to the state, usually in fighting foreign invaders. Following the English invasions of Buenos Aires in 1806 and 1807, a number of slaves were granted their freedom by the town council, though the councilmen reneged on their original promise to free every slave who distinguished himself in fighting the English.[4] This offer, made in the panicky weeks preceding the second invasion, was later scaled down to a lottery in which 22 of the 688 slaves who had fought the British were freed. The royal government and a number of white militia officers contributed money to free 48 more, also chosen by lottery, to make a total of 70, 10 percent of the slaves who had participated in the fighting.[5] The town council also resolved to buy the freedom of all slaves maimed or mutilated in the fighting and pay them a lifelong pension of six pesos per month, but it is not clear whether this magnanimous project was ever realized.[6] Other cases of slaves' winning freedom through extraordinary service to the state occurred in 1812, when a slave named Ventura was freed and was granted a pension for having informed the authorities of a counterrevolutionary conspiracy led by Martín de Alzaga, and in 1813, when the town council freed the daughter of the free black Captain Antonio Videla after Videla was killed while fighting the Spanish in Uruguay.[7]

Such manumissions were rare, however, and most slaves won their freedom through the more conventional and less risky means of either buying it or persuading their owner to grant it to them. The previously cited study of manumissions in Buenos Aires between 1776 and 1810 sets the approximate number of such freeings during that period at 1500. The study also concludes that the annual rate of manumission (percentage of slave population obtaining its freedom each year) tripled between those years, from 0.4 percent in 1776 to 1.3 percent in 1810.[8] This increasing frequency was probably due to the growing commercial activity of the city. Comparative studies have found that periods of economic expansion provide greater opportunity for slaves to earn the money to buy their freedom, and the increasingly prosperous Buenos Aires of 1801–10 seems to have conformed to this pattern.[9] The high number of manumissions was also probably associated with the quantity of slavers that docked at Buenos Aires after 1790, assuring a steady supply of new slaves and thus making owners more willing to part with their old ones, especially if those slaves had earned freedom by good service.

Still, Buenos Aires's slave regime was in little danger of being extinguished by the practice of manumission. Eugenio Petit Muñoz stated the situation with melancholy accuracy when he observed that the most frequent means by which slaves acquired freedom in colonial Uruguay and Argentina was by dying; only a limited percentage of each slave generation succeeded in acquiring that most precious of commodities, freedom.[10]

A 1-in-7 sample of the black population taken from the 1810 municipal census showed that by the last year of the colonial period 22.6 percent of the city's black people were free. (Data from that census presented in this and the following chapter are taken from this sample.) This is an intermediate figure on the scale of other eighteenth- and nineteenth-century slave regimes. Free people made up 59.7 percent of the black population in Caracas as of 1783.[11] By 1821, 54.5 percent of the black population of the Brazilian mining state of Minas Gerais was free.[12] And by 1850, 35 percent of the Afro-Cuban population was free.[13] On the other hand, in the city of Rio de Janeiro free people composed only 7.7 percent of the black population in 1808 and 12.0 percent in 1849.[14] At no point in the antebellum American South did free people form more than 9 percent of the Afro-American population.[15]

Female slaves in Buenos Aires acquired freedom significantly more frequently than male slaves. As of 1810 the sexual ratio in the slave population was 110.9 males per 100 females. The sex ratio among slaves manumitted between 1776 and 1810 was 70.1 males per 100 females; as a result, the ratio among Buenos Aires's free black population, as documented in the census of 1810, was 97.9 males per 100 females.

The city's slave and free black populations also displayed considerable differences in age structure. While 13.4 percent of the slaves were 40 years of age or older, 28.9 percent of the free blacks were in that age group. This produced a median age of 20.9 for the slave population and 27.0 for the free. This probably reflects a tendency observed in other slave societies for owners to free older slaves who were no longer of service and constituted a financial burden.[16] This impression is reinforced by the fact that children under 15 made up roughly equal proportions of the slave and free population, 30.9 and 28.3 percent respectively. Thus the higher median age of the free population is due mainly to the preponderance of individuals over 40.

It is in the area of race that the free and slave populations were most sharply differentiated. While pardos composed only 18.5 percent of the slave population of known race, they made up 48.7 percent of all slaves freed between 1776 and 1810 and 71.1 percent of the free black population resident in the city in 1810. To put it another way, 63.2 percent of Buenos Aires's pardos in 1810 were free; only 13.3 percent of the morenos were. Clearly, Afro-Argentines of mixed ancestry were much more fortunate in the pursuit of freedom than were Afro-Argentines of pure African descent. These data are very similar to figures for Brazil and the United States, which demonstrate a hemisphere-wide tendency for mulattoes to acquire freedom more frequently than pure blacks.[17] The primary reason for this was that mulattoes were almost always creoles, natives of the society, who better understood its customs and practices than did the foreign-born African blacks. Thus mulattoes were more adept at recognizing and exploiting legal, economic, and social opportunities to escape from bondage.[18] Furthermore, the next chapter will demonstrate that Buenos Aires's Afro-Argentines tended to lighten in color over the generations. The mulattoes benefited from the fact that their parents or grandparents may already have purchased their own freedom decades previously, enabling part of the mulatto population present in 1810 to have been born free. Certainly the percentage of pardos with free parents must have been significantly higher than the percentage of morenos with free parents, though the census does not provide data to prove this point.

But even those Afro-Argentines who were nominally free never enjoyed the same kind of freedom that was the birthright of every white person in Spanish America. Colonial legislation imposed a lengthy series of restrictions on the free blacks' liberties, some of them dating from medieval Spanish legal usage, others of them new limitations created in response to New World realities. These controls, known as the *Régimen de castas*, were instituted in order to slow or halt the process of race mixture in the New World and to reserve the highest social and economic positions in the society for European- and American-born whites. The legislation proved spectacularly unsuccessful in realizing the first goal, and very successful indeed in realizing the second. Subject to innumerable restrictions on their freedom, the castes—morenos, pardos, Afro-Indians, and mestizos; Indians were a separate racial category governed by special legislation—acquired a legal status midway between that of the whites and the slaves. The Afro-Argentines of Buenos Aires, along with the blacks of the rest of the empire, were forbidden to carry arms, wear certain types of clothing such as silks, lace, or pearls, walk through city streets after nightfall, hold civil, ecclesiastical or military office, buy or sell alcohol, be educated in the same schools as whites, and so on and on in a list that must have seemed *ad infinitum* to the people who lived under its dictates.[19]

One of the most irksome aspects of this system was that an Afro-Argentine born of a family that had been free for generations was the legal equivalent of an Afro-Argentine who had acquired his freedom the day before: both were equally disadvantaged under the caste regime. Nor did an admixture of white ancestry make any legal difference. Under the Spanish doctrine of *limpieza de sangre*, purity of blood, lines of descent tainted by "unclean" blood (African, Arab, Jewish, and Indian) were socially and legally irredeemable. Thus even in cases in which Afro-Argentines could claim European ancestry, as long as they showed obvious physical evidence of their African heritage they remained part of the castes and therefore of a different legal status from their white kinsmen.[20]

Such discrimination was not always easy to enforce, however, and the statutory rigidities of the caste regime acquired a certain flexibility when put into practice. The institutionalization of the Régimen varied considerably from one part of the New World to another, adapting itself to conditions in different parts of the empire. In Buenos Aires several aspects of this legislation were quietly dispensed with. For instance, blacks and mulattoes were generally allowed both to buy and to sell liquor, despite occasional protests on the part of the town council, which alleged that it contributed to black criminality and rebelliousness, and by white storekeepers, who did not mind if the Afro-Argentines bought the stuff but did not want black tradesmen competing in its sale.[21] Free morenos and mulattoes were legally required to pay annual tribute to the Crown in the form of money or service. Though this law was enforced in some parts of the colonies, it was ignored in Argentina and Uruguay, as was the requirement that free blacks were to live with a white person who would be responsible for their good behavior.[22]

Another way to loosen the restrictions of the caste system was to ease the racial criteria by which membership in the castes was determined. This is a very difficult phenomenon to isolate, discover, and describe, since an essential part of allowing mulattoes and mestizos to assume white racial status was the destruction of all evidence of their "unclean" ancestry. This problem of falsification of racial background in order to escape from caste status will be dealt with in detail in the next chapter. Suffice it for now to say that such deception did take place on a significant scale in colonial Buenos Aires.

But on the whole it seems that the government and society of the city were reasonably conscientious in observing the laws that denied Afro-Argentines their full freedom. Morenos, mulattoes, and Afro-Indians were barred from the city's schools and from service in municipal, royal, and ecclesiastical government.[23] Craft guilds prohibited nonwhites from voting or holding office in the organizations.[24] Free blacks' freedom of assembly and association was abridged by a series of ordinances banning *candombes*, their street dances.[25] In some areas Buenos Aires's officials actually led the rest of the empire in their zeal to enforce discriminatory legislation. A royal decree of 1805 ordered that whites and other people "of distinguished birth" could marry casta women with official permission from the viceroy or the *audiencia*, the local royal tribunal. Upon receiving this decree, Viceroy Sobremonte of Buenos Aires announced that under no circumstances would he grant such permission.[26]

EMANCIPATION: SLAVERY DIES A LINGERING DEATH

Such was the legal and social situation of the blacks of colonial Buenos Aires: the bulk of them enslaved, and the free persons among them enjoying only a partial liberty. Then came the revolution of 1810, and with it bold new calls for an end to racial discrimination. Actually, such talk in the Río de la Plata predated the revolution. In 1801 the *Telégrafo Mercantil* had attacked the caste system as an irrational, counterproductive regime that "deprives the Church of priests and religious laborers who could be extremely useful under a different system, [that deprives] the Arts and Sciences of learned Professors, the King of valiant and devoted Soldiers, and the State and Country of Citizens who could serve it most usefully and splendidly." Dwelling at length on the miserable state in which he found the nonwhites submerged, the editor argued that the elimination of the caste system would enable them to rise from their depressed level to a position of equality with the whites, "and perhaps the time would come in which we would see ruling over the Universities and leading soldiers into battle the very people whose grandfathers had been our Slaves."[27]

Such buoyantly optimistic expressions were representative of the current of liberal Enlightenment thought then running strong in Buenos Aires. As expounded by porteño thinkers such as Mariano Moreno, it stood for free trade, the overthrow of aristocratic privilege (and by extension racially discriminatory legislation), and occasionally the abolition of slavery, though the liberal enshrining of the rights of property frequently nullified this last. Indeed, shortly after the town council assumed power from the viceroy in 1810, officially beginning the Argentine revolution, it resolved that the immediate abolition of slavery was out of the question: "It is not possible to extinguish slavery at once without attacking the sacredness of our property and exposing the country to grave dangers caused by the sudden emancipation of a race that, brought up in servitude, would use freedom to do harm to itself."[28]

The same argument was used in an 1812 newspaper article directed to
the city's slaves which informed them that

> your longed-for liberty cannot be decreed right away, as humanity and reason
> would wish; because unfortunately it stands in opposition to the sacred right of
> individual liberty [i.e., the right of the slaveowners to own slaves]; and because
> having grown up and become aged in subjection and servitude, you are of course
> almost incapable of managing your own affairs, unless you are first prepared in
> some way for this abrupt change.[29]

Employing this double justification of the rights of property and the
slaves' alleged inability to function on their own, the city's
revolutionaries evaded the abolition that nobody except the Afro-
Argentines wanted. They hit instead on two more gradual processes of
terminating slavery. The first shall be described briefly here; it is
discussed in detail in Chapter 7. Faced with a shortage of men eligible
for military service, the government instituted a series of conscription
decrees aimed directly at the slave population. Slaves became free as
soon as they were drafted, though they were required to serve a
minimum term of enlistment in exchange for their freedom. Between
1813 and 1818 some two thousand Africans and Afro-Argentines
resident in Buenos Aires province entered the army under this
program.[30]

Able-bodied males were the only members of the slave population
eligible to win freedom in this way, and of course the children of such
men remained slaves, since legal status was passed on through the
mother rather than the father. Much more universal in its scope,
therefore, was the 1813 *Ley de libertad de vientres*, loosely translatable
as the Law of Freedom by the Womb. Very similar to laws declared in
Chile, Venezuela, Paraguay, and other Spanish American countries, this
decree provided that all children born of slave mothers in Argentina
after January 31, 1813, were free, though their freedom was limited by a
number of conditions. These children, known as *libertos*, were required
to live in the house of the owner of their mother until they married or
reached the age of majority (20 for males, 16 for females), whichever
came first. Only at that time would they become completely free. They
were required to serve their patron, as the law termed their mother's
owner, without salary until the age of 15, after which they were to be
paid one peso per month until they won their full freedom. The monthly
peso would be deposited in an account kept for them by the police, the
accumulated amount to be turned over to them when they reached
majority. Subsequent legislation established programs to provide the
libertos with land grants and loans when they attained majority, so that
they could become productive citizens of the state.[31]

Table 4.1. Children Living with and without Parents, from a Sample of the 1827 Municipal Census of Buenos Aires

	White	Black	Total
Children living with at least one parent	340	164	504
Children living without parents	57	111	168
Total	397	275	672

phi = 0.60
chi square = 58.296
sig. at .00 for 1 df

Source: Author's sample of the 1827 municipal census of Buenos Aires, discussed in Appendix B. Census manuscript located in Archivo General de la Nación, 10 23–5–5, 23–5–6.

Along with the decree concerning libertos, the revolutionaries early in 1813 enacted a sweeping abolition of the commerce in humans. Any slave entering the country from abroad, either freely or under compulsion by a trader or owner, would be free as soon as he or she set foot on Argentine soil.[32]

These were the initial efforts, generated by the Argentine revolution, to end slavery. Even as originally conceived, the Libertad de vientres offered striking resemblances to the old slave regime. The law specifically allowed libertos to be bought and sold almost exactly like slaves. In theory it was the right of patronage and the right to the liberto's services that changed hands, but in practice it was a human being who was being sold, despite the fact that he might be theoretically free. This reality was tacitly recognized by legislation establishing a procedure by which libertos could buy their freedom before reaching the age of majority. In an attempt to introduce a humane element into this system, the law also provided that liberto children could not be separated from their mothers until the age of 2; after that age they could be sold apart, and they frequently were, as a sample of the 1827 municipal census reveals. The phi measure of Table 4.1, which indicates the strength of association between the variables tabulated, shows that black children under the age of 15 (born, therefore, in 1813 or after) tended much more strongly than whites of the same age to live apart from their parents. To put it in percentage terms, 85.6 percent of white children lived with one or both of their parents; 59.6 percent of black children did so. Sixteen of the 275 black children were listed as slaves in the census, despite the fact that under the 1813 laws they should have been free.

Under Argentina's confederate system, enforcement of the liberto laws could and did vary considerably from province to province. In Mendoza, for instance, the age of majority for libertos was raised to 25, and

Table 4.2. Legal Status of Afro-Argentines Included in a Sample of the
1810 Municipal Census of Buenos Aires

	Free	Slave	Total
Male	92	345	437
0–14	29	89	118
15–44	46	209	255
45–up	14	29	43
unknown	3	18	21
Female	94	311	405
0–14	21	92	113
15–44	44	186	230
45–up	19	23	42
unknown	10	10	20
Total	186	656	842
0–14	50	181	231
15–44	90	395	485
45–up	33	52	85
unknown	13	28	41

Source: Author's sample of the 1810 municipal census of Buenos Aires, discussed in
Appendix B. Census manuscript located in Archivo General de la Nación, 9 10–7–1.

Table 4.3. Legal Status of Afro-Argentines Included in a Sample of the 1827
Municipal Census of Buenos Aires

	Free	Slave	Unknown	Total
Male	222	140	19	381
0–14	118	9	2	129
15–44	71	104	14	189
45–up	33	27	3	63
Female	390	213	48	651
0–14	147	7	1	155
15–44	195	184	36	415
45–up	48	22	11	81
Unknown	1	—	—	1
15–44	1	—	—	1
Total	613	353	67	1,033
0–14	265	16	3	284
15–44	267	288	50	605
45–up	81	49	14	144

Source: See Table 4.1.

cases of owners' retaining the services of libertos illegally past that age were not unheard of.[33] Enforcement of the decree in Buenos Aires seems to have been more scrupulous—every one of the cases involving libertos' suits for freedom that I encountered in the archives resulted favorably for the plaintiff, providing that he or she was able to supply the necessary proof of birth date. The government could be very sticky on this point: in 1831 a ruling was handed down in which an Afro-Argentine baptized on April 11, 1813, but actually born on January 19 was denied liberto status and required to go on serving his master as a slave.[34]

A comparison of data from samples of the 1810 and 1827 municipal censuses suggests the impact of the liberto legislation on the Afro-Argentines. As will be discussed in Chapter 5, the figures in Tables 4.2 and 4.3 represent samples from those two censuses, the manuscripts of which survive in incomplete form only. They should therefore not be taken to represent absolute changes in the black population during those 17 years, but rather should be interpreted as indices of the directions of demographic change.

It has already been noted that in 1810, at the close of the colonial period, 22.6 percent of the black population in the sample was free. By 1827 that percentage had almost tripled, rising to 63.4 percent. This figure is deceiving, however, since the free population in 1827 included the libertos born after 1812, all of whom were still in bondage in 1827, even though in line for eventual freedom. Children 14 and under made up 43.2 percent of the free black population. Of course, not all of these children were libertos. Some of them were children of free mothers and therefore had no obligations to any patrons or owners. Others were children who had had their freedom bought for them or granted to them by their owners and were similarly exempt from service obligations. To determine the approximate number of children who were libertos, I calculated child-woman ratios (number of children aged 0 to 4 per 1000 women aged 15 to 44) for the slave and free black populations in 1810. The ratio for the free population was found to be 1.31 times that for the slave population. In 1827 the proportion of black women aged 15 to 44 (potential childbearing ages) who were free was 51.5 percent; slaves accounted for 48.5 percent. Multiplying that free black proportion by 1.31 to establish the same relationship between the two groups that held true in 1810, we find that 67.5 percent of black children under 15 could be expected to be the children of free mothers and therefore themselves completely free, while 32.5 percent were libertos who would not win their freedom for another two to twenty years, depending on their age at the time of the census. This calculation suggests that 45.2 percent of the municipal black population was still in forced servitude by 1827, whereas 54.8 percent of the Afro-Argentines in Buenos Aires enjoyed more or less complete freedom, almost 2.5 times the proportion registered in 1810.

The program that permitted black men to win their freedom through military service seems at first glance to have had a certain amount of success. In 1810, 18.0 percent of black men in the sample between the ages of 15 and 44 had been free; by 1827 that percentage had more than doubled, to 40.6. However, black men had paid a cruel price for this freedom: in 1810 males aged 15 to 44 had formed 30.3 percent of the city's Afro-Argentine population; by 1827 their representation had dropped to 18.3 percent. The incomplete nature of the two censuses precludes reliable calculation of absolute population figures, but a comparison of the two samples suggests an absolute decline in the black male population aged 15-to-44 of between 10 and 20 percent between 1810 and 1827. We shall return to this point in Chapter 5.

Adult black women acquired freedom in the 1810–27 period more frequently than black men did, despite the fact that no special program or mechanism existed by which women could acquire freedom. As previously mentioned, in the 1827 sample 51.5 percent of black women between 15 and 44 were free; in 1810 only 21.4 percent of that age group had been free. We may speculate that, in a phenomenon similar to that which occurred in the United States during and after the Revolution, slaveowners were sufficiently moved by libertarian ideology to see the contradiction in the continued existence of slavery in a society fighting for its freedom from a colonial power.[35] This apparent willingness to manumit Afro-Argentines who had no legal claim on freedom seems to have cooled in the 1830s, as we shall see shortly.

Thus the period from 1810 to 1827 saw undeniable improvement in the Afro-Argentines' legal status. In terms of some socioeconomic indicators the Afro-Argentines also made progress. Table 4.4 shows that in

Table 4.4. Percentage of Black Population Living in White-Controlled Social Units, from a Sample of the 1810 and 1827 Municipal Censuses of Buenos Aires

	Families	Households
1810	68.4% (N = 803)	82.9% (N = 543)
1827	51.5 (N = 1,031)	73.7 (N = 890)

Source: See Tables 4.2 and 4.1.

1810, 82.9 percent of the black population in the sample lived in households headed by white people; by 1827 that percentage had dropped to 73.7 percent. More progress was made at the family level: in 1810, 68.4 percent of Buenos Aires's blacks were living in families headed by whites, but by 1827 only 51.5 percent were in that category. By point of comparison, in 1810, 99.4 percent of the white population lived in families headed by whites. In 1827 the figure was 99.0 percent.*

The increasing ability of black people to form their own household and family units seems strongly correlated with their escape from slavery. Indeed, the percentage of blacks enslaved and the percentage of blacks living with white families are fairly close in both censuses. It seems clear that as the Afro-Argentines left slavery they immediately formed their own family units, contradicting contemporary observations alleging a lack of family feeling among the black population.[36]

The increase in black-controlled households might have been even more substantial had it not been for two factors: the dearth of black males caused by the wars for independence, and the continuingly disadvantaged occupational structure of the black population. As we have just seen, the 1827 census documents a sexual imbalance among the Afro-Argentines: females heavily predominated, whereas black males had outnumbered females in 1810. Regardless of their racial composition, households in Buenos Aires were headed predominantly by males (68.9 percent of the city's households had male heads in 1810, 76.1 percent in 1827). The removal of a large portion of the black male population seems to have dealt a heavy blow to many families striving to form their own households. Among black households, 67.7 percent had been headed by males in 1810, a figure in keeping with that for the city as a whole; in 1827, 56.8 percent of black households were headed by males. That the number of black households increased at all between 1810 and 1827 seems to have been due to the determination of the community's newly freed women to establish independent households whenever and wherever they could. In a period during which the percentage of the city's population that was black declined from 29.5 to 19.5, the percentage of households headed by Afro-Argentines rose slightly, from 4.8 to 5.5.

Tables 3.2 and 3.3, discussed in the previous chapter, revealed the concentration of Afro-Argentine workers at the lowest levels of the city's

---

* "Household" is here defined in terms of housing: all of the individuals listed by the census taker as residing in an independent living unit are considered to belong to that household. "Family" is defined in terms of kinship, i.e., a nuclear family and those relatives, slaves, servants, employees, or persons of undefined relationship listed as living with the family.

occupational pyramid. The provincial government was conscientious in granting libertos their freedom once majority was reached, but it did little else to aid them to escape their subordinate socioeconomic position. For instance, no attempt was made to institute the land grant and loan programs envisioned by the original Libertad de vientres legislation and which would have enabled Afro-Argentines to become independent small farmers. Lacking the economic basis to buy or even rent houses on their own, black family heads established independent living arrangements far less frequently than white family heads did. This was not a matter of choice: research on the city's free black master artisans, the most prosperous segment of the community, has shown that their rate of home ownership was almost as high as that of white master artisans.[37] Whenever Afro-Argentines could afford to become household heads, they did so. Unfortunately, their position in the city's economy seldom gave them that opportunity.

Despite its many shortcomings, however, the legislation concerning libertos did allow more Afro-Argentines than ever before to acquire freedom. The law abolishing the slave trade did not fare so well. In fact, it remained in effect less than one year. Early in 1814 the revolutionary government ordered that any slaves entering Argentina from Brazil were to be returned to their owners. This decree was issued in response to Brazilian protests concerning the number of slaves who had fled south upon hearing that they could win their freedom there.[38] The abolition of the slave trade was further modified that same year to provide that slaves who entered the country accompanying their masters as domestic servants would not win their freedom. This generated such a traffic in slaves imported under this rubric that in 1824 the provincial government found it necessary explicitly to outlaw the sale of domestics brought into the country by foreigners. Citizens of Buenos Aires, however, especially those belonging to elite families, won numerous special permits to bring slaves into the country for their own use. This occurred in spite of the 1813 legislation outlawing the trade, an executive decree by Governor Las Heras in 1823 that declared the commerce in humans an act of piracy, and an 1825 treaty with Great Britain to stamp out slaving. Another violation of the law that usually went unpunished was the taking of pregnant slaves outside the country to give birth so that the babies would be permanent slaves rather than libertos. Legislation passed in 1816 that outlawed this practice was seldom enforced.[39]

The loopholes in the 1813 law are amply illustrated by some data from the 1827 census. That census included a question asking how long individuals had resided in Buenos Aires province. From the answers to

Table 4.5. Legal Status of Africans by Date of Entry into Buenos Aires Province, from a Sample of the 1827 Municipal Census of Buenos Aires

	1760–1812	1813–27	Unknown	Total
Free	56	12	16	84
Slave	79	23	36	138
Unknown	0	0	25	25
Total	135	35	77	247

Source: See Table 4.1.

this question it is possible to calculate dates of entry. According to my sample of that census, as of 1827 two-thirds of the Africans who had entered the city after 1812 were slaves, a higher proportion than among Africans brought to the city during the slaving years prior to 1813. Caution is in order in interpreting these figures due to the very small number of cases in the 1813–27 column. Still, they demonstrate that by no means all of the blacks entering Buenos Aires after 1813 automatically won their freedom as soon as they stepped on Argentine soil. The proportion of slaves was even higher among Africans with no known date of entry. This group may well have included Africans brought to the country after 1813 whose owners did not want them to fall under the *liberto* legislation and therefore withheld their dates of entry from the census taker.

These data also show that the slave trade declined considerably in volume after 1812. Even allowing for the imports of the early 1820s, the impressed labor brought into the city was inadequate to meet the demand for it, and the government was forced to consider new methods of allowing slaves to enter the country without openly violating the earlier legislation, to which it had ideological, if no longer practical, attachments. The 1825–28 War with Brazil provided a perfect opportunity. Under the conditions of war, Argentina empowered privateers, the *corsarios*, to fight under the Argentine flag, capture Brazilian ships, and sell the contents of such prizes in Buenos Aires. Since Brazil continued to maintain a thriving slave trade at that time, one of the most important commodities captured by the privateers was Africans.

In March 1827 the provincial government handed down a set of regulations to govern the sale of this booty.[40] Recalling that under the 1813 law any slave who set foot on Argentine soil was free, the government announced that those fortunate enough to be captured by Argentine vessels were also free, though it was freedom of a most peculiar sort. First, all blacks would be sold by the privateers to the government for fifty pesos apiece—this apparently failed to satisfy the privateers, since seven months later the government raised its price to two hundred pesos.[41] All the men fit to bear arms would be sent to service in the armed forces for a four-year term, following which they would be free. The remaining men, women, and children would acquire liberto status, would be rented out by the state to patrons, and would be required to serve them either for six years or until the age of twenty, whichever came later. Subsequent legislation established staggered terms of service depending on the liberto's age upon entering the country.[42] The patron paid the government one peso per month for a liberto, certainly a reasonable price in the city's perpetually labor-hungry market. Also, since the libertos could be bought and sold like slaves, it was possible for their patrons to make a profit on them. In April 1830, Federico Guittarde bought a liberta, María, for four hundred pesos, and three months later he sold her to a new patron for seven hundred pesos.[43]

Though this legislation empowered the police to handle the distribution of the libertos and the collection of rent, it is clear that this procedure was frequently violated. Police files contain numerous documents in which patrons record having received their libertos directly from privateer captains, sometimes paying as much as four hundred pesos for them.[44] Any distinction between this system and slaving was purely academic, though it is true that the libertos were obligated to serve only a limited period of time and thus escaped the probably permanent slavery that awaited them in Brazil. Or at least one hopes that they did: in 1831 the police registries of the libertos brought into the country by privateers were somehow lost, and libertos and patrons were requested to report together to their local precinct headquarters to inform the police how much time remained to be served and to draw up new documents. Though the police sought "a method that will protect the rights of the Patron, and at the same time prevent the frauds that he could perpetrate on his libertos," one wonders how many libertos performed extra years of enforced and unpaid service because of the loss of those lists.[45]

The Africans brought to Buenos Aires by the corsarios were apparently inadequate to supply the city's demand for impressed labor, and in 1831 Governor Juan Manuel de Rosas reopened the trade in domestic servants brought into the country by foreigners, making it perfectly legal for them to be sold to Argentines as slaves. Two years later this decree was revoked, though the law superseding it provided that anyone who turned in a black who could not prove his freedom became the patron of that black, who became a liberto.[46]

The slave trade, which had been terminally outlawed in 1813, finally began to wind down in the 1830s under persistent British pressure. The signing of the Anglo-Argentine anti-slave-trade treaty of 1840 seems to have marked its termination, though as late as 1853 a cargo of one hundred Africans were brought ashore in Patagonia by the corsario *Lavelleja* and either drafted into the army or farmed out as libertos under the still-existent 1827 legislation.[47]

It only remained, then, finally to abolish slavery, a legal system which had still not yet been officially overturned in Argentina. The never-ratified constitution of 1819 had contained an abolition clause, but it was not until 1853 that the national constitution announced that "there are no slaves in the Argentine Confederation; the few that now exist are free upon the ratification of this Constitution."[48] Even at this late date Buenos Aires contrived to preserve the existence of its slave regime: since Buenos Aires was the only Argentine province not to join the confederation and ratify the constitution, slavery continued there until 1861, when the province finally joined the confederation and became subject to its charter. Buenos Aires's provincial constitution of 1854 banned the slave trade but carefully refrained from abolishing slavery.[49]

It remains an open question exactly how many slaves were freed in Buenos Aires by the 1861 emancipation, though it seems clear that by that point slavery in the city was a dying institution. By 1850 advertisements concerning the sale of slaves had completely disappeared from the newspapers. The 1840 antislaving treaty with Great Britain seems to have effectively cut off the entry of slaves from abroad. While the municipal census of 1855 included no information on race in its questionnaire, several census takers marked down race on their own initiative: the foreign-born blacks included in that census were an extremely elderly group, having a median age of 62.4.[50] Certainly slaves as old as these would have been of little economic benefit to their owners.

Leaving the numerical question aside, it is important to note that there is considerable doubt as to whether emancipation was ever enforced. The article of the Constitution of 1853 providing for abolition also called for the establishment of commissions to reimburse owners for their freed slaves. Although such a commission was established in the province of Santa Fé, where slaves continued to form the backbone of the agricultural labor force,[51] none ever was in Buenos Aires, or in most of the other provinces. Since the constitution also provided that no property could be expropriated by the state without previous indemnization, it appears as though the slaves remaining in Buenos Aires in 1861 probably never received the benefits of emancipation.[52] Leslie Rout nicely summarizes the Argentine emancipation when he observes that slavery in Argentina was never really abolished—it just died of old age.[53]

FREE AT LAST

We have already discussed the severely circumscribed freedom that was the lot of free blacks in colonial Buenos Aires. To what extent did the Argentine revolution realize the *Telégrafo Mercantil's* vision of black professors and generals ruling over the country's affairs in a society free of racial restrictions? The reader will not be unduly shocked to learn that the vision remained a vision, existing only in the realm of imagination. Although the legal status of free black people did improve with independence, it would be decades before Afro-Argentines were the legal equivalent of Euro-Argentines. The following discussion will be limited to the first half of the nineteenth century, the five decades between the revolution of 1810 and the ratification by Buenos Aires province in 1861 of the Constitution of 1853.

To a certain extent the antidiscrimination rhetoric expressed during the early stages of the revolution was probably genuine, but it also had an obvious ulterior motive: winning black support for the struggle against Spain. The form of support most immediately needed was military, and to hearten the black soldiers in their fight against the Spanish the revolutionary government laid the inspirational language on strong and made some genuine concessions. In June of 1810, the revolutionary junta had officially elevated Indian soldiers and officers to a position of equality with the whites. The black troops were justifiably resentful—in the colonial militia they had served side by side with the Indians in the Battalion of Castes. Now suddenly the Indians were equal to the whites, while the blacks remained in an inferior position. The junta became aware of this resentment and responded to it. In December of 1810, in recognition of the outstanding performance of the free black troops in the expeditionary force to Bolivia, black officers and soldiers were declared the equal of whites and Indians, black officers now being allowed to append the coveted *Don* to their names, and soldiers to term themselves *distinguido*.[54] A few months later Agustín Sosa, an Afro-Brazilian who had migrated to Argentina and risen to the rank of lieutenant colonel in the colonial militia, was reconfirmed in that rank by the junta, thus becoming the first black lieutenant colonel in the Argentine army.[55] Sosa's military experience and gifts were both great, but we may speculate that he earned his promotion as an example to the black troops of how high a black man could rise in the new revolutionary army. When in October 1811 the Sixth Regiment of

Pardos and Morenos was elevated from the status of militia to that of a regular line unit, with the corresponding increases in status, pay, and privileges, the junta took advantage of the occasion to advertise its antidiscriminatory philosophy:

The present government . . . must especially direct its efforts against those prejudices that diminish the mass [of people] working for the grand cause of liberty. Such prejudices are responsible for the degradation to which the accidental difference of color condemned until now a part of our population as numerous as it is capable of any great enterprise.[56]

In an 1813 communiqué to the government of the interior province of Córdoba, the central government in Buenos Aires discussed the necessity of convincing the masses that the revolution truly was dedicated to overturning the caste regime. The Supreme Government ordered the Cordobans to appoint civil and military officials solely on the basis of talent and ability, choosing candidates who were capable administrators "even though their extraction and genealogical descent may not be the most accredited." All their revolutionary policies would be useless, it was argued, "if the People do not experience the good effects of the promises made by this Government," i.e., the promises of an end to discrimination.[57]

As it turned out, the Cordobans did exactly the opposite, relieving of duty all the black officers when the province's black militia company was sent off to war. This was an accurate forecast of what was to come. Throughout the period from 1810 to 1850, free Afro-Argentines and Africans remained severely disadvantaged, both officially and unofficially. A series of discriminatory laws or practices that assumed the force of law set Afro-Argentines apart from the greater society. Black civil servants were almost unheard of. Though many free blacks rose to officer rank in the armed forces, the step between colonel and general proved an unbreachable barrier, and the number of blacks who became officers was in no way proportionate to their representation in the ranks (see Chapter 7). From 1810 to 1821 only the sons of free blacks could vote in Buenos Aires—a man who had been a slave or the son of slaves was denied franchise, as of course were all black women. In 1821 this rule was overturned: free black males were allowed to vote and hold office in the province providing they met the necessary property requirements, which only a small percentage of Afro-Argentines could do.[58]

In the area of education, Afro-Argentines became gradually better off as the national period went on, but the struggle toward equality was a long and exasperating one. It was especially difficult in the interior city of Córdoba, where blacks were first admitted to the public schools in 1829, with a quota of two Afro-Argentines per year allowed to enter the high school. As late as 1852 Afro-Argentines were still officially barred from the University of Córdoba by rules left unchanged from the colonial period.[59]

Educational opportunities were only slightly better in Buenos Aires. It is not clear at what point the city's public schools were opened to blacks. Certain it is that when the government authorized the establishment of black mutual aid societies in 1820, one of the obligations that it imposed on the societies was the establishment and maintenance of schools for the children of the members, a requirement which would have guaranteed a segregated school system in the city.[60] It is known that the city's Beneficent Society established a segregated school for mulatto and moreno students sometime around 1830, and in 1852 it opened two more segregated schools for black girls.[61] These two girls' schools continued to operate into the 1860s, containing at their height, in the 1850s, 17 percent of the city's female students.[62] Though by 1853 the boys' schools were open to black students, informal discrimination prevented the Afro-Argentines from occupying an equal place in them. *La Crónica* of July 15, 1855, carried an article on the discriminatory treatment of blacks in Buenos Aires's public schools, to which one of the accused teachers retorted that since black children had to earn their living as domestic servants, they could never come to morning classes, and it was for this reason that they did so badly in school. The rector of the University of Buenos Aires expressed regret that as yet no black students had entered the university, to which he added his profound hopes that he might soon have the pleasure of teaching such students.[63] As late as 1882, no black student had yet graduated from the university.[64]

A more subtle but equally effective form of discrimination was the greater society's assumption, usually unspoken but occasionally explicit, that the city's black population existed solely to serve the white. This assumption emerges clearly in official documents such as the annual reports of demographic statistics made by parish priests to the provincial government, in which black births are listed in a column headed "blacks and people of service" *(morenos y gente de servicio)*.[65] As the libertos began to win their freedom and a resulting shortage of domestic labor hit Buenos Aires in the 1830s, angry editorials appeared in the porteño papers proposing the conscription of black people into domestic service. An 1830 editorial painted the melancholy picture of well-to-do families begging free Afro-Argentines to come to work for them, offering them staggering salaries, and still being unable to find help. The servants "know the demand that there is for them, and they lay down the law to their employers. Though this is reasonable from time to time, it shows the urgent need of taking corresponding measures to remedy in some way an evil that so clearly affects the delicacy, consideration, and respect required among the classes of society." After attacking the Afro-Argentines for taking unfair advantage of the market conditions of heavy demand and low supply, the editor suggested the passage of laws to force blacks into contracting as domestic servants and to govern their behavior while on the job.[66] He apparently failed to perceive any discrepancy between this stand and the name of his paper, *Martyrdom or Freedom (El Mártir o Libre)*, the same issue of which carried a long paean to "Liberty," "the sacred voice that forms the dignity of humanity . . . that precious gift."

The government did not enact such laws, however, and the shortage of help grew ever more acute. In October 1853 *La Tribuna* ran a two-part article on the problem, blaming the recently overthrown Rosas dictatorship for the blacks' refusal to enter service:

Domestic service since then has been converted into a genuine martyrdom; the good habits of the people of color corrupted, their extravagance, laziness, and licentiousness encouraged; families have had to resign themselves to putting up with their libertinism or performing the various household chores themselves. Fifteen years of disorder and immorality have completely ruined domestic service in Buenos Aires, so that it is now easier to find ten schoolteachers to educate one's child than it is to find an honest and punctual servant who performs her duties according to the law.[67]

The editor went on to propose remedies considerably harsher than those suggested in 1830: he argued for the establishment of a House of Correction to which all people arrested for vagrancy, minor crimes, or who simply showed "certain faults that could still be corrected" would be sent. There they would be trained in domestic service and then hired out by the city.[68]

La Tribuna thereby suggested a patently illegal violation of the black population's civil rights. Individuals innocent of any crime except "certain faults" would be forced to go to work against their will. Even more sinister was the paper's equation of African descent with automatic candidacy for domestic service. A similar rationale, though this time referring to military service rather than domestic service, was employed to justify a series of racially discriminatory draft decrees in the 1820s and 1830s. An 1831 edict calling for the enlistment of libertos 15 and over argued that the patrons were of course entitled to their libertos' service, since the libertos were born to serve, but the state had an even more pressing claim. "If the patrons are entitled to enjoy the service that the libertos give them, the State cannot be considered less entitled, when the land that has distinguished them [i.e., given them freedom] calls equally to all to come to its service."[69] A month later the government decided that in fact the state was not calling equally to all its citizens, but rather was beckoning especially insistently to the Afro-Argentines: "This duty common to all especially affects the pardos and morenos, who should have been born slaves due to the status of their mothers, but who were born free through the generosity of the State."[70] Similar justifications were employed for a draft of free blacks in 1826 and for the formation of a slave militia in 1816.[71]

A discussion of the limitations on the Afro-Argentines' freedom would not be complete without mentioning the legislation and practices that, while not racially discriminatory, hit particularly hard at the Afro-Argentines because of their low socioeconomic status. The period from 1810 to 1860 saw a concerted effort on the part of the commercial and landholding elites of Buenos Aires province to acquire ever more complete control over the society's non-elites, transforming them from an underemployed, vagrant mass of people into an organized, regimented proletariat, tied and rooted to their workshops or estancias. Progressively stiffer laws governing vagrancy, the necessity of having employment, and service in the military, combined with the illegal exploitation of forcing them into disadvantageous contracts or outrageous terms of military service, struck equally at poor whites, mestizos, Indians, and blacks, and severely limited their freedom to go where they wanted when they wanted, to work or not to work.[72] The grim irony of this increasing control of the lower class by the elite was that it was necessitated by the ending of slavery and the slave trade, which had removed a readily exploitable source of labor that could be employed in any way desired by the owner. The Afro-Argentines could not win: they no sooner began the transition from slavery to freedom than they saw their freedom besieged by the social and economic demands of the greater society, a siege that would not be lifted until the century was nearly over.

The Spanish historian Nuria Sales de Bohigas suggests a five-stage process model for analyzing the progress of Spanish American abolition.[73] The first stage is that of prerevolutionary growth of abolitionist sentiment among the colonial liberals, lasting until 1810. The second is the stage in which the revolutionary governments proposed bold, sweeping measures to do away with the colonial structures of privilege and slavery. This initial ardor soon cooled, however, and was replaced by a more cautious, gradual approach exemplified by the concept of the Libertad de vientres. Toward the end of the independence wars, around 1820, full-fledged reaction set in as the landed and commercial elites began to face the reality of the end of slavery and the slave trade. Confronting the prospect of losing their impressed labor forces, the Spanish American governments began studiously to ignore the earlier antislavery legislation, either failing to enforce it or, as in Peru, actually repealing it. Then, beginning in the mid-1820s to 1830, one sees an attempt actively to prolong slavery and peonage by renewing the slave trade and reducing the postrevolutionary freedoms temporarily enjoyed by the blacks and Indians. This stage lasted in all the Spanish American countries well into the second half of the century, and large portions of this resurrected colonial system survive more or less intact in various parts of the continent.

Buenos Aires fits into Bohigas's scheme quite nicely. Neither significantly better nor worse than the rest of the Spanish American republics, the city consistently ignored the rights of its black citizens whenever it was economically or politically convenient, and handed out concessions only when it felt that it had something to gain in the bargain.

As part of the 1815 celebration of Buenos Aires's Independence Day, May 25, four statues were erected in the city's central plaza: one represented the newly free Americas, another Europe admiring America's freedom, a third showed Asia still in chains, and a fourth represented Africa, her chains just broken. The inscription on the base of the African statue was a poem.

> Until now Africa cried
> For her children
> So cruelly imprisoned.
> Her bitter sobbing ceased
> When the American,
> Proud with liberty,
> Compassionate and generous,
> Bestowed this precious gift
> On the miserable African.[74]

The porteños' self-congratulations were premature and undeserved. The gift of liberty proved to be no gift. Freedom was a commodity like any other, kept off the market by its owners to drive the price up and then purchased very dear by the Afro-Argentines on an installment plan stretching over decades.

5

How the Afro-Argentines Disappeared

The decline and disappearance of the black population of Buenos Aires is one of the most striking events of Argentine history; it even qualifies as one of the more curious footnotes to world demographic history. Historians began commenting on the phenomenon as early as the 1830s, and it has continued to attract attention and arouse puzzlement among Argentines and foreigners. That attention and puzzlement is by no means confined to historians: even *The 1975 South American Handbook*, a comprehensive travel guide to the continent, included a brief aside on the problem. Discussing the population of Argentina, the editors commented that "a curious sidelight of the racial composition is that up till 1850 about 40% of the population of Buenos Aires was black. This element has completely disappeared."[1] And, as was mentioned in Chapter 1, the North American magazine *Ebony* became sufficiently intrigued by the disappearance to send a reporter to Buenos Aires to gather material for a story on the phenomenon. The disappearance might be dismissed as an unusual but insignificant curiosity of world history were it not that similar developments have occurred in other Latin American countries. The black population of Uruguay, Argentina's neighbor, has dropped significantly during the country's history, falling to 2.3 percent of the national population by 1954.[2] Similar declines have occurred in Chile, Paraguay, Peru, and Mexico, where today it is unusual to see people of African descent.[3] Somewhat more surprisingly, such strongly Afro-American countries as Cuba, Puerto Rico, and Brazil have also reported proportional declines in their black populations.[4] Thus an examination of the decline of Buenos Aires's Afro-Argentine community is relevant to an understanding of a pattern that seems to affect Latin America as a whole.

The first writer to comment on the decline of the Afro-Argentines was Woodbine Parish, a British diplomat who served in Buenos Aires from 1825 to 1832 and became a friend and intimate of Governor Rosas. Parish's lengthy work, *Buenos Aires and the Provinces of the Río de la Plata*, appeared in 1839 and contained several pages on the black demographic decline. Lumping together Afro-Argentines, Indians, and mestizos under the label "people of color," Parish observed that according to the census of 1778 they composed a third of the city's population, whereas by 1825 their representation had shrunk to only a quarter. Pointing out that this nonwhite caste was composed almost entirely of Afro-Argentines, he explained their relative decline as due to two factors: the abolition of the slave trade in 1813, which ended the influx of black people to the city, and a high mortality rate among the Afro-Argentines. He cited the province's Statistical Register to show that black births between 1822 and 1825 barely exceeded black deaths, which would result in a negligible rate of growth, while the white population regularly enjoyed a high surplus of births over deaths. Parish concluded that these factors, combined with steady European immigration into the city, would have to result in an eventual extinction of the black population.[5]

This process was apparently well advanced by the 1860s, according to José Manuel Estrada, who wrote at that time that "today there are almost no blacks in Buenos Aires." Estrada made it clear that he was speaking not of mulattoes but of people of pure African descent, as he went on to say that race mixture had produced "gradual improvements" in the black population and the disappearance of "those genuine examples of the Ethiopian race."[6] By 1883 Domingo Sarmiento could write that very few people of color remained in the city, and he ventured the prediction that within twenty years they would have disappeared completely.[7] The national census of 1895 reported the existence of only 454 individuals "of African race" in a country of almost 4,000,000, leading the writers of the census report to conclude that "the race question, so important in the United States, does not exist in the Argentine Republic." This report blamed the disappearance of the Afro-Argentines on their participation in the nation's wars. They were recruited heavily "and nearly all died on the battlefields, in the camps, or in well-deserved retirement after their patriotic struggles."[8] Nevertheless, when in 1905 the popular magazine *Caras y Caretas* sent a reporter to search for the remnants of the black population, he was able

Table 5.1. Results of Eight Censuses of the City of Buenos Aires, 1778–1887

Year	Whites	Indians or Mestizos	Afro-Argentines	Unspecified	Total	Percent Afro-Argentine[a]
1778	16,023	1,104	7,236	0	24,363	29.7%
1806[b]	15,078	347	6,650	3,329	25,404	30.1
1810[b]	22,793	150	9,615	0	32,558	29.5
1822	40,616	1,115	13,685	0	55,416	24.7
1827[b]	34,067	152	8,321	0	42,540	19.5
1836	42,445	—	14,906	5,684	63,035	26.0
1838[b]	42,312	—	14,928	5,717	62,957	26.1
1887	425,370	—	8,005	0	433,375	1.8

Sources: *1778*, José Luis Moreno, "La estructura social y demográfica de la ciudad de Buenos Aires en el año 1778." *Anuario del Instituto de Investigaciones Históricas* 8 (Rosario, 1965): 151–70; *1806*, Marta B. Goldberg, "La población negra y mulata de la ciudad de Buenos Aires, 1810–1840," *Desarrollo Económico* 16 (April-June 1976): 75–99; *1810*, Goldberg, "La población negra"; *1822*, Goldberg, "La población negra"; *1827*, figures provided by Karla Robinson while writing a Ph.D. dissertation, "The Occupational Structure of Post-Independence Buenos Aires"; *1836*, Goldberg, "La población negra"; *1838*, Goldberg, "La población negra"; *1887*, *Censo general de población, edificación, comercio e industrias de la ciudad de Buenos Aires* (Buenos Aires, 1889), 2:56–57.

[a] Column calculated excluding unspecified column from total.

[b] Incomplete results.

to find a community whose social activities and economic progress furnished material and photographs for an article on "The People of Color," though the tone of the piece was distinctly elegiac: "Little by little, this race is dying. Slowly . . . the black race of the children of the sun marches toward its death."[9] Similar articles have appeared in Argentine magazines as recently as 1971.[10]

THE CENSUSES

Table 5.1 is a summary of the results of eight censuses of Buenos Aires taken between 1778 and 1887. They reveal that the Afro-Argentines comprised roughly 30 percent of the city's population from 1780 to 1810. There was then a gradual decline to 25 percent in 1822 and 20 percent in 1827. The 1830s witnessed an apparent recovery to 26 percent, followed by a precipitous drop during the fifty-year period ending in 1887. The proportional decline that occurred over that half-century is so marked that it is hardly surprising that the bulk of the nineteenth-century observations concerning the decline of the community should come from this period. But all too easily passed over in this comparison is the tale told by the actual population figures, the absolute numbers representing the men, women, and children present in the city on census day. A comparison of the years for which census figures are complete, 1778, 1822, 1836, and 1887, reveals a pattern of steady growth between 1778 and 1836, a period during which the city's Afro-Argentine population more than doubled in size. The decline in absolute numbers did not occur until the second half of the century. Even in absolute terms this drop was an extraordinary one: the 1887 black population was 53.7 percent of the 1836 black population. The Afro-Argentine community had declined by almost half, though it still remained larger than the population of 1778.

The half-century between 1838 and 1887 is clearly crucial in understanding what happened to the Afro-Argentines, but by an irony of history neither of the city's censuses of that period (the municipal census of 1855 and the national census of 1869) recorded race as a category of information. The censuses of 1836 and 1838 also recorded very little information on the city's inhabitants—the only data gathered were the name of the household head in each living unit and the number of white people and black people living in the house. Thus it is impossible to obtain age-sex characteristics of the population, data on professions, or information other than mere totals. If one plans to use municipal censuses to analyze the demographic history of the city, he is thrown back on the earlier censuses of 1806–7, 1810, and 1827. The original canvassing sheets of the census of 1822 do not survive, though the published totals are available.[11]

For the purposes of this study, stratified samples were taken of the 1810 and 1827 municipal censuses of Buenos Aires and then analyzed. A description of those samples may be found in Appendix B. Since the samples are stratified, they cannot and should not be used to discuss the relative racial composition of Buenos Aires's population over time. Readers seeking that information should refer to the published census totals summarized in Table 5.1.

The 1810 and 1827 censuses were selected for analysis because they represent the city at two very different points in its nineteenth-century development. The census of 1810 (the manuscripts of which are much more complete than those of the census of 1806–7) portrays the city at the end of 230 years of colonial development. It offers a picture of the extent of race mixture, of the respective characteristics of the slave and free black populations, and of the demographic differences between whites and blacks. The 1827 census provides similar data for the city at the end of the independence wars which it had fought against Spain. The intervening 17 years had witnessed a substantial relative decline in the black population, from roughly 30 percent of the city's total to 20 per-

Table 5.2. Results by Race of the Samples of the 1810 and 1827
Municipal Censuses of Buenos Aires

Nonblacks	1810	1827	Blacks	1810	1827
Whites	944	1,256	Pardos	201	436
Indians	13	37	Morenos	372	597
Mestizos	8	13	Unknown	269	0
Total	965	1,306	Total	842	1,033

Source: Author's sample of the 1810 and 1827 municipal censuses of Buenos Aires,
discussed in Appendix B. Census manuscripts located in Archivo General de la Nación,
1810: 9 10-7-1; 1827, 10 23-5-5 and 23-5-6.

cent, suggesting that the causes of the decline and eventual disappearance of the Afro-Argentines were already present and taking effect.
An examination of the demographic trends revealed by the two censuses,
therefore, should bring to light the underlying causes of that disappearance.

The two samples produced the totals listed in Table 5.2. A word of explanation is in order concerning the "unknown" Afro-Argentine category in the 1810 sample: many of the census takers simply left the race
category blank whenever they counted a white person. Some also left
that space blank when they counted black people, but they entered
"free" or "slave" to denote the person's legal condition. When either of
these words appeared, the individual was coded as a slave or free person
of unknown Afro-Argentine race.

As summarized in Chapter 1, the decline of Buenos Aires's black population has usually been explained in terms of four factors: the abolition
of the slave trade; high mortality rates and relatively low fertility rates
among the Afro-Argentine population; very high death rates among
black males during the wars of the 1810–70 period; and race mixture
and gradual lightening, which was exacerbated by the shortage of black
males produced by wartime casualties. We shall now turn to the census
samples and the other demographic sources available to see what light
they shed on these four explanations.

The previous chapter discussed the abolition of the slave trade in 1813
and the subsequent amendments to that legislation. Data contained in
the censuses of 1810 and 1827 suggest, though they do not conclusively
demonstrate, that the 1813 decree did have a significant retarding effect
on the slave trade to the city. Table 4.5 demonstrated that, of those Africans resident in Buenos Aires in 1827 whose date of arrival was recorded
in the census of that year, 79.4 percent had arrived in the city prior to
1813. The decline of the post-1813 traffic in humans becomes even more
apparent when one takes into account the mortality that by 1827 had

Table 5.3. Afro-Argentines by Birthplace in the Samples of the 1810 and 1827
Municipal Censuses of Buenos Aires

	1810			1827			
	Males	Females	Total	Males	Females	Unknown	Total
Buenos Aires	33	37	70	210	433	1	644
Rest of Argentina	3	2	5	30	60	—	90
Unknown location in Argentina	20	28	48	0	0	—	0
Africa	34	28	62	120	128	—	248
South America	0	0	0	15	22	—	37
Other	2	2	4	6	8	—	14
Unknown	345	308	653	0	0	—	0
Total	437	405	842	381	651	1	1,033

Source: See Table 5.2.

greatly shrunk the African population that had entered prior to 1813. It
is important, however, to recognize that almost a third of the Africans
recorded in that census had no date of entry listed, making it impossible
to extrapolate from those figures with any great degree of certainty.

An alternative approach to the question of how much the slave trade
declined is to compare the African representations in the city in the two
census years (see Table 5.3). Again the shortcomings of those documents
pose problems. The officials encharged with the 1810 census often failed
to record birthplace, especially when counting black people. Place of
birth remains unknown for over three-quarters of the Afro-Argentines
canvassed in 1810 and for 20 percent of the whites. Of 189 Afro-
Argentines whose birthplace was listed, 62, or 32.9 percent, were
Africans. By 1827 the percentage of Africans in the black population
had declined to 24.0 percent.

As will be discussed later in this chapter, the frequent failure of the
1810 census to list race (pardo or moreno) or birthplace for Afro-
Argentines appears to have resulted in an undercount of the African and

Table 5.4. Birthplaces of Afro-Argentine Enlistees, 1810–20 and 1850–60

	1810–20			1850–60		
	Pardos	Morenos	Total	Pardos	Morenos	Total
Buenos Aires	22	11	33	139	127	266
Rest of Argentina	28	48	76	60	30	90
Africa	2	149	151	2	12	14
South America	5	16	21	23	43	66
Other	1	9	10	3	6	9
Total	58	233	291	227	218	445

Source: Archivo General de la Nación, 3 59-1-1, 59-1-6, 59-2-1, 59-2-4, 59-2-7.

moreno populations. Certainly the results obtained from the 1810 census are at sharp variance with those obtained by tabulating Afro-Argentine army enlistment records (in which the recruiter was required to record birthplace) for two decades, 1810–20 and 1850–60 (see Table 5.4). Africans made up somewhat over half of the enlistees between 1810 and 1820 but had dwindled to 3 percent by mid-century. It seems highly likely that those Afro-Argentines listed in the census of 1810 with unknown birthplaces included large numbers of Africans whose origins were of little or no interest to the census takers.

But for the purposes of this discussion, the significant question is not whether the trade declined, but whether that decline in the number of African migrants to the city had any adverse effect on the growth of the Afro-Argentine population. To cite the case of the United States, the

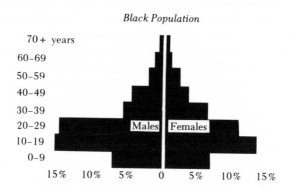

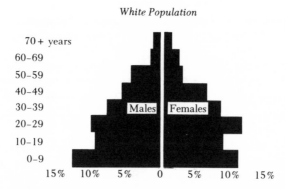

Figure 5.1. Age-Sex Pyramid Constructed from a Sample of the 1810 Municipal Census of Buenos Aires

termination of the slave trade to that country in 1807 had little or no impact on the continued expansion of the black population, which since the early 1700s had enjoyed a substantial excess of births over deaths. Natural increase served to maintain its average annual growth rate at more than 2 percent throughout the 1800–1860 period.[12]

Figure 5.1 is an age-sex pyramid constructed from the 1810 sample. An immediately striking difference between the black and white populations is the concentration of blacks in the young adult category. Among the white population the modal age category is the 0–9 group, exactly what one would expect in a preindustrial society in which birth control was probably little practiced. Among the blacks, however, the modal category is the 10–19 age group. And 56.4 percent of the blacks fall into the 10–29 age category, while only 38.4 percent of the whites do. This predominance of young adults is even more marked in the slave population than in the free: 61.5 percent of the slaves were between 10 and 29, while 38.2 percent of the free blacks were between those ages, a figure essentially the same as that of the whites.

The slave trade was clearly responsible for the high proportion of young adults in the black population. The years from 20 to 35 were those in which slaves experienced maximum productivity.[13] When the Uruguayan government sought to reopen the abolished slave trade on a limited basis in 1832, it stipulated that Africans imported under the new legislation were to be 16 years of age or younger.[14] The 1827 census shows that, of the Africans living in Buenos Aires that year, their median age when they had arrived in the city was 15.8. The demands of the market dictated that slaves be brought to the New World as teenagers. This had the effect of swelling the 10–29 age group among black males and females alike.

The concentration of black people in the 15–29 age category should have provided an ideal childbearing population. The proportion of females in the childbearing years, 15 to 44, was 59.7 percent of all black females in the sample, 53.0 percent of all white females in the sample. Furthermore, the median age of black women in the childbearing years was 24.7; for white women in those years it was 28.1. Nevertheless, black replacement rates proved significantly lower than white. The lack of comprehensive birth registers for the colonial period precludes the calculation of birth rates from vital register data, but an alternative index is the child-woman ratio, the ratio between children aged 0–4 and women aged 15–44. This ratio, generally expressed in number of children per 1000 women, is a fairly sensitive indicator of fertility performance in the previous five years, and is especially useful for examining fertility in small geopolitical areas such as states, counties, or

Table 5.5. Ratio of Children Aged 0 to 4 per 1000 Women Aged 15 to 44 in the Samples of the 1810 and 1827 Municipal Censuses of Buenos Aires

	1810	1827
Whites	400.8	365.9
Blacks	256.5	183.1

Sources: See Table 5.2.

cities. In the case of the 1810 census, the ratio given in Table 5.5 shows that the black population lagged far behind the white in reproducing itself. The ratio of white children to white women aged 15–44 was 400.8 per 1000; among the blacks, the ratio was 256.5 per 1000. The ratio was especially low among slaves, 231.2, while among free blacks it was 363.6. This is partly explained by the manumission strategies of slave families. Studies of manumission have found that when families had saved enough money to buy the freedom of some of their members, there was a tendency to purchase the freedom of children first. Infants could be bought out of slavery fairly cheaply due to the high probability of their dying before reaching adulthood.[15] Thus, many children of slave mothers were doubtless free by 1810 and served to raise the child-woman ratio for free blacks. What is important to recognize is the fact that the ratio for the black population as a whole was almost 40 percent lower than for the white.

In fact, the number of black children was barely adequate for replacement purposes. By way of comparison, the child-woman ratio for the United States in 1960 was 488 per 1000; in Costa Rica it was 875; in England it was 336. The nation to which the Afro-Argentine child-woman ratio was closest was Sweden, which in 1960 had a ratio of 286 per 1000. At that time Sweden had one of the lowest growth rates in the world.[16]

High infant mortality severely reduced the reproduction rates of the black community. In 1815 the city published a report on births of libertos since 1813, i.e., children born to slave mothers. The figures yielded by that report indicate a male infant mortality rate during the first two years of life of 399 per 1000 live births, and a female infant mortality rate of 352 per 1000 live births.[17] Similar figures are not available for the white population at that time, but research by the Argentine historian Marta Goldberg has demonstrated that infant mortality between 1827 and 1831 was significantly higher among the black population than among the white. The mean annual infant mortality rate (deaths during the first year of life per 1000 live births) was 284.3 for the white population, 350.4 for the black.[18]

Black fertility was slightly higher than white, but not enough to overcome the differential between the two races' infant mortality. In 1822 the number of live births per 1000 black women aged 15 to 49 was 50.5, while the white rate was 48.3. By 1837 these figures had risen slightly to 53.9 per 1000 for the black population, 50.8 for the white.[19] Roughly equal fertility, combined with significantly higher infant mortality among the Afro-Argentines, resulted in a widening of the gap between child-woman ratios recorded in 1810. According to the census of that year the white ratio was 1.4 times higher than the black; by 1827 it was twice as high, and the black ratio had dropped below the level required to sustain the Afro-Argentine population.

The deteriorating demographic position of the black population documented in these statistics is further demonstrated in calculations

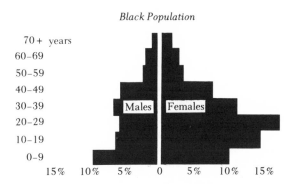

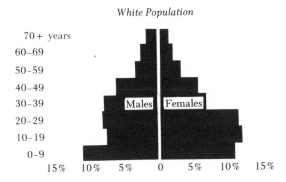

Figure 5.2. Age-Sex Pyramid Constructed from a Sample of the 1827 Municipal Census of Buenos Aires

made by Goldberg. Utilizing published totals from the census of 1822 and from vital statistics registers of that year, she sets total black mortality in 1822 a third higher than white, 40.9 per 1000 as compared to 30.2 per 1000. She computes the net reproduction rate for the black population in that year as 0.96; in another calcuation, she uses the admittedly incomplete birth and death totals for the decade between 1822 and 1831 to arrive at an even lower rate of 0.19.[20] A net reproduction rate of 1.0 implies that a population is maintaining itself at a stable and constant level; a rate less than 1.0 indicates that the population is declining; a rate of 0.19 implies that the population would virtually disappear within two generations.

More evidence of the black population's grave prospects may be found in Figure 5.2, age-sex pyramids for the black and white populations taken from the sample of the 1827 census. The most immediately striking characteristic of these pyramids is their sexual imbalance. In 1810 the masculinity index, the number of males per 100 females, was 107.9 in the black population, 103.4 in the white. By 1827 that index had plummeted to 58.5 for the black population and declined to 90.3 for the whites. This imbalance was especially marked in the 15–34 age group, where the ratio was 40.5 black men per 100 black women, and 74.9 white men per 100 white women. Clearly the years of war had taken their toll, lending credence to the traditional explanation that the black population disappeared because its males were killed in the wars. Bereft of its men, the community lacked the earning power to buy the food, clothing, and shelter which might have lowered the mortality rates registered during the 1820s. Also, the removal of a large portion of the adult male population would be expected to impair the community's ability to reproduce itself.

All of the indicators are in agreement: the censuses of 1822 and 1827, combined with the partial vital statistics available for the period, paint a picture of a community in sharp decline and heading inexorably toward extinction. It is surprising, then, to find the 1836 and 1838 censuses reporting the existence of the largest black population yet registered in any municipal census, nearly 15,000. The deficiencies of these documents, which recorded very few data on the city's population, do not permit detailed investigation to determine the causes behind this unexpected increase. If Goldberg's calculations are correct and the 1822 reproduction rate of 0.96 held for the 1822–36 period, one would expect the black population at the end of those fourteen years to have been slightly under 8000. Instead it was almost double that figure.

One possible explanation for the increase is the post-1827 privateer traffic in slaves and Governor Rosas's reopening of the slave trade between 1831 and 1833. The nineteenth-century historian Vicente Fidel López estimated that by 1840 Buenos Aires contained between 12,000 and 15,000 Africans brought into the city during the War with Brazil and after.[21] This estimate is equal to the entire black population registered in the 1836 and 1838 censuses and therefore seems excessive. It is true that one not infrequently encounters post-1827 African arrivals in official records of the 1830s and 1840s.[22] And the vigorous activity of the African mutual aid societies in those decades (see Chapter 8) may well have been due to the recent arrival of slaves and libertos whose African allegiances were still strong. But even if López's estimate was as much as double the actual number of Africans in the city, the black community would have been more heavily African than at any time in its history. This does not seem possible, given the previously cited enlistment records that show the African percentage of the city's black enlistees dwindling from 50 percent in the 1810s to 3 percent by the 1850s, and the median age of 62.4 recorded for foreign-born black people in the municipal census of 1855 (see Chapter 4).

Internal migration seems to have contributed somewhat to maintenance of the city's black community. It is clear that by the late 1820s there was a flow of migrants to Buenos Aires from Uruguay and the interior of Argentina. The 1827 census indicates that 10.3 percent of the black population and 8.4 percent of the white population had been born either in the Argentine interior or in Uruguay. Examination of census returns from several Argentine provinces and the Uruguayan capital of Montevideo suggests that the only significant stream of reverse migration was from Buenos Aires to Montevideo; population exchange between Buenos Aires and the interior seems to have redounded to the advantage of the capital.[23]

It is unclear to what extent migration within Buenos Aires province added to or subtracted from the city's population. The province's Statistical Register reveals that by the 1850s the bulk of the black population in the province resided in the ranch country outside the capital, but this urban-to-rural transfer of population appears to have been due not to migration but to natural increase. During the 1820s the register showed a consistent excess of deaths over births among the urban black population, while in the countryside black births exceeded deaths by almost 25 percent. By the 1850s black urban births exceeded deaths by 29 percent, while in the countryside black births were more than double the number of black deaths. Clearly the rural areas of the province formed a more healthy environment for black people than the capital. This resulted in a shift of Afro-Argentine population from the city to the hinterland, as may be seen in a comparison of birth and marriage figures from the register. In the years 1822–25 city births made up 62.4 percent of Afro-Argentine births in the province; by the 1850s city births accounted for only 40.9 percent of black births in the province. In the 1820s 64.3 percent of the province's black marriage partners were from the capital; between 1856 and 1875 only 31.1 percent were from the capital.

Lacking any sort of data concerning intraprovince migration, we can only speculate about whether the province's rural areas attracted black migration from the city or whether they served as a generating area to replenish the city's population by sending a stream of in-migrants to the capital. World demographic experience, which has shown a steady pattern of rural-to-urban migration over the last one hundred fifty years, would argue for the latter. So does the black experience in the United States, where black migration to the cities has been a constant since the Civil War. As in Buenos Aires, unhealthier living conditions in the cities produced higher urban death rates than rural; they also reduced black fertility, so that black birth rates were higher in rural areas than in urban ones.[24] Black urban natural increase rates in the 1860–1920 period were negative, migration being the only force that sustained the black urban populations.[25] The Brazilian province of São Paulo is another example. The black population of São Paulo city experienced negative or very low growth rates following emancipation, but was sustained by constant migration from the rural areas of the province, where conditions for blacks and whites alike appear to have been healthier.[26]

But would migration and the continuation of the slave trade have been sufficient to account for the remarkable rebound in the black population documented in the 1836 and 1838 censuses? And as we question this unexpected reversal of black population decline, we might also consider the period encompassed by the 1810 and 1822 censuses. The 1810 census showed a community suffering from very low replacement rates. Nevertheless, extrapolation of the incomplete results of the 1810 census suggests that the black population of the city in that year was 11,837, and by 1822 that population had grown to 13,685.[27] This growth occurred despite a sharp reduction in the slave trade and the drafting of almost 2000 slave troops and an unknown number of free black troops to fight the Spanish. How, then, does one account for the registered growth?

The question is unanswerable. Use of the official demographic records available would inevitably lead us to conclude that the Afro-Argentines should have disappeared completely by the 1850s or 1860s, if not earlier. Plagued by high mortality, even higher infant mortality, and, by

1827, an extraordinary sexual imbalance, the community should logically have faded away to nothing over the course of the first half of the century. The censuses of 1822, 1836, and 1838 reveal that this was not happening.

ALTERNATIVE EVIDENCE

Other data further suggest that the decline of the black community simply did not occur to the extent that historians have traditionally thought it did. If the logic of the demographic rates were true, one would expect to find that by 1900 the Afro-Argentines simply did not form a visible element within the city's population. Yet the frequency with which Afro-Argentines appear in random newspaper and magazine photographs of the period is truly startling. Photos of crowds are not of sufficiently high quality to allow one to pick out individual Afro-Argentines, but pictures of individuals or small groups include black people with unexpected regularity. A 1900 photo of five firefighters injured at a fire includes one black man, Corporal Enrique Muñoz. A photo of three policemen who distinguished themselves during the great heat wave of the same year shows two white sergeants and a black corporal. A shot of a political candidate's office during the election of 1900 caught a well-dressed young black man standing behind the desk of the candidate. A 1902 advertisement for a faith healer included several testimonials, one of which was from a black man named José González, who attested that he had been cured of rheumatism, stomach trouble, and deafness in five sessions. An 1899 article on Buenos Aires's insane asylum was illustrated with photographs of nine "psychotic types," two of whom (the kleptomaniac and the compulsive) were black. When the Beneficent Society presented its annual Prizes for Virtue in 1900 to nine deserving women, one of them was black. Another annual ceremony in the city occurred during Holy Week, when a delegation of town worthies washed the feet of twelve needy men chosen at random. A 1901 photograph of those twelve men showed one of them to be Afro-Argentine. A portrait of seven soldiers who won prizes for marksmanship in a 1900 competition included a black sergeant. A 1901 feature on a Spanish American holiday, the Day of the Dead, contained pictures from festivities at the Recoleta cemetery. Several of the people in the accompanying photos were black youths working as flower vendors. Most interestingly, an article on the first six babies to be born in Buenos Aires in the twentieth century included one black girl, Rosita Rosales, born at 11:30 a.m. on New Year's Day, 1900.[28]

Another inexplicable phenomenon is that of the Afro-Argentine press, treated in detail in Chapter 10. Of the twenty newspapers and magazines published by Afro-Argentines in the nineteenth century, only four were published prior to 1870. The black press in Buenos Aires did not really flourish until the final decades of the century, a period in which the black community had supposedly dwindled to nothing. Even more peculiar, two of those papers, *La Igualdad* and *El Tambor*, published during the 1860s and 1870s, were subsidized by political parties seeking black support in the presidential elections of 1868 and 1874.[29] Afro-Argentines must have accounted for a significant part of the voting population to draw this kind of political patronage.

The contradictions are compounded when one compares the census totals of the 1800–1830 period with the comments of European travelers on the racial composition of the city. Table 5.1 showed that none of the censuses of the period placed the white population at less than two-thirds of the city's total. This is in striking contrast to the observations recorded by writers like Alexander Gillespie, a British officer captured by the Argentines during the English invasions. Writing in 1807 on his several months' captivity in Buenos Aires, he estimated the population of the city at 41,000: "A fifth were white, the rest being a caste composed of various states of mixture and progressive alteration, from the black man to the blondest European. Though color may improve, even in the most refined cases there persists a trace of the features that recall the true origin of many of them."[30]

Gillespie's observations were corroborated by Samuel Haigh, another Englishman who lived ten years in Buenos Aires during the 1820s. Writing in 1827, he reported that the city and its environs contained 100,000 inhabitants. "Pure whites are not numerous, and the most common is a caste of white, Indian, and black, so mixed that it would be difficult to fix its members' true origins."[31] Compare Haigh's comments to the census of 1827, conducted the same year he was writing, in which over three-quarters of the city is described as white—the conflict is striking. Furthermore, the French traveler Mellet wrote in 1809 that Buenos Aires was one-third white, while John and William Robertson put the white population in the 1810s at one-fifth of the total.[32] Woodbine Parish was the only European visitor to Buenos Aires whose observations agree with the censuses.

It is essential to keep in mind that these sources were all European; their concepts of race had been formed in a Continental environment rather than a creole American one. Insensitive to the etiquette of the New World, they labeled an Afro-European a mulatto, while in Buenos Aires or Caracas such an individual, especially if he had acquired personal wealth and prestige, might well be accepted as white. At the same time it is essential to remember that Latin Americans, and especially the Argentines, swore allegiance to the same racial concepts and mores held by the Europeans, holding white skin and European ancestry to be the most valuable asset a person could have. As the Swedish traveler Jean Graaner found when he visited Buenos Aires in 1816, the porteños "pride themselves, even today, on how their ancestors' blood has remained tolerably pure or with little mixture of African blood."[33] However, although the Argentines sought to adhere as closely as possible to European racial standards, the evidence presented by European visitors to the capital suggests that in fact they had deviated from them significantly, especially in the area of assigning race in censuses. One finds occasional evidence of such deviation in Argentine sources as well as European. In an 1853 editorial on the shortage of domestic servants in the city, the newspaper *La Tribuna* made the startling observation that in Buenos Aires "for every one hundred white people, there are that many or more of color."[34] This comment, made fifteen years after a municipal census had set the black population at only a quarter of the city's total, is puzzling indeed.

At this point a new factor must be introduced into discussion: the possibility that the city's censuses and vital statistics registers do not accurately reflect racial realities in the city. The reliability of censuses taken in preindustrial, largely illiterate societies is notoriously problematic. Deficiencies in coverage, consistency, and accuracy of information are endemic in nineteenth-century censuses taken throughout Europe and the Americas.[35] Buenos Aires's municipal censuses displayed all these failings and others besides. The census of 1806–7 was administered so poorly that eventually it had to be abandoned in an uncompleted state.[36] The census was conducted again in 1810, but several precincts were never canvassed, and the categories of information collected varied so widely from one part of the city to another that the results had to be published separately by precincts rather than in comprehensive totals. The results of the 1827 census were never tabulated.[37] The 1854 municipal census produced such an undercount of the population that it was officially repudiated and a new census taken in 1855.[38] This was particularly unlucky for the purposes of this study, since the 1854 census forms asked for information on race, while the 1855 forms did not.[39]

In addition to these basic failings, North and South American censuses have demonstrated a consistent tendency to underenumerate black people. To take the example of the United States, the census of 1870 was found to have undercounts of the Southern population as a whole, and especially the black population. The census of 1890 was found to have undercounted the national Afro-American population. Postcensus surveys have revealed that as recently as 1960 Afro-Americans were undernumerated by about 10 percent. Larger miscounts occurred in 1920, 1940, and 1950.[40]

These underenumerations of Afro-Americans in the United States were not a chance phenomenon. Rather, they were due to causes found throughout the Americas. Traditionally black people tended to occupy the least desirable houses and neighborhoods. This was particularly true in cities; nineteenth-century descriptions of urban housing in the United States recall how black people sheltered themselves in basements, abandoned shacks, and run-down buildings, habitations not considered fit for whites.[41] Census takers often found it difficult to locate these out-of-the-way, ramshackle housing units. Reluctant to venture into the noisome alleys of the black neighborhoods and unwilling to face the hostility of the inhabitants, they missed many residents of such areas. The result was the consistent underenumeration of Afro-Americans registered in United States censuses until the present.

Similar conditions existed in Argentina. Though black housing in Buenos Aires does not seem to have been as squalid as in United States cities, Afro-Argentines tended to inhabit the least desirable buildings in the city. One center of black settlement was the parish of Monserrat, a "gloomy and filthy" neighborhood overrun by thieves, prostitutes, and underworld characters.[42] The infamous *conventillos*, a barrack-like form of lower-class housing, first appeared in Buenos Aires in Monserrat and other black neighborhoods and were inhabited mainly by black people until the 1860s and 1870s, when the Afro-Argentines were pushed out by immigrants from Europe.[43] Many black people then lodged themselves in shacks in the southside neighborhood of Barracas, along the polluted Riachuelo River. To take an analogous case, North American census takers showed little diligence in canvassing such neighborhoods. There is no evidence to suggest that census takers in Buenos Aires were any more conscientious.

Of particular importance in considering the sexual imbalance registered in the 1827 census is the demonstrated tendency of North American censuses to underenumerate Afro-American males between the ages of 15 and 35. Undercounts of the black population have traditionally been especially severe for that age and sex group. Postcensus analysis of the 1960 census, for example, showed undercounts of almost 20 percent for 25-to-29-year-old males and 18 percent for 30-to-34-year-olds.[44] The reasons for an undercount of this dimension are several, but the primary ones are the high mobility of young black males and their frequent reluctance to get involved with official government representatives of any sort, be they census takers, tax collectors, policemen, or others.

There was ample reason for young black males to have been wary of Buenos Aires census takers throughout the period from 1810 to 1870. We have already discussed the discriminatory draft decrees which placed a disproportionately heavy burden on the Afro-Argentines. Virtually all the censuses taken in the city during this period had as one of their purposes the determination of the manpower pool from which military recruits could be drawn.[45] Indeed, three slave censuses taken between 1813 and 1820 had that as their sole object and did not even bother to count women.[46] The same was true of an 1833 census of the city's males.[47]

Though black men were initially more than willing to take up arms in defense of the province, as the years of warfare rolled on and the toll of Afro-Argentine dead went higher and higher, it is not unreasonable to presume that a certain number of black men may have sought to avoid the census takers and thus the draft. This would have been especially true with the census of 1827, taken during the War with Brazil, after seventeen years of almost uninterrupted warfare. Also, as will be seen in Chapter 7, desertion rates among black and white units in the 1810s and 1820s were extremely high, much higher than death rates. Deserters at large in the city would certainly have done their best to avoid the census enumerators in 1827, further helping to account for the decline in masculinity indices registered among both races.

A final consideration in evaluating the reliability of census data on the Afro-Argentines is the complex question of defining exactly who is black and who is not. Historians have long recognized the flexibility employed in Latin American societies in assigning racial labels. To say that an individual is white is not necessarily to say that the individual is of more or less pure European descent. Numerous cases have been documented of economically or politically successful Latin Americans of mixed race experiencing an informal lightening of their social race in recognition of their higher status.[48] A classic anecdote from Brazil illustrates this phenomenon. A European visitor to a colonial Brazilian town was surprised to see a noticeably dark-skinned man serving as a local official. He asked a townsperson if the official, also a man of considerable personal wealth, was not a mulatto. Replied the townsperson, "he was, but he's not any more."[49]

Though Brazil is the Latin American society most frequently cited for the variability of its racial labels, the same tendency existed and exists throughout Spanish America to a greater or lesser degree. In fact, in the closing years of the colonial period, the royal government established a procedure whereby nonwhites could legally purchase the racial labels and prerogatives of white people. *Gracias al sacar,* as this system was known, was Spain's attempt to generate revenue from a practice that had proceeded quietly and informally for centuries in the New World.[50]

Bernardino Rivadavia (1780–1845), Argentina's first president. Rivadavia's family was rumored to include African ancestors, and "Dr. Chocolate" was one of the unflattering sobriquets applied to him by his political opponents. This portrait probably dates from around the period of his presidency (1825–27). Photograph courtesy Archivo General de la Nación.

A number of important individuals in nineteenth-century Argentina seem to have been men of mixed Afro-Indio-European descent who were accepted by the society of the time as white. The Taboada family, one of the pillars of the ruling oligarchy in the province of Santiago del Estero, was known throughout Argentina for its numerous dark-skinned members.[51] José Bernardo Monteagudo, an early patriot and subsequent Minister of War and Navy for Peru, is believed to have had black ancestry.[52] Argentines are familiar with the debate over the racial background of Bernardino Rivadavia, Argentina's first president. Labeled as white in the 1810 census of Buenos Aires, he also served as an officer in a white militia regiment. Still, rumors concerning his African ancestry were sufficiently persistent to earn him the nickname of Dr. Chocolate among his political opponents. An Englishman who wrote an anonymous memoir of his own residence in Buenos Aires during the 1820s described the president as dark-skinned, observing in passing that Rivadavia's appearance "offers some peculiarities" which would have made him an easy victim of English caricaturists.[53] The historian J. A. Rogers included Rivadavia as one of eight Latin Americans in his biographical anthology *Great Men of Color*.[54]

The stigma of black ancestry was a heavy cross to bear in the society of Buenos Aires; whenever the possibility arose of shrugging it off and walking away as white, only a rare person would have failed to take advantage of it. It is exceedingly difficult to document the process by which Afro-Argentines left the black racial category and entered the white, since an integral part of such a process was the destruction or obscuring of records concerning one's African descent. Only exhaustive and tedious research into the ancestry of hundreds of individuals could definitively establish the rate at which people of mixed race experienced an alteration of their social and legal racial status. However, there is a good deal of indirect evidence which serves to suggest both the mechanism by which this process occurred and the frequency with which it happened.

TRIGUEÑO: NEITHER BLACK NOR WHITE

Shortly after independence was declared in 1810, a new term to denote racial background began to appear in the official records of Buenos Aires province. That term was *trigueño*, literally "wheat-colored." The racial sense of the word is vague, perhaps purposely so. Consultation of two nineteenth-century Spanish dictionaries failed to produce any racial definition. Conversations with four Argentine historians specializing in the period resulted in a consensus that it means "dark-skinned" and may be applied to mulattoes, mestizos, Afro-Indians, swarthy-complexioned Europeans (e.g., Sicilians, Andalusians, or Portuguese), or any combination of the above. Thus the word has a very broad application and does not necessarily or automatically imply African descent, which the terms mulatto and pardo always do.

The term *trigueño* virtually never appears in colonial records, but following independence it was used frequently in such documents as lists of prison inmates, city employees, and, above all, army recruits. Chapter 7 contains a tabulation of the racial composition of several Argentine regiments recruited during the decades of the 1810s, 1820s, and 1850s. Although these figures are not representative of the racial composition of the Argentine army, since they are taken only from regiments in which significant numbers of Afro-Argentines served, they show that trigueño was a commonly used racial label in army enlistment records. In three regiments recruited between 1813 and 1818, 32.0 percent of the enlistees were trigueños. During the 1820s this proportion rose to 37.8 and then dropped slightly to 35.8 in the 1850s.

The extensive use of this term would inevitably result in a decrease of an officially documentable Afro-Argentine population. When individuals were labeled trigueño, they had escaped the automatic assumption of African ancestry which applied to a pardo, moreno, mulatto, or negro. They had succeeded in passing over to an intermediate category, which included more than a few native Europeans.[55] The question that must be answered is to what extent it is possible to document the application of this racial term to Afro-Argentines. Data from Argentina and other Spanish American societies suggests that the tendency was strong and widespread. Let us first examine the evidence from other countries.

The only Spanish American society for which extensive documentation on the use of the word trigueño exists is Puerto Rico, a society in which race mixture is probably even more prevalent than in nineteenth-century Buenos Aires. One Puerto Rican writer, Elena Padilla, offers an explanation of the term.

The term *"trigueño"* (brunet) is applied both to white persons who have brown or black hair and tan or light olive skin color, and, by extension, to persons whose physical appearance would place them as Negroes if that were the only criterion of race. This not being so, *trigueño* is used to avoid the term "Negro" for persons of respect, because, besides race, there are other social and personal factors, such as wealth and education, which determine a man's worth and social position. It is not proper to call persons of respect "Negro."

She goes on to add that "persons who are being talked about in their absence may be referred to as Negroes, but they will probably be described as *trigueños* in their presence."[56] Other autobiographical literature reinforces this impression of trigueño as a social device by which black people avoid the stigma of their African ancestry. One of the characters in Oscar Lewis's *La Vida* comes from Puerto Rico to live in Florida, where she finds that though she was considered a trigueña in Puerto Rico, she is black in the United States and is unable to visit her white sister when the sister is interned in a segregated hospital.[57] The central conflict of an autobiographical novel by Piri Thomas, born in the United States of Puerto Rican parents, is his anguish over being the only mulatto sibling in a family of five children. Piri eventually embraces his own blackness and urges his mulatto father to do the same. "Poppa, what's wrong with not being white? What's so wrong with being *tregeño*?"[58]

Could the use of trigueño be one cause of the steady and inexplicable decline of Puerto Rico's black population registered in censuses from 1860 to the present? This evidence suggests the desire of both the blacks and the whites in the island politely to ignore the extent of African ancestry in the population; has this desire found expression in Puerto Rico's demographic sources as well?[59] Leslie Rout provides evidence linking the term trigueño with underenumeration of Afro-Peruvians. Surveys in Peru in 1931 and 1935 discovered that large numbers of Indians and mestizos described themselves for census purposes as white, while Afro-Peruvians tended to describe themselves as trigueño. These surveys provided material for several scholars to question the accuracy of the 1940 Peruvian census, in which less than 2 percent of the population was counted as *negro*.[60] In its 1920 census Nicaragua explicitly established a trigueño category to include Afro-Europeans and Afro-Indians.[61]

The porteños' use of the term trigueño seems to have paralleled its use in the countries discussed above. Trigueño slaves appear regularly in sales and manumission documents and are prominent in military records. Of 121 enlistments encountered for the Seventh Battalion of Libertos, 6.6 percent were trigueños, and another 1.7 percent were light enough to be classified as white.[62] Enlistment records contain other interesting cases, such as Francisco José Albarao, a Buenos Aires–born trigueño who was assigned to Company Two of Free Pardos in the Second Regiment of Patricios.[63] Victor Luques, a porteño who joined the First Battalion in 1854, has two surviving enlistment records: one describes him as a trigueño, the other as a pardo.[64]

Another indication exists that although trigueño could be applied to whites and nonwhites alike, it was more closely associated with African descent than was generally admitted. In annual reports on the state-run

Women's General Hospital, death figures were published in two columns, white and *de color*. Throughout the 1856–75 period, black deaths regularly outnumbered white, but beginning in 1873, the margin by which black deaths exceeded white became quite striking. That year there were 166 black deaths to 70 white ones, the following year 186 black deaths to 98 white ones, and in 1875, 180 to 50. Since in previous years the excess had never been so marked, the hospital officials apparently felt obliged to offer an explanation, and in 1875 they appended to the bottom of the table, "in the books of the Hospital the trigueñas have been considered as colored."[65] This admission is of great importance, for it strongly suggests that though trigueños were of a racial class that made them liable to be counted as nonwhite, in fact they seldom were in official records. In an unusual case in which trigueños were counted as black, the record keepers apparently felt it necessary to stipulate that this was being done, which implies that the more normal procedure was to class them as white.

It is also important to note that for 1868, 1869, and 1872 (in 1870 and 1871 death figures were not divided by race), black deaths reported by the hospital represented 320 out of 634 total deaths, 50.4 percent. From 1873 to 1875, black deaths represented 532 out of 750, 70.9 percent. Adding trigueñas to the black category had increased its representation by 40 percent and its absolute number of deaths by two-thirds.

Finally, logic dictates that trigueño would in fact be more closely associated with black racial status than with white. It is unreasonable to assume that, in a society as race-conscious as nineteenth-century Buenos Aires, any individual who was entitled to white racial status would settle for being termed a trigueño. The term could occasionally be applied to low-status Sicilian and Andalusian immigrants who might not have been aware of its connotations, but it does not seem plausible that a white porteño would willingly have consented to the same racial label that was being applied frequently to black people. It is much more likely that the term would in fact serve primarily as a label for those upwardly mobile and lighter-skinned Afro-Argentines and mestizos who, for one reason or another, were unable to enter the white category.

The available evidence suggests that the Afro-Argentines readily acquiesced in the use of the term, taking advantage of it in an attempt to leave their African ancestry behind, just as the black Peruvians, Puerto Ricans, and Nicaraguans did. In social columns of the black newspapers one finds references to "charming trigueñitas."[66] Estanislao Maldones, an Afro-Argentine lieutenant colonel who began military service as a fourteen-year-old soldier in Governor Rosas's black Restorer Battalion, was described on his death certificate as a trigueño, and the enlistment record of Maldones's son, Estanislao junior, also describes him as a trigueño. The elder Maldones's enlistment papers, which would have served to show us how his race was designated at the age of fourteen, unfortunately do not survive.[67] A similar case occurred in another Afro-Argentine military family, the Mauriños. Captain Federico Mauriño was a pardo, born in 1828, the son of pardo Major Feliciano Mauriño. However, when Mauriño's son Federico junior joined the army in 1882 he was entered on the rolls as a trigueño.[68]

In his classic comparative study of race relations in Brazil and the United States, Carl Degler proposed the concept of the "mulatto escape hatch," an informal social mechanism by which lighter-skinned Afro-Brazilians of special gifts, capabilities, or social prestige were allowed to enter the ranks of white society and escape their African ancestry.[69] The category of trigueño served a similar function in Buenos Aires; indeed, the sense of trigueño is captured by the title of Degler's book, *Neither Black nor White*. This intermediate racial status provided an avenue of escape, an exit through which Afro-Argentines could leave the black category completely. When official demographic statistics were compiled and published in dichotomized form, these Afro-Argentine trigueños were eligible to be tabulated as whites instead of blacks. Though for obvious reasons this process cannot be documented, we may hypothesize that it occurred in the annual statistics published in the Statistical Register in the 1822–25 and 1854–80 periods, in which demographic data were published separately for the white and colored populations. The same thing could have occurred with the municipal censuses of 1836 and 1838, in which the two racial categories were whites and pardos-morenos, and in the census of 1887, in which the two categories were whites and de color. Therefore, while the racial category of trigueño never appeared in any of Buenos Aires's demographic publications, I submit that in fact the existence of the term had a direct effect on the accuracy of racial data contained in those publications, and that that effect was one of consistent underenumeration of the Afro-Argentine population, both in vital statistics registers and in censuses.

This new terminology of course corresponded to the racial realities in Buenos Aires society. Let us not forget the English writers' observations concerning the degree of race mixture in the city. A glance at enlistment records from the first half of the century reveals a bewildering array of racial terms. Besides the usual white, pardo, mulatto, negro, moreno, Indian, mestizo, and trigueño, there is Indianish, dark brown, medium white, somewhat white, ugly black, *zambo* (a mixture of Indian and black), and others.[70] Given the process of race mixture suggested by these terms, it seems undeniable that increasing numbers of porteños could claim both African and European ancestry and perhaps Amerindian as well. As the races became more intermingled, racial barriers became increasingly ill-defined. The white slaves that were not uncommon in the southern United States were no rarity in Buenos Aires either. Newspaper ads and documents concerning slaves and libertos occasionally refer to *mulatos blancos*, white mulattoes. An 1803 manumission of a two-year-old slave boy labels him as a "little mulatto" but then goes on to describe him as blond-haired and white in color. His mother was a parda.[71] A similar case occurred in 1806, when a widow freed two young mulatto slaves, both white, with straight hair.[72] An 1840 newspaper ad requested information on the whereabouts of the runaway liberta Ulalia, who was described as white in color.[73] Another ad appeared in 1835 concerning a runaway liberta "de color pardo blanco."[74] Lina Beck-Bernard recalls an anecdote involving "a white mulatta of rare beauty."[75]

A comparison of the censuses of 1810 and 1827 shows a definite lightening of the Afro-Argentine population. Referring again to Table 5.2, above, and excluding Afro-Argentines of unknown race from the calculations, we find that pardos composed 35.1 percent of the Afro-Argentine population in 1810 and 42.2 percent in 1827. These figures are, however, somewhat misleading, since the weight of the available evidence suggests that the unknown Afro-Argentines in 1810 were in fact heavily moreno. The pardo population in 1810 was predominantly free, while the morenos were predominantly slave: 63.2 percent of the pardos were free, while only 13.3 percent of the morenos were free. Among Afro-Argentines of unknown race, only 5.6 percent (15 out of 269) were free people, strongly suggesting that these unknowns were in fact morenos. Of the 62 Africans registered in the sample, 29 did not have race listed. They were presumed to be morenos and were counted as such for purposes of analysis. Since the bulk of Afro-Argentines had no birth-places listed, we can reasonably assume that many more Africans lie hidden in the unknown Afro-Argentine racial category. Finally, the age-sex distribution of the unknown Afro-Argentines corresponds much more closely to the morenos than to the pardos. Among morenos and unknowns, males outnumbered females, while among the pardos the opposite held true. The masculinity index for morenos was 116.6, for unknown Afro-Argentines it was 108.5, and for the pardos it was 88.7. Among the morenos and the unknowns the teen-age category of 10–19 was the modal 10-year age bracket, while among pardos it was the young adult category of 20–29. In short, the characteristics of the unknown population suggest that it was composed mainly of people of more or less pure African descent, and that therefore pardos actually composed a smaller percentage of the Afro-Argentine population in

1810 than the census indicates. The lightening process among the black population was therefore proceeding at a more rapid pace than is suggested by a simple comparison of the censuses.

This conclusion is borne out by enlistment records. Table 5.4 (above) indicates that between 1810 and 1820 pardos formed only 19.9 percent of the Afro-Argentine enlistees. Forty years later they made up a majority, 51.1 percent. This lightening of the Afro-Argentines can be seen in process in the 1827 census, in which 20 percent of the children of moreno family heads were described as pardo. Two percent of the children of white family heads were pardo.

It appears, then, that race mixture was occurring on a significant scale and that, in conjunction with the use of ambiguous racial terminology, it led to correspondingly large numbers of Afro-Argentines being counted as white in official demographic records. This point can only be argued, however—it can never be irrefutably proven, since the only conclusive proof, exhaustive family histories which would demonstrate racial change in porteño society over several generations, is unobtainable. All one can do is attempt to point out oddities and discrepancies in the official sources, and make occasional deductions using official data as the basis. Those records do reveal a steady lightening of the black population, but of course they do not tell us anything concerning the transition of Afro-Argentines to the white racial category. Once an Afro-Argentine left the black category, it became impossible to reassign him statistically to that caste. For demographic analytical purposes, he or she had become a white person.

It is therefore my contention that, although the Afro-Argentine population was in demonstrably poorer demographic health than the whites during the first half of the nineteenth century, the differentials between the demographic indices for the races are partly explained by suspected, probable, and demonstrated shortcomings in the documents themselves, particularly in the area of underenumeration. These shortcomings are most strikingly evident in the fact that, despite the lugubrious conclusions that must be drawn from the 1810 and 1827 censuses, the black community grew steadily throughout the 1800–1840 period, defying the indicators yielded by those two censuses. We may suspect, then, that the most important determinant behind the absolute decline of the population in the 1838–87 period was not low birth rates or high death rates (though these unquestionably contributed to the decline), but rather the statistical transference of a large segment of the Afro-Argentine population from the black racial category to the white.

Several additional pieces of evidence support this conclusion. First, the 1838–87 decline occurred after a fifty-year period in which the city's

Table 5.6. Number of White and Black Births and Deaths in
Buenos Aires City, 1822–25 and 1854, 1856–57

	1822–25			1854, 1856–57		
	Births	Deaths	B/D	Births	Deaths	B/D
Whites	8,337	6,463	1.29	12,834	5,578	2.30
Blacks	3,192	3,517	0.91	1,671	1,147	1.46

Source: Registro Estadístico de la Provincia de Buenos Aires, 1822–25, 1854, 1856–57. The year 1855 was not included in this table because death figures were not published by race that year.

black population had registered steady growth, in absolute numbers. There is no apparent reason to think that this pattern of growth should have altered in subsequent decades. In fact, the post-1850 Afro-Argentines displayed markedly better corporate health than did those of the 1820s. Although the community had experienced a surplus of deaths over births in the 1820s, it appears that by 1837 the corner had been turned. In that year black births exceeded deaths, resulting in a modest growth rate of 0.6 percent. The white growth rate that year was 1.7 percent.[76] In the 1850s there was a healthy surplus of black births over deaths. In fact, by the 1850s the Afro-Argentine community had a higher growth rate than the white population had had during the 1820s, as the ratios of births to deaths indicate (see Table 5.6). The failure of the Statistical Register to publish birth statistics by race after 1857 precludes the calculation of ratios for the 1860s and 1870s. It is clear, however, that the white growth rate exceeded the black, and this difference, combined with the massive European immigrations, meant that the black population was destined to form a steadily dwindling proportion of the city's population as the years went on. In the 1820s the Afro-Argentines had accounted for 27.7 percent of the city's births and 35.2 percent of the city's deaths; in the 1850s they accounted for 11.5 percent of the births and 17.1 percent of the deaths. A phenomenon with graver implications for the Afro-Argentines was the fact that their absolute number of births and deaths had declined markedly over the intervening thirty years. Multiplying the 1850s totals by 1.33 to add an extra year (since the 1820s totals represent four years) shows that while white births had more than doubled since the 1820s, the number of black births had fallen by 30 percent. Deaths had fallen by more than half. Though the community was growing, it seems to have declined in size since the 1820s. We may note this anomaly as another of the troubling contradictions that so bedevil porteño statistical sources in the area of race. One wonders whether the pattern of growth registered by the black population in the 1854–57 reports was in any way connected with the decision of the province's record keepers in 1858 to stop publishing annual birth totals by race. Beginning in that year, only death and marriage statistics continued to be separated into white and "de color" categories. We therefore have no way of knowing whether the Afro-Argentine growth trend continued at the same level, intensified, or declined.

Those death and marriage totals (see Tables 5.7 and 5.8) indicate that the city's Afro-Argentine population held fairly steady in size throughout the period from 1850 to 1870, though it dropped noticeably in percentage terms. The post-1870 decline in black deaths and marriages coincides with the observations of Argentine historians, who label the 1865-70 Paraguayan War and the 1871 yellow fever epidemic in Buenos Aires as the twin coups de grâce to the Afro-Argentines. No statistical documentation is available concerning the impact of either of these events. The 1853 integration of the Argentine army meant that only two all-black battalions served in the Paraguayan War, and I was unable to obtain their roll calls, if in fact the documents survive. As far as the disastrous yellow fever epidemic is concerned, of the 23,748 people who died that year, 17,729 had race listed, and of these, an

Table 5.7. Marriage Partners by Race in Buenos Aires City, 1856–76

	White	Black	Unspecified	Total	Percent black[a]
1856–60	8,207	448	153	8,808	5.2%
1861–65[b]	8,073	308	585	8,966	3.7
1866–70	14,592	427	1,169	16,188	2.8
1871–75	18,297	155	—	18,452	0.8

Source: *Registro Estadístico de la Provincia de Buenos Aires*, 1856–75.

[a] Column calculated excluding unspecified column from total.

[b] 1862 figures missing.

Table 5.8. Deaths by Race in Buenos Aires City, 1856–76

	White	Black	Unspecified	Total	Percent black[a]
1856–60	11,539	2,084	1,820	15,443	15.3%
1861–65[b]	12,588	2,283	3,248	18,119	15.4
1866–70	26,526	2,375	3,346	32,247	8.2
1871–75	37,137	1,953	7,184	46,277	5.0

Source: See Table 5.7.

[a] Column calculated extending unspecified column from total.

[b] 1862 figures missing.

unusually small number, only 268, were listed as Afro-Argentines.[77] It is of dubious statistical significance, but nevertheless interesting, to note that a small yellow fever outbreak in 1858 took 141 lives, of which only two were black.[78] Afro-Argentines do not seem to have had a special vulnerability to the disease, and their allegedly heavy death rates during the epidemic cannot be documented through any source. Nevertheless, two of the community's vital events, death and marriage, showed marked absolute declines after 1871, so perhaps the epidemic did damage the community badly.

By 1887 the Afro-Argentines of Buenos Aires had supposedly been reduced to 8005 individuals. Women still heavily outnumbered men, 4700 to 3305.[79] The published census totals include no information on age distribution, so we can say nothing concerning the community's health, number of children per women, and so on. There seem to have been enough active young men and women to staff the community's newspapers, social clubs, and mutual aid societies, and to provide substantial turnouts at black dances and social functions. Indeed, as shall be seen in Chapter 10, the Afro-Argentine newspapers and writings of the 1880–1900 period display remarkably little concern over the community's eroding demographic situation, though they were deeply preoccupied with its continuingly subordinate socioeconomic position. So indifferent do they seem to have been to their demographic decline that one must again wonder whether in fact the community was disappearing as fast and as completely as the censuses, vital registers, and white Argentine writers claimed it was. This chapter has sought to demonstrate that it was not, and that in fact the Afro-Argentines continued to exist even while labeled as trigueños and whites. The question must then become not why did the Afro-Argentines disappear, but rather why was there so much writing and talking about black people dying off and their community dwindling away to nothing, when in fact it continued to grow throughout the period during which census records were kept for it? Why was a disappearance claimed at all when in fact the black community was still very much alive? The answers to these questions will be found in the next chapter.

6

Why the Afro-Argentines Disappeared

In the previous chapter it was argued that the demographic decline of the black population in Buenos Aires was artificially accelerated by the deceptive use of official statistics. Those statistics find confirmation, however, in the frequent observations of Argentine historians and writers in the second half of the century. Discussions of the imminent extinction of the city's black community appeared regularly in the writings of the period, just as reflections on the *fait accompli* of the disappearance have appeared regularly to the present day in Argentina. As in the case of the statistics, one must suspect historical perjury. The evidence against such observations has already been cited in Chapter 5: the frequent appearance of Afro-Argentines in photographs, the continued vitality of the community as expressed in its numerous newspapers and mutual aid societies, and so on. (The history of the community in the second half of the century will be dealt with at length in Chapters 8–10.) What remains to be established is a motive for these efforts to make the community disappear before in fact it had done so. The search for that motive requires one to delve deeply into the city's history and to examine closely how it was written, by whom, and for what purposes.

It is also important to consider the degree of esteem, or lack of it, with which the Afro-Argentines were viewed by their white compatriots. In Chapter 4 it was seen that, just as throughout the rest of the Americas, porteño society's association of black skin with inferior social status proved impossible to break. Even when free, the Afro-Argentines occupied a distinctly subordinate position in the city, and only in rare cases did individuals succeed in rising above the social and economic status to which their color consigned them.

Fear enhanced this prejudice. White society recognized that the victims of such discrimination could not fail to harbor resentments against those who enforced and benefited from the slave and caste regimes. Buenos Aires regularly received news of slave and free black risings from abroad.[1] The nervousness of the local officials and oligarchs over the possible occurrence of such a rebellion in Buenos Aires emerges clearly in the frequent complaints concerning the Afro-Argentine street dances. Protests by the town council to the viceroy, one of which is quoted extensively in Chapter 9, argued that the dances provided an opportunity for the free and slave blacks to gather and plot rebellion against the whites. The elite's uneasiness also surfaced during the English invasion and occupation of the city in 1806. With the coming of the British the rumor spread among the black community that the end of slavery was at hand. Worried by the consequent restiveness among the slaves, the town council delegated one of their number to persuade the British commander to put down the potentially rebellious blacks. General Beresford obligingly issued a communiqué informing the city that he had no intention of abolishing slavery and that all slaves should go on serving their masters as before. Thus, when the Argentines expelled the British from the city six weeks later, they did so assisted by hundreds of free black and slave troops, who fought with arms issued them by the town council (see Chapter 7). But after the fighting was over, the councilmen grew uneasy at the thought of so many potential rebels wandering around armed. They therefore announced a decree thanking the slaves for their services to the city and requesting the return of all weapons the city had issued. A fee of one peso was offered for the return of each sword, two pesos for each gun.[2]

The councilmen's fears were not unreasonable, especially after the slave revolution in Haiti in 1789. Slave revolts had gone on throughout the Americas since the 1500s, but Haiti was the biggest, the bloodiest, the most successful, and therefore the most intimidating to slave owners everywhere. Inspired by the principles of the French Revolution, the Haitian revolt sent shockwaves running through the entire hemisphere. In 1790 the viceroy forbade the further importation into Buenos Aires of any slaves from French colonies or ports for fear that they might be infected by the contagion of revolution. This precaution apparently proved ineffective, since in 1795 Buenos Aires was shaken by a so-called "French Conspiracy." Several Frenchmen, Italians, and an Argentine mestizo were accused of sowing revolutionary propaganda among the city's slaves, free blacks, and Indians. At their trial for treason, the prosecution was able to prove only that one of the Frenchmen had taught his slave to read and write, that the Europeans had toasted liberty, equality, and fraternity in front of their slaves, and that an unknown person had posted placards around the city proclaiming a coming revolution that would make all men equal. Notwithstanding the lack of evidence against them, the Europeans were found guilty and banished from the empire, while the Argentine was sentenced to ten years hard labor.[3]

Despite the whites' fears, Buenos Aires's black population displayed a seemingly imperturbable tranquillity throughout the period of the slave regime. Other than the brief restiveness of 1806, there was not a single revolt or attempted revolt among the city's slave or free blacks. Why this should have been true is not clear. No contemporary observers ever felt compelled to explain the lack of revolts in the city, but if they had, they probably would have singled out the relatively benign treatment given slaves there. Argentines and foreigners alike repeatedly exclaimed over the mild nature of the capital's urban slavery, especially as compared to the horrors of the Brazilian and Caribbean plantations. The Englishman Emeric Vidal reported that "slavery at Buenos Aires is perfect freedom compared with that among other nations." Vidal informed his readers that the city's slaves were frequently better clothed, housed, and fed than the poor whites, and that he had seen several cases of slaves' refusing freedom rather than leave the comfort of their masters' homes.[4] Woodbine Parish enthusiastically seconded Vidal, arguing that throughout Spanish America "the slaves were always slaves more in name than in reality."[5] Argentine writers and historians repeated this theme throughout the nineteenth and twentieth centuries. President Bartolomé Mitre (1862–68) described the slaves as "colonists" who were treated indulgently by their masters and were seldom made to work hard. In an 1883 article on the Afro-Argentines, writer Vicente Quesada described the relations between Buenos Aires's masters and slaves as "almost affectionate"; fifty years later, sociologist José Ingenieros characterized slavery in Buenos Aires as a benevolent institution.[6] Writing in 1930 about his visit to Harlem, one Argentine journalist explained the Afro-Argentines' failure to produce any music akin to North American jazz in terms of their never having endured real hardship in Argentina. The blacks of Argentina had nothing in common with Harriet Beecher Stowe's slaves, he asserted, for "they never ever suffered."[7]

The debate over the relative cruelty or benevolence of different slave regimes has been carried on for centuries. One of the most influential participants in the debate was the North American historian Frank Tannenbaum, who argued in his celebrated book *Slave and Citizen* that

Spanish and Portuguese colonial societies were significantly milder in their treatment of slaves than the English, French, or Dutch.[8] This theme was taken up by a number of Spanish American historians, each of whom argued that his or her country's slave regime had been more benign and humanitarian than any other.[9] It is by now generally recognized that the relative harshness or mildness of treatment accorded slaves was determined not so much by the nationality or cultural heritage of the slave owners but rather by the economic use to which the slaves were put.[10] Booming plantation economies produced brutal, dehumanizing conditions; less active economies, in which the incentive to wring the maximum utility possible out of each slave was not so pronounced, tended to produce more relaxed conditions. Writing shortly after the appearance of Tannenbaum's book, the Argentine historian José Luis Lanuza made precisely this point: "I do not think we are any better than the people of other countries. It was lucky for the blacks—and for us—that we had no plantations or sugar mills. There was no need to treat them like workers and exploit them. Excepting a few lamentable incidents, we treated them like humans, and now we are at peace."[11]

In any case, to explain the lack of slave revolts in terms of the benevolent treatment received by porteño slaves would be clearly fallacious. Montevideo, the Uruguayan capital across the Río de la Plata, a city in which conditions for slaves were virtually identical to those in Buenos Aires, was disturbed by several nearby *cimarrón*, or runaway slave, communities during the first decade of the nineteenth century and by a full-scale attempted revolt by free blacks and slaves in 1832.[12] There seems to be no way to explain the lack of similar incidents in Buenos Aires except to say that perhaps the Afro-Argentines were conserving their insurrectionary energies for the Rosas years, when their relationship with the governor made them a political force to be reckoned with.

ROSAS AND THE UNITARIANS

The reader received a brief introduction to Governor Juan Manuel de Rosas in Chapter 2. The importance of this personage in Argentine history, and the impact on Buenos Aires of his twenty-year rule, would be difficult to overestimate. As described earlier, probably his greatest offense, at least in the eyes of the unitarians, was his active recruitment of the non-elites into the political system of the province. Prominent among those non-elites were, of course, the Afro-Argentines. As soon as Rosas recognized the advantage to be obtained by organizing the masses on his behalf, he directed special attention toward the black population. Like the later populist Perón, Rosas was greatly assisted by his wife,

Doña Encarnación Ezcurra de Rosas. In 1831, in an uncanny forecast of Eva Perón, Doña Encarnación reported to Rosas that she had been busy organizing the workers in his favor. "I have called together the *paisanos*, I have spoken to them, as well as to the presidents of all the black nations."[13] In 1833, when Rosas was out of office but was laying the groundwork for the coup that would restore him to power, he instructed his wife to redouble her efforts.

You have already seen what the friendship of the poor is worth, and how important it is to nurture it and not miss ways to attract and cultivate their allegiance. Do not neglect your correspondence. Write them frequently, send them gifts, and don't worry about the expense. I say the same concerning the mothers and wives of the pardos and morenos who are faithful. I repeat, do not fail to visit those who merit it and to invite them to your parties, as well as to help them in their misfortunes in any way you can.[14]

Rosas's daughter Manuelita was another link between the governor and the Afro-Argentines. She regularly attended the dances of the African nations, at which she scandalized the unitarians by dancing with black men. The government organ *La Gaceta Mercantil* came to her defense in 1843.

The pardos and mulattoes are in no way unworthy; on the contrary, they are needed and considered by General Rosas, just as are the morenos and the Africans, as sons of the Fatherland, valiant defenders of liberty who have won fame and glory in a hundred battles in which they have bravely maintained the national independence against all foreign domination and against the savage unitarians, who are unworthy to rub shoulders with the honored pardos and morenos. . . . General Rosas so appreciates the mulattoes and morenos that he has no objection to seating them at his table and eating with them; for which *El Nacional* [a unitarian paper in Montevideo] has attempted to mock him, reproaching him because his daughter Doña Manuelita de Rosas y Ezcurra shows no reluctance to dance on certain occasions with the honest and hard-working mulattoes, pardos, and morenos.[15]

In 1848 the women of the Congo nation (a mutual aid society composed of slaves and free blacks born in that region of Africa; see Chapter 8) reaffirmed their loyalty to the governor and his daughter by composing a length "Hymn to Doña Manuela Rosas" in honor of her birthday.[16]

Although Rosas was greatly aided by his wife and daughter, he did most of his wooing of the Afro-Argentines himself, employing a deft combination of propaganda, flattery, and genuine concessions to win support for his cause. In a characteristic move, he named his suburban mansion after the black Saint Benito of Palermo, the patron of one of the city's black religious brotherhoods. Rosista propagandists were instructed to write pro-Rosas poems and literature in Afro-Argentine dialect, to be distributed to the populace. An irregularly published newspaper called *La Negrita* (The Little Black Girl) was a prime example of this public relations tactic. The persona of the paper was the black woman Juana Peña, who declared in the first issue that

> My name is Juana Peña,
> And I'm proud to be able to say
> —I want everyone to know—
> That I'm a federalist all the way.

Put out during the pre-coup days of 1833, *La Negrita* exhorted the Afro-Argentines to stand firm behind their leader Don Juan Manuel [de Rosas], and not to tolerate the outrages committed by "a few political aspirers / Who wish to sacrifice the nation / So that they can come out higher."[17]

Another paper, *El Avisador*, sought to rouse the Afro-Argentines against Felix de Alzaga, commander of the black militia and a political figure who assumed an increasingly anti-Rosas stance as the 1830s wore on. *El Avisador* warned its readers that "he is counting on the BLACKS because he commands them . . . , but the BLACKS will abandon him, they will leave him, and when the time comes they will tell him, TRAITOR, die like your *father*."[18] The reference to Alzaga's father is to Martín de Alzaga, executed in 1812 after his counterrevolutionary conspiracy was uncovered by a slave.

Rosas also made genuine concessions to the Afro-Argentines. In 1836 he overturned earlier legislation requiring the automatic drafting of libertos over the age of fifteen, and in 1839 he finally abolished the slave trade that he had reinstituted in 1831. After both these events the Afro-Artentines staged demonstrations to show their gratitude to the governor.[19] Occasional grants of money were made to the African mutual aid societies.[20] The bans on the candombe dances that had been imposed in the 1820s were lifted, and in 1838 the nations were even invited to hold an all-day dance in the central plaza to celebrate Independence Day. Just as the revolutionary government had done in the 1810s, Rosas promoted carefully chosen black men to high military position, thus cementing the loyalty of his black troops. Certain others became close personal retainers. The black man Domiciano was an especially feared executioner; the mulatto Zabalía was a prominent figure in the secret police, the Mazorca, as was the black Lieutenant Colonel José Narbona.[21]

In other ways, however, Rosas was no more a promoter of Afro-Argentine interests than earlier administrations had been. He did, after all, renew the slave trade in 1831 and allow it to function openly.

Though he made a policy of courting the nations, he was also capable of abandoning them when it suited his interests. In 1833 the headquarters of the Cambundá nation was confiscated and sold to pay debts contracted by the society. Rosas might have stepped in to forestall the confiscation or to lend the society the money, but he failed to do so.[22] His government did end the obligatory draft of native-born libertos, but in 1834 he established the automatic conscription of all foreign-born libertos, i.e., those brought in by privateers during the War with Brazil.[23] Educational opportunities for Afro-Argentines remained almost nonexistent, and the governor's heavy reliance on black males to fuel his war machine did the Afro-Argentine population little good.

As a result, black support of Rosas was by no means unanimous. Some Afro-Argentines, especially those more comfortably placed in the city's society, sided with the unitarians against the dictator. Colonel José María Morales, Argentina's highest-ranking black officer, began his military career fighting on the unitarian side at the Siege of Montevideo. Doña Encarnación repeatedly warned her husband of plots to assassinate him; the suspected instigator of one of them was a mulatto named Carranza, "very unitarian."[24] Another mulatto named Felix Barbuena was alleged to have been a leader of the 1839 anti-Rosas revolt in the south of the province.[25]

The governor's enemies did whatever they could to undermine Afro-Argentine support for the dictator. In 1836 an informant wrote the chief of police that the former officers of an old black military unit, the Fourth Battalion of Cazadores, had infiltrated the African nations and were spreading unitarian subversion.[26] Letters written in 1839 by the unitarian Petrona Acosta de Sinclair to her husband in exile reported on attempts to turn the blacks against Rosas. She gleefully informed her husband that

> we have succeeded in getting the blacks mad at him [Rosas]. The washerwoman, President of the blacks, is mine, and we lose no opportunity to advise them until we have succeeded in making them hate him. . . . We tell them many things and they have believed them. The blacks say that they [the government] must be the worst, because they are tired of the [French] blockade [of 1838–40]. I told the black woman President that it is shameful that he made them dance in the plaza to make fun of them, and they are very angry. Even if he kills them, they say they will never dance again.[27]

Doña Petrona's claims proved unduly optimistic. Up until the very end, Afro-Argentine support for Rosas seems to have stayed firm. The city's blacks prominently displayed the red federalist insignias, and they loyally stepped forward to serve in Rosas's armies. The candombe dances unfailingly began with several verses honoring the governor, written either by the blacks themselves or by Rosas's propagandists.

> You all see how at the candombe
> The black people shout and call,
> "Long live our Father Rosas,
> The best Governor of them all!"[28]

Bands of black musicians paraded through the streets after each federalist victory.[29] On at least one occasion, forty-two African societies joined together to make a special contribution to the provincial treasury when extra money was needed for military expenses.[30]

After the fall of Rosas, several unitarian writers claimed that the city's black servants had formed a spy network for the dictator. Domestics in unitarian households allegedly reported on their employers to Rosas and his secret police, with usually disastrous results for the families involved.[31] There is no evidence of this at all in police or government documents from the period, but the charge was repeated so frequently that there may be some truth in it. In 1853, shortly after Rosas's flight into exile, *La Tribuna* cited as an example of his misdeeds the fact that slaves who had denounced unitarian tendencies on the part of their owners to the Rosista police had been automatically granted their freedom.[32] The newspapers' having said this openly so soon after the fact, when memories were still fresh, argues that perhaps domestic espionage was another way in which the Afro-Argentines demonstrated their support for the dictator. It was clearly a frequently repeated charge: an 1878 editorial in the black press attacked white ignorance of Afro-Argentine history in general and expressed particular irritation at the widespread belief that black people's only role in Argentine history had been as soldiers and spies for Rosas.[33]

The Afro-Argentines and Rosas thus became inextricably linked in the mind of the unitarians. The racism of the white unitarians combined with their hatred of Rosas and the federalists to transform black people into a recurring symbol of the alleged barbarism and savagery of the Rosas years. When in 1838 Rosas invited the African nations to dance in the central plaza to celebrate Independence Day, the fury of the unitarians knew no bounds. The anti-Rosista poet Juan Cruz Varela commemorated the event in his poem "To the 25th of May, 1838."

> To the jeers of a proud people,
> African bands of low-born slaves
> Go rambling through the streets and squares.
> Their barbarous cries, their savage dances,
> On that day are a purposeful outrage
> Of the new Caribbean, an abortion of the South.[34]

The previously quoted Petrona Acosta de Sinclair must have been filled with anger as she penned a letter to her husband describing the event: "He [Rosas] has arrived at the ultimate disgrace imaginable. The 25th, a day that has been so respected and should be as long as Buenos Aires exists, arrived at the last degree of vileness and disgrace by being lowered to the level of putting nations of blacks that day in the plaza."[35]

In recalling the worst aspects of the Rosas years, the unitarian historians often depicted the confrontations between respectable unitarians and black Rosistas. José María Ramos Mejía recalled how bands of Afro-Argentine musicians used to stop in front of unitarian homes to sing scurrilous songs about the "filthy unitarians" and then demand money in return for their serenades.[36] José Wilde alleged that black people, who up until that time had always known their place in society and kept to it, were transformed by the Rosas years. "The *time of Rosas* came and upset everything, ruined and corrupted everything, and many blacks turned against their protectors and best friends. In the spy system established by the tyrant, they performed an important service, denouncing various families and accusing them of being *savage unitarians*; they became haughty and insolent and their masters came to fear them as much as the Mazorca."[37] Several authors singled out the weekly candombes as times of particular fear and uneasiness among the whites, for it was on those days that the blacks were especially likely to run amok. The spectacle of the dances "aroused the presentiment of what those poor animals would do once stimulated by drink or the hunger for loot, encouraged and protected by the guardianship of the Restorer."[38] V. F. López echoed this, recalling how the families would shudder when they heard "the sinister sounds from the streets of the center, like a threatening invasion of African tribes, black and naked. Lust and crime ruled the city, with the African drums underlying all."[39]

The Afro-Argentines had been extraordinarily quiescent during the whole colonial period and the first decades of independence. Almost alone among the major Latin American cities, Buenos Aires had suffered no attempted or realized uprisings by its free and slave blacks. But, at least in the perceptions of Rosas's opponents, the twenty years of the Restorer's administration more than made up for the previous centuries of peace. The Afro-Argentines had shown their true colors and had been revealed to be a potent force for federalism—or, in the unitarian lexicon, barbarism. It was a revelation that the unitarians would not soon forget.

THE GENERATION OF 1880

It will come as no surprise that Rosas's fall in 1852 was greeted with the most profound relief and rejoicing by the unitarians. The province was now free to resume the path of development that the liberals planned for it. All memories and holdovers from the Rosas years were to be ruthlessly expunged. Inevitably, the Afro-Argentines lost the somewhat favored position they had held in Rosas's Buenos Aires. But more profound than that, and ultimately much more damaging to the Afro-Argentines, were the philosophy and policies enshrined by the unitarians when they took power. A basic part of liberal Argentine ideology since 1800 had been an orientation toward the "progressive" nations of Europe, particularly Great Britain and France, and a desire to exchange the traditionalism of the Spanish colonial past for the modernity of Europe. The unitarians professed a strong and unwavering faith in the innate superiority of the European republics as manifested in their industrialization, economic expansion, a historical development in which enlightened monarchies were succeeded by republicanism, and the beginnings of empire in Asia and Africa. If only Argentina could follow the path taken by western Europe and the United States, argued the capital's new rulers, it could become the greatest nation in South America.

An integral part of this set of beliefs was the assumption that in order to form a nation on the European model, one needed a European population. It was undeniably true that European modes of economic, social, and political development occurred only in areas where there were European peoples. The unitarians extrapolated from this fact to conclude that if one were to populate a given region or country with Europeans and their descendants, European modes of "progress" would inevitably follow. This conclusion was further supported by the "scientific" racism that ruled European and North American thought during the second half of the century. As articulated by Louis Agassiz, Joseph Arthur de Gobineau, Houston Stewart Chamberlain, and a host of followers, the various schools argued the innate superiority of the white race and the inferiority of Africans, Amerindians, and other nonwhite races. These theories held sway over Europe and the United States in the post-1850 period and had an equally powerful impact on the Latin American intellectuals, who obligingly adopted whatever ideas were current in Europe.[40]

Combining indigenous strains of racist thought with this potent variety imported from abroad, the unitarians looked with disdain on the highly variegated Afro-Indio-European population of their country. The irredeemable inferiority of the "subservient races" doomed Argentina, along with the rest of Latin America, to secondary status in the world. The only hope for the modernization and future greatness of the country was immigration. The encouragement of European immigration had been a basic plank of the unitarian platform since the 1820s, but it was only in the 1850s and after that the Generation of 1880, as these men have come to be called in Argentine history, could begin freely promoting their projects. We may examine several representative Argentine ideologues to see how heavily the example of Europe and the necessity of European immigration weighed on their minds.[41]

President Domingo Sarmiento (1868–74) was the author who perhaps most clearly expressed the assumptions underlying the unitarian philosophy. His *Civilization and Barbarism: The Life of Juan Facundo Quiroga* (1845) was a lengthy treatise on the conflict between the cities of Argentina and the countryside, between urban civilization and rural barbarism.[42] In subsequent works Sarmiento refined this theme and presented it in explicitly racial terms. His characterizations of the races left little to the imagination. In describing black people he dwelt on "their musical ability, their childlike happiness, their stupid maliciousness, their candid stupidity, their primitive imagination."[43]

Sarmiento was enormously dismayed by the process of race mixture that had occurred in Argentina; in one of his books he quoted Agassiz, "the most distinguished North American theorist of mulatto degeneracy," on the baneful effects of such mixing.[44] An admirer of the United States, Sarmiento attributed that country's progress to its white settlers' not having permitted the "servile races" (or "secondary races," as he also termed them) to join with them and become part of the society. The North Americans had instead pushed the Indians and blacks aside, not allowing them to participate genetically, socially, or politically in the formation of the country, and that was what had made the United States great. The Spaniards in Latin America had followed a different path of development, mixing with the Indians, "a race of prehistoric servility," to produce an irredeemably inferior population. The only hope for Argentina, and for the region as a whole, prescribed Sarmiento, was European immigration, which would "correct the indigenous blood with new ideas ending the medievalism" in which the country was mired.[45]

Sarmiento's thinking was profoundly racist. Despite the fact that he was the father of Argentina's educational system, he paradoxically believed that ideas and enlightenment are not so much learned as inherited genetically. Thus, instruction alone would not be enough to pull Argentina out of its barbarism; an actual infusion of white genes was required.

Juan Bautista Alberdi, the political philosopher most responsible for the ideas embodied in the Constitution of 1853, expressed sentiments almost identical to Sarmiento's. "Put the bum, the gaucho, the peasant, the basic element of our population, through all the transformations of the best systems of education; in one hundred years you won't make of him an English worker, who works, consumes, and lives in dignity and comfort."[46] Alberdi's choice of an English worker as the model citizen was not accidental; while Sarmiento took his inspiration from the United States, Alberdi looked to the British Isles. He pronounced the English "the most perfect of men," and demanded that English, "the language of liberty, industry, and order," be taught in the Argentine public schools in place of Latin.[47]

Alberdi agreed with Sarmiento that the successes of the United States were due to its predominantly European population, but he felt that the South American republics possessed a similar potential for progress. Writing in 1852, at a time when the population of South America was overwhelmingly Indian, mestizo, and black, Alberdi showed astonishing ethnocentrism by proclaiming, in an essay titled "The Civilizing Action of Europe on the South American Republics," that "we who call ourselves Americans are nothing more than Europeans born in America. Cranium, blood, color, it's all from abroad." He went on to proclaim that every city in Spanish America had been founded by Europeans (apparently forgetting such settlements as Cuzco and Mexico City) and that "America itself is a European discovery."[48]

Alberdi was an enthusiastic exponent of race mixture, since he felt that history had demonstrated that the superior white genes would always prove dominant over those of the inferior races. Arguing that race mixing would produce "the unlimited betterment of the human race," he proposed numerous measures to promote European immigration, several of which were later incorporated into the constitution. Religious tolerance was officially established in order to encourage Protestant immigration from northern Europe. Immigrants were granted most of the privileges of citizens with few of the obligations, and one article of the constitution specified that one of the duties of the government was to expedite immigration from Europe. Alberdi further suggested that any president who failed to double the country's population every four years should be dismissed as incompetent.[49]

Elementary calculations would have demonstrated that a doubling of Argentina's population every four years would have meant demographic catastrophe by the end of the century. But such calculations were of little interest to the unitarians, who tirelessly promoted the concept of a totally Europeanized Argentina. The government's efforts from 1850 to 1870 to attract immigrants had middling success, but it was the economic boom of the last decades of the century that sparked massive immigration to the country and came close to making Alberdi's dream a reality. By 1914 it was time for José Ingenieros, perhaps the most influential of all Latin American sociologists, to take a retrospective look at what had happened to Argentina's population during the last half century.[50] He was pleased by what he saw. Ingenieros went further than either Sarmiento or Alberdi in formulating a racial theory of history. Borrowing heavily from Social Darwinism, he asserted that history is not a record of class or institutional struggle but rather of race struggle. Latin America was a clear example of this phenomenon, argued Ingenieros, since the white race had taken over an area previously dominated by members of an inferior race. He generously credited Sarmiento with having been among the first to recognize this, but said that the state of the social sciences several decades previous had not permitted Sarmiento to develop his theories as they deserved.[51]

Ingenieros differed from Alberdi in expressing grave reservations concerning the efficacy of race mixing. He once declared that the inevitable result of mixing inferior races with superior ones was a "rickety, simian offspring, with all the defects of the noble race accentuated by the inferior blood."[52] To him, a mulatto was basically "an African who has reinforced his blood with European elements."[53] Rejecting race mixture as an undesirable development, Ingenieros instead argued that the white and nonwhite races should develop separately, and in the resulting competition for dominance the blacks and Indians would inevitably lose. Dismissing the Afro-Argentines as "beings who seem to be closer to anthropoid apes than to civilized men," Ingenieros argued that "all that is done in favor of the inferior races is anti-scientific. At most, one might protect them so that they die out agreeably."[54]

Europeanization is not, in our opinion, a hope . . . ; it is an inevitability which will come to pass even if the Spanish Americans wished to impede it. It is born of determinants that exist independent of our wishes: by an inevitable law of sociology the more highly evolved social organisms overcome the less evolved. . . . We will Europeanize ourselves, as Sarmiento foresaw. . . . Sociology can affirm that future transformation of Latin America.[55]

Sarmiento's and Alberdi's faith in the eventual triumph of the white race was echoed throughout porteño society. José Manuel Estrada's observation concerning the "improvements" introduced among the Afro-Argentines by their transformation from morenos to mulattoes was mentioned in the previous chapter. President Bartolomé Mitre concurred that mulattoes were superior to morenos because of their white admixture. The mulattoes, announced Mitre, "have assimilated the physical and moral qualities of the superior race."[56] An 1883 article in the Buenos Aires newspaper *El Nacional* reported that in the interior city of Córdoba "there are no pure blacks, and many of the old mulattoes have become gentlemen, following the natural evolution and progress of the times."[57] A 1901 magazine article on the blacks of North America observed that the United States suffered from race problems for the reason that the whites refused to mingle with the blacks. "Sociologists who concern themselves with these matters do not think it unlikely that the blacks will eventually merge completely with the whites, forming a mixture beneficial to Mankind. The great difficulty presently consists of those whites who resist the crossing of black with white."[58] The same magazine carried a story several months later on a black woman in Córdoba who had given birth to triplets, two of whom were white and one of whom was black. The article congratulated the woman on her good fortune and praised her for contributing to "the enlarging of the Fatherland."[59] A 1905 article on Buenos Aires's black community reported that it was occasionally shaken by news that yet another of its youths was planning to marry a white. "As is logical, they think that this offends the dignity of the race. But they should be philosophical . . . the race is losing its primitive color through mixing. It is turning gray. It is dissolving. It is lightening. The African tree is giving forth white Caucasian flowers."[60]

THE WHITENING OF BUENOS AIRES

The unitarian dream was being realized. In terms of population, Argentina was becoming increasingly differentiated from her sister South American republics, which, with the exception of Uruguay, remained numerically dominated by a racially mixed population of Afro-Indio-Europeans. Citizens of the only "truly white" nation in South America, the Argentines compared themselves to such "mongrelized" countries as Brazil, Peru, Paraguay, and Mexico, and were well pleased. By the 1880s Domingo Sarmiento could write that the banners of the African nations that one used to see at the old Carnival celebrations had been replaced by the flags of the various French, Italian, and Spanish clubs and societies.[61] The published summary of the 1895 national census included an announcement that black people had almost disappeared from the country, "where very soon the population will be completely unified, forming a new and beautiful race which is the product of all the European nations made fruitful on American soil."[62] A special issue of the magazine *Caras y Caretas* commemorating the Argentine centennial carried articles on the ethnic groups that had built the nation: "France and the French in Argentina," "The Italians in Argentina," "Argentina and Great Britain," and so on. There was no mention of the Afro-Argentines.[63]

Pride in Argentina's European heritage became even more intense in the twentieth century. A 1973 essay on the country's demographic development stressed the similarities between Argentina's demographic rates and those of "Western Europe, Canada, the United States, and others that have been in the vanguard of economic and social progress." The author drew special attention to the fact that Argentina was one of the major recipients of European immigration, whereas the nineteenth-century growth of other Latin American countries, such as Brazil and the Caribbean nations, was due primarily to the slave trade. The article placed special emphasis on Brazil's alleged failure to receive European immigration.[64]

The author thus demonstrated a surprising ignorance of Latin American demographic history. Between 1800 and 1913 Brazil received about 3.5 million European immigrants.[65] Between 1870 and 1900 in particular, Brazil gained almost as many foreign-born residents as Argentina, 732,000 versus 795,000.[66] By erroneously singling out Brazil for deleterious comparison to Argentina, the author was following a time-honored Argentine tradition of contrasting Argentina's allegedly white population with Brazil's racially mixed people. As early as 1883, Sarmiento had gleefully predicted that by 1900, if an Argentine wanted to see what a black person looked like, he would have to go to Brazil.[67]

The Argentine desire to set itself apart from its miscegenated sister republics is evidenced in a 1976 article in an Argentine tourist magazine which drew its readers' attention to a pleasant hotel in the small town of Puerto Rico, in the province of Misiones, near the Iguassú Falls and the Brazilian border. The editors cautioned readers not to confuse the Argentine town of Puerto Rico with the Caribbean island of Puerto Rico.

In this Puerto Rico you won't find any black men or juicy mulatta women dancing tropical dances and shouting, "ae, ae, chébere, oba oba, a little water, baby, I'm burning up!" You will find a purely European village settled by Germans, Swiss, and their children. The total population of Puerto Rico is 12,000 inhabitants (not counting eight Brazilian infiltrators), all of them blond, with blue eyes and perfectly white skin.[68]

In order to eliminate any possible confusion, the editors included a cartoon showing a pair of Argentine tourists descending from a plane. As they watch a voluptuous black woman with an Afro and a gigantic grin dance with a black man under a palm tree (both of them shouting "oba oba" and "chévere"), the husband turns to the wife and asks, "but where have you brought me? I wanted to go to Puerto Rico, in the province of Misiones." Nevertheless, during a drive through the Argentine town of Puerto Rico in 1975, I saw as many Guaraní-speaking Indians and mestizos as blue-eyed, blond-haired Europeans.

These cases of erroneous information concerning Brazil and the town of Puerto Rico are but two examples of the blinders that race pride imposes on the Argentine perceptions of reality. Another is a 1965 history of the Buenos Aires parish of San Telmo, which asserted that the city's blacks had settled mainly in the parishes of Monserrat, Concepción, La Piedad, and Balvanera: "In our neighborhood the statistics indicate a minimum percentage [of black settlement] in comparison with the neighboring parishes. . . . In San Telmo the black population constituted a tiny minority."[69] The author, who was the long-time parish priest of San Telmo, made the mistake of including population totals from the census of 1836 to prove his point. Those statistics show that in fact blacks composed 20 percent of San Telmo's population, a larger percentage than Balvanera's, and roughly equal to La Piedad. Apparently the author had not examined his own sources before giving vent to his desire not to have Afro-Argentines associated with his parish.

Porteño race pride was at times carried to ridiculous extremes, as in the frequent claim that Buenos Aires's blacks were racially superior to those found in Africa and the rest of the Americas. Writing in 1883, Vicente Quesada described the physical repulsiveness of the Africans, and then went on to say that

it is not possible to verify the law by which the black slaves of Buenos Aires were superior, physiologically speaking, to those savages of Africa, who go about almost naked. The fact is that by changing the form of the head, their features seem to become more regular, and even though they retain the color, the flattened nose, the big mouth, and the kinky hair, in general the body had improved so much that there were very good-looking black men and women [in the city].

The Afro-Argentines had advanced so far, said Quesada, that many of them were now fit to acquire the culture and refinements hitherto monopolized by the white race.[70] Manuel Bilbao, who wrote in 1902, echoed Quesada: "The African race in the Republic did not have the repellent aspect of certain races of Africa, being, physiologically speaking, superior to those of the continent."[71] Alfredo Taullard calmly asserted in 1927 that Argentina's blacks were physically and mentally superior to blacks anywhere else in the New World—"if it had been otherwise, nobody here would have bought them."[72]

Race pride has come to form part of the very core of the Argentine identity, and especially of the porteño identity. We have just seen how it has produced startlingly obvious errors of fact, observation, and thought in recent writings. Let us turn back a few pages to Sarmiento and the other writers analyzed earlier. Recall Alberdi's assertion that Latin Americans are really Europeans born in America, and Ingenieros's iron law that the Europeanization of Latin America is an inevitability. Those statements betray a complete disconnection from reality, a crippling tendency to view the world through the lenses of these men's own theories and dreams. In talking and writing as they did, Ingenieros, Alberdi, and other authors demonstrated that the racial theories they had borrowed from Europe blinded them to the reality that surrounded them, just as race pride would blind later Argentine scholars and writers to evidence that directly contradicted their statements.

The United States has had ample opportunity to see the corrupting, corroding effect that racism has on every aspect of a nation's life. This is particularly true in intellectual activities. The inescapable and grinding contradictions between constitutionally guaranteed civil rights for all and the reality of racial discrimination produced a sort of societal schizophrenia, a desperate effort to reconcile two systems that cannot be reconciled. Similarly, racism and race pride had a comparable effect in nineteenth-century Buenos Aires. The city's whites had long disdained and scorned the nonwhite castes, but following the trauma of the Rosas years the unitarians' fear of and aversion toward the nonwhites was more intense than ever. Those people formed *la plebe*, the mob, the supporters of Rosas and barbarism. Given the opportunity to rebuild the province and the country after Rosas's fall, the liberals put their faith in European immigration and racial mixing to eliminate this undesirable element and rescue the country from its malaise. The Europeans did come, and the mixing did occur, but when it did not proceed as quickly as the elite wanted, they hurried the process up a bit by the statistical devices described in Chapter 5—transferral of Afro-Argentines from the pardo-moreno racial category to the white via the intermediate status of trigueño—and oft-repeated assertions that the black population had disappeared. To a certain extent those assertions reflected reality. If one uses "disappear" in the sense of "to become invisible," then the Afro-Argentines had disappeared. Forming less than 1 percent of the capital's population by 1900, they were indeed a miniscule fragment of the city's population. But if one uses "disappear" in the sense of "to cease to exist," it would be completely mistaken to say that the Afro-Argentines were gone, as will be seen in subsequent chapters.

A PARALLEL CASE

The "disappearance" of the Afro-Argentines is a statistical and historical phenomenon by no means unique to Buenos Aires. The previous chapter contained a reference to the falsification of racial data in twentieth-century Peruvian censuses. A study of colonial Guatemala has argued that large numbers of Guatemalan mulattoes were counted as mestizos or whites in censuses of the area.[73] More than one country has yielded to the temptation to use false or distorted demographic data to make ideological statements concerning its racial minorities. For instance, the United States census of 1840 contained figures indicating that insanity rates among free blacks were eleven times higher than among slaves. Proslavery spokesmen promptly seized on them as proof that blacks were naturally fitted for slavery and that freeing them was inhumane cruelty. Investigations by the American Statistical Association demonstrated that the figures were fraudulent and utter fabrications, leading the House of Representatives committee that was in charge of the census to announce officially that the figures on black insanity were useless. Nevertheless, those data continued to form ammunition for anti-abolitionists up until the Civil War.[74]

A case that is uncannily similar to that of Buenos Aires is the "Negro deficit" of the southern Brazilian city of São Paulo. Like Buenos Aires, São Paulo was a neglected and isolated colonial backwater. In the second half of the nineteenth century it entered a period of intense economic development which eventually resulted in its becoming the industrial and commercial center of the nation. Like Buenos Aires, its development attracted large numbers of immigrants—by 1897 there were two Italians for every native-born Brazilian in the city, which at that date contained 65,000 inhabitants.[75] During the opening decades of this century it was frequently observed that the Afro-Brazilians formed a steadily decreasing percentage of the city's population and that if existing trends continued black people would eventually disappear from São Paulo. In 1938 the demographer Samuel Lowrie demonstrated that in absolute terms the black population was actually increasing and suggested that many of its members were being statistically transferred from black to white racial categories. The *paulistanas*, as the inhabitants of the city are known, nevertheless continued to congratulate themselves on the impending disappearance of the black population. In 1961 Raul Joviano do Amaral noted in passing that "the *pardo* group—constituted by numerous shades of pigmentation—tends to become integrated not only statistically but also *de facto* into the ruling group, the white one, robbing the black population even more."[76]

Florestan Fernandes's discussion of the "deficit" argues that conditions very similar to those in Buenos Aires held true for the black population of São Paulo: while black fertility was as high or higher than white, black infant mortality kept reproduction rates below those of the whites. Therefore, while the black population continued to increase, it did not do so as rapidly as the white population, which was further bolstered by European immigration.[77] Fernandes concluded that although "it is clear from the statistical data that the natural growth rates of the Negro and mulatto groups of the *Paulistana* population do reveal a certain decrease deriving from purely ecological, economic and social circumstances,"

everything indicates that it would be wise to view the opinions held during the first quarter of this century regarding the widely publicized Negro deficit of the capital of São Paulo with reservations. The inconsistency of statistical data and the complexity of the demographic problems that underlie the comparisons (and which cannot be investigated or resolved objectively by means of those data) make this approach mandatory.[78]

In short, we have the same situation that held for Buenos Aires: statistical integration of the black population into the white, the resulting statistical anomalies and inconsistencies, and societal denial of the absolute increases registered for the black population, all in the face of the continuing existence of that population. The motives behind the invention of the "Negro deficit" may be found in Thomas Skidmore's study of racial ideology in postindependence Brazil.[79] The same schools of European and North American racism that circulated in Argentina took firm root in Brazil, producing the "whitening thesis" that Skidmore discusses at length. The Brazilian intelligentsia and elite placed their faith in the superiority of white genes over black, hoping that an influx of European immigrants and their mating with Afro-Brazilians would eventually whiten the population. The case of São Paulo was gratifying evidence that those theories were correct and workable, even if the evidence had to be doctored a bit.

Afro-Brazilians in São Paulo reacted to these policies more vocally and angrily than did the Afro-Argentines of Buenos Aires. Speaking in 1951, an Afro-Brazilian voiced the kind of outrage that was seldom expressed in Buenos Aires.

We aren't against miscegenation. But we are against the policies of forced miscegenation because they want to make the Negro race disappear. White policy is really to make the Negro race disappear. First through miscegenation. Second, by drowning it in a torrent of white immigrants. It's because the white doesn't want to hear anything about us. There's the police policy to degrade the Negro in order to see him disappear with tuberculosis, syphilis, and prostitution. What we want is to be recognized as citizens like everybody else and have a right to be educated. We should be brought into society and not be voluntarily abandoned in the hope that we'll disappear.[80]

There is clearly something peculiar in the writing concerning the black people of São Paulo and Buenos Aires, although, as Fernandes correctly observes, existing data can only be used to reveal inconsistencies. They cannot be used to demonstrate the true history of the cities' black people. In the final analysis the demographic part of the Afro-Argentines' "disappearance" can only be subjected to intense questioning. The theory of the statistical transfers of people from the black to the white racial category can only be argued; it cannot be proven.

There is, however, another disappearance of the Afro-Argentines that can be unquestionably demonstrated to have been a false one created by the writers of the country's history. That is the disappearance of the Afro-Argentines from the pages of Argentine history. The following chapters are an examination of how the Afro-Argentines were excised from their country's past in the areas of military, social, and cultural history. Perhaps those chapters will serve as the most compelling evidence that the Afro-Argentines did not disappear or die off at any point in the nineteenth century; rather, they were quietly written out of the record by census takers and statisticians, by writers and historians cultivating the myth of a white Argentina. Though it may be a hundred years too late, the time has come to write them back in.

7

The Black Legions

The phenomenon of armed black men has always been a troublesome one for the multiracial societies of the Americas. The spectacle of present or former bondsmen, or their descendants, organized into disciplined fighting units inevitably suggests the possibility that those units may acquire institutional autonomy and strike against the very government and society that created them. Armed forces always present this threat, but especially so when the members of those forces belong to a class or social group consistently exploited and confined to a subordinate position. Even if the black soldiers never use their power to redress their legitimate grievances, the fear that they will do so is a constant in the mind of the greater society.

Another drawback of black participation in the armed forces is that the services rendered the state by its black soldiers entitle those men, and the rest of the black population as well, to recognition and repayment of the collective debts owed them by their nation. Black assistance in defending the country against invasion can form the basis for demands that official and unofficial discrimination against black people be ended. This assistance, plus the potential of mutiny or rebellion if the demands are not met, can provide black people with the bargaining power to force societal change.

Thus, while black military units have proved useful and even irreplaceable as defenders of various North, South, and Central American states, their very existence has implied a force potentially hostile to the social bases on which those states rest. The problem of black men serving in the armed forces has therefore proved to be an extremely complex and delicate issue, not only for military policy

113

makers, but for historians as well. To acknowledge black participation in a nation's military history is to acknowledge the contributions which entitle black citizens to equality with whites. Such acknowledgment is obviously undesirable in societies dedicated to maintaining racial inequality.[1]

Perhaps it is for these reasons that the role of the Afro-Argentines in fighting their country's wars remains so little known and poorly understood. Few Argentine historians have failed to mention the importance of black soldiers in the nation's military past, but their participation in that past has been misrepresented in a variety of ways. Inaccuracies abound in the writings on Afro-Argentine military history, ranging from fairly innocuous mistakes concerning which regiments were black and which were white to far more serious misconceptions concerning the nature of segregation in the armed forces, death and desertion rates, and the very existence of the black officer corps. This chapter is an effort to set straight the confused and confusing record of Buenos Aires's black legions.

It is particularly important to correct these inaccuracies because of the pervasive influence of military activity and institutions in the life of Buenos Aires as a whole and its black community in particular. Embroiled in an almost continuous series of foreign and civil wars between 1810 and 1870, Buenos Aires underwent the "militarization" of its society and political system common to most Spanish American states in the postindependence period.[2] Military institutions assumed tremendous importance in the social and political affairs of the province, and black men were disproportionately represented in those institutions, though seldom at very exalted levels. Afro-Argentines were subject not only to the racially discriminatory draft decrees discussed in Chapter 4, but also to other laws aimed at rounding up as many of the province's non-elite masses as possible and impressing them into service. Legislation in effect between 1823 and 1872 required all men convicted of vagrancy, gambling, carousing, idleness, or carrying a firearm to serve four-year terms in the regular army, twice as long as terms for volunteers. The embattled Rosas administration, straining to fight simultaneous wars in Uruguay and the interior of Argentina, stretched those terms considerably: its courts regularly handed down sentences of ten to fifteen years of military service, while women convicts could receive sentences of ten years or more as military seamstresses, sewing uniforms for Rosas's troops.[3] Once enlisted, soldiers could be sentenced to additional years of service for infractions of military discipline, and cases of soldiers being illegally forced to reenlist were common.[4]

Given the province's never-ending quest for men to fuel its war machine, military service was an experience that virtually every black man who reached adulthood in nineteenth-century Buenos Aires could count on having. Few indeed are the memoirs of life in the city that do not include a vision of the province's black troopers, and one cannot help but be struck by the way in which the Afro-Argentines themselves dated events in their lives in relation to military happenings. The will of Federico Mendizábal recalled how his wife Ermenegilda deserted him in 1851 to follow Rosas's army in the Campaign of the South. Mendizábal himself died in 1867 while fighting as a lieutenant in the Paraguayan War.[5] In an 1852 lawsuit brought by the female members of the Mayombé nation against the males, the women recalled that the origins of their dispute dated from the calling up of the men for the 1840 campaign.[6]

BATTALIONS AND REGIMENTS

Afro-Argentines served in a succession of units in colonial and nineteenth-century Buenos Aires. As early as the 1660s, black men formed segregated militia units in the province; by 1801 black troops formed 10 percent of the city's 1600-man militia.[7] These troops were easily overcome by a British expeditionary force which occupied the city in 1806, but when the British were driven out six weeks later, free and slave Afro-Argentines fought side by side with white militiamen. A second British invasion a year later was defeated by a defending force of some 5000 men, of whom 876 belonged to the Corps of Indians, Pardos, and Morenos.[8]

Officers and enlisted men from these black militia units went on to fight in the independence wars. Free black troops from Buenos Aires constituted two all-black units in the revolutionary army—the Sixth Infantry Regiment of Pardos and Morenos, and the Battalion of Pardos and Morenos of Upper Peru. Both units distinguished themselves against the Spanish in Uruguay, Bolivia, and northwestern Argentina before being mauled at the Battle of Sipe-Sipe in November 1815. In the worst defeat suffered by Argentine arms during the revolution, over 1000 men were killed, wounded, and captured, while the Spanish suffered 20 dead and 300 wounded. The surviving Afro-Argentines were sent back to Buenos Aires to recuperate; they saw no further action against the Spanish.[9]

Another black unit, the Seventh Infantry Battalion, also fought at Sipe-Sipe, but the Seventh was of a very different type from the free black units, being composed entirely of slaves bought by the state or donated by their owners. As mentioned in Chapter 4, in 1813 the government initiated the first of a series of *rescates* (possible translations of this word include ransom, redemption, and exchange), decrees by which owners were required to sell their able-bodied slaves to the state in varying proportions, depending on the economic use to which the slaves were being put. Owners of domestic slaves were to contribute one-third of their holdings, owners of bakeries and *fábricas* one-fifth, and owners of slaves engaged in agriculture one-eighth. In Buenos Aires province, this draft produced 1016 slave soldiers, who were organized into two battalions, the Seventh and the Eighth Infantry. Subsequent rescates in 1815, 1816, and 1818 yielded 1059 more libertos, who were aggregated to the Eighth Infantry and the Second Battalion of *Cazadores* (literally Hunters).[10]

When Englishman Emeric Vidal wrote an account of his trip to Buenos Aires, as part of his discussion on the humaneness of porteño slavery he mentioned a particularly benevolent government program by which slaves could be sold to the state as soldiers, whereupon they would be free men.[11] In one respect Vidal was quite right: slaves were free as soon as they entered the armed forces, acquiring liberto status which they would retain for the duration of their military service, afterwards becoming completely free men. This program therefore had obvious attractions for Buenos Aires's male slaves, though there is no record of their responding to it as enthusiastically as the slaves of Santiago, Chile, three hundred of whom hired a lawyer in 1813 to sue the government for their right to enter the army and win their freedom.[12] Instances of slave resistance to the rescate program in Buenos Aires were rare, much rarer than those of owner resistance. After an initial flurry of enthusiasm in which a number of porteño families donated slaves to the state as a patriotic gesture, slave owners began to flood government offices with petitions for exemptions for their slaves, usually based on their economic dependence on the slave's labor. Many owners resorted to the crime of spiriting their slaves out of the city and hiding them in the countryside, where law enforcement was looser. By 1816 the government had decreed the uncompensated expropriation of slaves belonging to any master caught illegally withholding eligible slave males, and an especially long term of service for any slave who failed to turn himself in when called for service. Slaves who informed on such recalcitrant owners would be released from service after a mere three-year term of duty, considerably less than the hitches served by the other libertos.[13]

Vidal's description of the rescate system as a benevolent one is a bit wide of the mark. The libertos' freedom came neither easily nor frequently. Those drafted earliest signed up for the comparatively short term of five years; later decrees required liberto troops to serve until two years after the cessation of hostilities before acquiring complete freedom.[14] To what extent these original terms were honored is unclear. Many libertos died during the campaigns and thus never lived to claim their freedom. The numerous libertos discharged for medical reasons before completing their term of service did not always win their freedom, but rather were frequently returned to their owners—whether as slaves or libertos is not clear.[15]

Many other libertos deserted to escape the miserable conditions of campaign life. Those who succeeded in this enterprise may have won a precarious freedom which conceivably could have proved permanent, but those who were recaptured were usually sentenced to lengthy terms of extra service as punishment.[16] In any case, deserting libertos forfeited hopes of legally winning their freedom through the originally established mechanism of service. There is even serious doubt that the remnants of the revolutionary regiments that made it back to Buenos Aires after years of campaigning were allowed to enjoy the freedom they so richly deserved. An official history of the liberto Eighth Infantry Regiment reports that when its few survivors returned to Buenos Aires in 1824 after eight years of campaigning in Chile, Peru, and Ecuador, they were promptly incorporated into regiments preparing for the approaching War with Brazil, an incorporation which must have been forced on them since it is impossible to imagine that those broken survivors would have gone off voluntarily to fight in yet another war.[17]

Despite the shortcomings of the rescate program from the Afro-Argentines' point of view, it was undeniably successful in furnishing the revolutionary armies with much-needed manpower. Following the destruction of the free black battalions at Sipe-Sipe, the Afro-Argentine representation in the armed forces consisted almost entirely of libertos. When General José de San Martín led his army across the Andes into Chile in 1816 to liberate that country from Spanish rule, half of his invading force consisted of ex-slaves recruited from Buenos Aires and the provinces of western Argentina and organized into the all-black Seventh and Eighth Infantry Battalions and the integrated Eleventh Infantry.[18] San Martín's conquest of Chile and Peru is the stuff of which military legend is made. Leading his small army with a rare combination of skill and luck, he succeeded in throwing off Spanish rule in two centers of royalist resistance and sympathy. Even more remarkable was the career of the black batallions that accompanied him. Between 1816 and 1823 they fought and won battles in Chile, Peru, and Ecuador in an odyssey of campaigning that took them as far north as Quito, thousands of miles from their homes in Argentina. By the time they were finally repatriated, fewer than one hundred fifty men remained out of the approximately two thousand black soldiers who had crossed the Andes with San Martín.[19]

No other black unit ever experienced a Calvary quite so long and difficult as that suffered by those ill-fated battalions. The only other liberto unit fielded by Buenos Aires, the Second Battalion of Cazadores, sat out the war doing garrison duty in the city. It later saw action against the federalists who invaded the province in 1819 and in the Indian wars of the 1820s.[20] The Fourth Battalion of Cazadores, established in 1826 at the outset of the War with Brazil, also spent the war in Buenos Aires, seeing minor service in the civil disturbances of 1829. Dissolved in 1831, its members were assigned to the Argentine Guard, an all-black battalion of the Rosas period.[21] Other black units prominent in Rosas's army were the Provisional Battalion and the Restorer Battalion, named after Rosas's self-imposed title of Restorer of the Laws.[22]

Following Rosas's fall in 1852, segregation was eliminated in the regular army by the national Constitution of 1853 and the provincial Constitution of 1854, but it continued to exist in the militia. Black militia units remained a constant in Buenos Aires's military establishment throughout the nineteenth century, evolving from the colonial Corps of Indians, Pardos, and Morenos and Battalion of Castes into the Civic Regiment of Men of Color (established in 1811), the Third Battalion of the Native Legion (1820), the Fourth Militia Battalion (1823), the Defenders of Buenos Aires (1830), various units established during the Rosas years, and the Fourth Battalion of the National Guard (established in 1852 and reorganized into the Second Battalion of the Third National Guard Regiment in 1858). A slave militia, the Argentine Auxiliaries, also served during the independence wars.[23]

A focus on the all-black regiments, however, obscures the importance of Afro-Argentines in integrated units. Though segregation of the military was more strictly observed during the colonial period than after independence, there is considerable evidence that even prior to 1810 black and white soldiers served side by side in the local militias. It was not unusual, for instance, for well-to-do merchants or professionals to send their slaves to substitute for them at militia drills and in actual combat, so that a de facto integration resulted through slaves' serving in supposedly all-white units.[24] Sometimes integration was officially condoned. During the English invasions a company of free mulattoes was attached to the First Squadron of Hussars, a prestigious white cavalry unit. At least two petitions survive from black officers in this company appealing to the viceroy to allow them to continue to serve in "this distinguished unit" rather than be transferred back to the Batallion of Castes. So badly did these two men want to stay in the white unit that they both offered to serve without pay, supplying their armament and horses at their own expense. Despite their pleas, both men were reassigned to the Castes.[25]

Given the liberal rhetoric of the revolution, integration of regular army units was almost inevitable. At first the revolutionary junta sought to keep Afro-Argentine companies in separate batallions, allowing only the Indians to serve with the whites, but eventually they relented, and in 1811 several companies of free Afro-Argentines were aggregated to the Second Infantry Regiment. These companies were later separated from the regiment to form the basis of the Tenth Infantry, another integrated unit.[26] The Eleventh Infantry, which accompanied the black Seventh and Eighth Battalions on their eight-year campaign through the Andean countries, was also integrated.

The true extent of integration in Buenos Aires's nineteenth-century regiments is only hinted at by official military legislation. Although several units were established by decrees that explicitly described their integrated or segregated racial nature, the majority were not. Only by studying enlistment records from the period and seeing to which regiments soldiers of given races were assigned can one arrive at an accurate impression of the racial composition of Buenos Aires's army. Such investigation indicates that the province did not field one single battalion or regiment in the 1810–60 period that did not have black soldiers. In some of these units black representation was minimal, 1 or 2 percent. Examples of these would be the Buenos Aires Artillery Division (1853–60),* the Ninth Infantry Regiment (1816), the Infantry Legion of Cazadores (1853–60), and the Artillery Regiment of the Fatherland (1814–17). But in other units the representation was substantial, especially when one takes into account the Afro-Argentines probably concealed among the trigueños that appear in the enlistment records. Table 7.1 is a tabulation of the enlistments recorded for ten units in the 1813–60 period. Those enlistments appeared in five volumes of such documents chosen at random from a total of about twenty.[27] The importance of black soldiers in integrated units, even before integration was instituted in Buenos Aires's army, is obvious. Black troops constituted more than a quarter of the soldiers in six of the ten units considered; in one of them, the Tenth Infantry Regiment, they made up three-quarters of the enlistments. The trigueño enrollment was even

* The numbers in parentheses indicate the years for which enlistment records survive.

Table 7.1. Enlistees in Selected Military Units from Buenos Aires Province, 1813–60,
Tabulated by Race

Unit	Enlistees			Total	Percent black
	Black	White	Trigueño		
Third Infantry Regiment (1813–17)[a]	14	25	36	75	18.6%
Second Infantry Regiment (1813–15)	23	28	37	88	26.1
Tenth Infantry Regiment (1814–18)	65	15	7	87	74.7
Seventeenth Cavalry Regiment (1826–28)	34	60	40	134	25.4
Buenos Aires Artillery Battalion (1824–28)	12	24	49	75	16.0
First Infantry Battalion (1853–60)	200	224	264	688	29.1
Second Infantry Battalion (1853–60)	43	97	80	220	19.5
Third Infantry Battalion (1853–60)	56	91	60	207	27.1
Second Cavalry Regiment (1853–60)	12	26	26	64	18.8
Fifth Regiment of Mounted Grenadiers (1853–60)	10	12	11	33	30.3

Source: Archivo General de la Nación, 3 59–1–1, 59–1–6, 59–2–1, 59–2–4, 59–2–7.

[a] Dates in parentheses indicate the years for which enlistment records survive.

larger, outnumbering the white in four of the ten units, including the largest, the First Infantry Battalion.

There is also evidence that units established as black were in fact integrated, though the number of whites in them was very small. Even the liberto Seventh Infantry Battalion of 1813–15 showed two white enlistees, as did the Fourth Cazadores. In the Rosas period there were instances of white criminals being sentenced to service in such black units as the Restorer Battalion and the Argentine Guard, just as there were black prisoners sentenced to serve in white units.[28] This accounts for a surprising incident in 1847, when the commander of the Restorer Battalion, asked to nominate noncommissioned officers for promotion to two vacant sublieutenancies in the battalion, nominated two white men, both of whom had served in the unit for ten years.[29]

DEATH, DESERTION, AND DISEASE

A potentially explosive question concerned with segregation and the existence of all-black units is the possibility that commanders used them as assault troops in preference to white units, consciously killing off Argentina's black population while achieving military objectives. No Argentine historian has suggested in print that such genocidal policy existed, but several mentioned it in conversation as one explanation for the demographic decline of the Afro-Argentines. Simón Bolívar, the liberator of northern South America, once argued frankly in favor of such a policy.

Is it right that only free men die to free the slaves? Would it not be just for the slaves to win their rights on the battlefield and diminish their dangerous number by this powerful and legitimate means? In Venezuela we have seen the free population die and the slaves remain; I do not know if this is politic, but I do know that if in [Colombia] we do not make use of the slaves [as soldiers] the same thing will happen.[30]

Let it stand to Argentina's credit that there is no evidence of such thought or practice in the country's military history. Although black males were drafted in numbers disproportionate to their representation in the population, it does not appear that they were singled out for consistently hazardous duty. It is true that the Seventh and Eighth Infantry Battalions eventually melted away to nothing during their years of campaigning, but the white units that accompanied them did no better. The First Cazadores was almost completely destroyed at the Battle of Maipú, and very few of the Mounted Grenadiers ever returned from Peru to Buenos Aires.[31] No casualty counts are available for the disaster at Sipe-Sipe but a list of officers killed and captured suggests that the mainly white Ninth Infantry suffered more heavily than the two black regiments combined. The Ninth lost fifteen officers, while the Sixth and Seventh Infantry between them lost six.[32] Or consider the Fourth Cazadores, which quietly sat out the War with Brazil in Buenos Aires while the integrated regiments battled Brazilians and the cold in Uruguay.

A comparison of the 1810–15 roll calls of several battalions on active duty against the Spanish indicates that the white units actually lost more men than the black.[33] Since these roll calls are fragmentary in nature and vary considerably in coverage from month to month, monthly death rates (number of deaths divided by number of men in the unit at the beginning of the month) were computed and the sum of those rates then divided by the number of months to produce a mean monthly death rate for the period in question. That mean monthly death rate was then multiplied by twelve to produce a yearly death rate.

Three units that campaigned together in Bolivia and northwestern Argentina from 1812 to 1814 were the Battalion of Pardos and Morenos of Upper Peru and the white Second and Eighth Battalions of Peru, all

Argentine units despite their names. During the 1810–13 period the Battalion of Pardos and Morenos suffered an annual death rate of 91.2 men per 1000, a very high rate indeed. However, the roll calls of the white Second Battalion, which survive only for 1813, show a death rate of 253.2 per 1000. By comparison, the black batallion's death rate in 1813 alone was 114.6 per 1000. The white Eighth Battalion also fought in the 1813 campaign in northwestern Argentina, but roll calls survive for only two of the twelve months of that year, so their results should be treated with caution. They produce an annual death rate of 201.6 per 1000.

Three other units that served together in the northwest were two Afro-Argentine units, the Sixth Infantry Regiment and the Seventh Infantry Battalion, and the white Ninth Infantry Regiment. These units had much lower losses. In an eighteen-month period in 1814–15 (a period which does not include the Battle of Sipe-Sipe; the army was so shattered after its defeat there that no roll calls were taken), the Ninth had an annual death rate of 38.4 per 1000, the Sixth slightly lower at 37.2, and the newly created liberto Seventh Battalion had 27.6.

These losses vary somewhat from the traditional image of Argentina's blacks dying in heaps on the battlefield, going to their deaths by the thousands in the cause of the *patria*, the fatherland. There is no writer on the subject of the Afro-Argentines who does not sound this familiar theme, and some carry it to ghoulish extremes. One Argentine poet and writer of popular history recalls at length how the Afro-Argentines served as cannon fodder from one end of the country to the other, leaving their bleaching bones, which he employs as a recurring image, everywhere they went.[34] The image of the bones is a striking one: as used by that author, who focuses on the contrast between the black skin of the Afro-Argentines and the whiteness of their bones, it becomes a subtle metaphor for the whitening of the Afro-Argentines. They did their duty to their country, died in the process, and left as their memorial a heap of bones, which redeem the memory of the Afro-Argentines not only through the heroism they represent, but also by the fact that the soldiers' blackness has disappeared, replaced by pure and gleaming white.[35]

The bone motif appeared in another of the many popular magazine features that have reinforced the theme of the Afro-Argentines' being killed in the wars. An 1898 interview with a veteran of the independence wars yielded the following grisly anecdote:

One time we were marching to San Juan, and with me in the advance guard was a black from La Rioja, a slave of the Bazán family. . . . One night he was on guard duty and he went to sleep forever when an enemy scout slit his throat.

Well, before leaving we got the body and to save it from the vultures we put it in a huge cave in the hillside, and there we left it, without so much as a wooden cross. After all, the black left nothing on this earth besides his bones—who would ever remember him?

As it turned out, the teller of the story did. Four years later he happened to be campaigning in the same area when a thunderstorm broke and he took refuge in a nearby cave. Surprise of surprises, it proved to be the same one in which they had left the black man's body. "Would you believe that the bones of that poor guy served as fuel to make our fire and keep us dry that night? See what some people are destined for, eh? Some are useful even after they're dead, and others even when they're living are worthless."[36]

Other feature stories on the Afro-Argentines were less gruesome, but they all agree on the recurring theme of the blacks' being killed in the wars. As recently as 1976 a Buenos Aires newspaper article recalling the end of the slave trade went on to discuss how "the blacks fell to the last man in all the battles of the young nation, in the Army of the Andes, in the wars against the Indians, in the marshes of Paraguay."[37]

To what extent is this image of the Afro-Argentines' dying en masse in the country's wars an accurate one? It has more than a kernel of truth, of course, as can be seen from the marked sexual imbalance in the city's black population, documented by the census of 1827. The low death figures registered for the regiments described above should not obscure the fact that all it took was one disastrous battle for a unit to lose more men in an afternoon than it had lost in three years. Though black losses at such battles as Salta (eleven killed), Tucumán, and Chacabuco (eight killed) were minimal, clashes such as Ayohouma, Sipe-Sipe, Maipú, Pichincha, Ituzaingó, Caseros, and a host of others levied a hideous toll on the Afro-Argentines, as well as on the whites, Indians, and mestizos unfortunate enough to be drafted into the armed forces.

Even more destructive was the sickness endemic among nineteenth-century armies throughout the world, Argentina being no exception. When the Argentine army invaded Bolivia in 1813 the worst enemy it faced there was the *soroche*, a crippling condition produced by prolonged exposure to the altitude and the bitterly cold weather of the Bolivian *altiplano*.[38] Between December 1811 and July 1812, when the Battalion of Pardos and Morenos of Upper Peru was stationed in the Argentine province of Jujuy, bordering on Bolivia, an average of 22.2 percent of the battalion was sick each month, the majority of them with soroche.[39] When the integrated Río de la Plata Regiment left Lima in 1823 for the Campaign of the Ports, it left behind over one hundred fifty sick men in the city's hospitals; almost all of them died.[40] During the anti-Indian campaign of 1824, the Second Cazadores lost hundreds of men dead or permanently crippled by freezing and frostbite.[41]

Given the miserable conditions of army life, it is amazing that Argentine historians have consistently overlooked the single most important source of losses in the Afro-Argentine regiments. Perhaps attracted by the drama and pathos of the subject, historians have ascribed the losses suffered by those units to battlefield deaths, though a minority do mention the living conditions that caused so many deaths from illness. Only one study has pointed to desertion as a factor in the losses suffered by black regiments, and that study concluded that desertion was relatively infrequent among black troops.[42] This is completely untrue. Blacks and whites alike deserted in droves in all of Argentina's wars, especially the early ones. General Paz's memoirs recalled that during an 1815 march from Buenos Aires to Bolivia, an army of five thousand men was reduced to three thousand by desertions. A draft sent to northwestern Argentina three years later lost two-thirds of its men in a matter of months as a result of desertions.[43]

Afro-Argentines did not hesitate to embrace discretion as the better part of valor, joining their white comrades in wholesale flight from the front. The debilitating effect that these desertions could have on a unit's manpower can be seen in the fact that while the roll calls of the Battalion of Pardos and Morenos of Upper Peru show it losing 47 men through death from 1810 to 1813, it lost 69 men through desertion. The Sixth Regiment lost 18 men dead between October 1814 and August 1815 but 98 men through desertion. Similar figures for the Seventh Battalion (March 1814 to August 1815) are 30 deaths, 189 desertions; the Ninth Regiment (September 1814 to August 1815), 27 deaths, 145 desertions; and the white Second Infantry Battalion of Peru (January through June 1813), 34 deaths, 64 desertions. An obviously discontented unit was the Afro-Argentine Fourth Cazadores, which between November 1827 and October 1829 lost 31 soldiers dead and an astonishing 802 in desertions, many of which must have been multiple, since the battalion at its largest numbered only 715 men. And the same military report that mentions that the Río de la Plata Regiment left one hundred fifty sick men behind in Lima when it departed the city in 1823 adds that it also had to leave behind some three hundred fifty deserters who had not been apprehended by the military police and who remained at large in the city.[44] Therefore, when one reads such accounts as Domingo Sarmiento's description of how he encountered the remnants of an Afro-Argentine regiment at the siege of Montevideo in 1851, reduced to 30 men and commanded by a sergeant,[45] one should not immediately draw the conclusion that Sarmiento implies—that the rest of the regiment was killed in fighting. It is entirely possible that they took the rational course of action and left for home rather than be killed or maimed in the grueling siege.

In searching for the motive behind this constantly reiterated message of the annihilation of the Afro-Argentines in the wars, one may return to the discussion of Chapter 6. By claiming an almost complete destruction of the black male population through military service, the nation's historians were able to ignore the fact that many of those soldiers returned alive from the wars to contribute to Buenos Aires's cultural, social, and demographic development. It is significant that the best-known Afro-Argentine military hero is not a historical figure like Colonels Domingo Sosa and José María Morales, who fought in a host of battles, served Buenos Aires heroically for forty or fifty years, and died quietly at home in bed, but rather the mythical Falucho, who, if in fact he ever existed, was killed while suicidally defending the flag of Argentina.[46] Emphasis on the heaps of white Afro-Argentine bones and the pools of red Afro-Argentine blood provides a convenient distraction from the continued presence of black Afro-Argentine skin in the nation's capital. This is not to belittle the disastrous effect that virtually continuous military service over six decades exerted on the city's black population. Many of those deserters clearly never made it back to Buenos Aires and thus were as effectively removed from the black community as they would have been if they had died. Several Argentines who visited Lima in the 1830s and 1840s reported encountering survivors of San Martín's expeditionary force there, and one of the more celebrated anecdotes of nineteenth-century Argentine literature concerns an old black deserter encountered living among the Ranquele Indians by the writer Lucio Mansilla.[47] And many more of the deserters who did make it back to Buenos Aires arrived broken in health, suffering from wounds or the rigors of campaigning. But it is clearly incorrect to say that the Afro-Argentines fell "to the last man" fighting for a country that consistently denied them the rights they were fighting for. To pretend that this was so is to deny them the most elementary common sense or instinct of self-preservation.

When one considers the meager rewards received by the black warriors for their services, the infrequent promotions, the miserable pay, the hardships, the grudging and long-delayed granting of rights promised them during the revolution, one must be amazed at the heroism and endurance the Afro-Argentines consistently displayed. The only major Argentine commander who ever criticized the Afro-Argentines' military performance was Manuel Belgrano, who after

A survivor of the wars. This photograph accompanied a profile of Juan Martínez Moreira which appeared in the picture magazine *Caras y Caretas* in 1900. A veteran of the Paraguayan War (1865–70), Martínez was presented in the article as one of the few Afro-Argentines who had survived service in that conflict—which, by 1900, he probably was. Photograph courtesy Archivo General de la Nación.

presiding over a series of defeats in Paraguay, northeastern Argentina, and Bolivia, wrote to General San Martín that "I'm not at all pleased with the libertos; the blacks and mulattoes are a rabble who are as cowardly as they are bloodthirsty, and in the five actions we have been in, they have been the first to break ranks and hide behind walls of bodies."[48] General Paz, a subordinate of Belgrano's who later made brilliant use of black troops in the civil wars, disagreed sharply, once remarking that one black soldier was worth at least three Europeans.[49] Paz and San Martín both preferred liberto troops, whose experience as slaves made them more amenable to military discipline than the whites. When the Seventh Infantry arrived in northwestern Argentina in 1813, Paz was extremely pleased with the way they had mastered their drills: "Along with the Mounted Grenadiers the handsome Seventh Battalion arrived to enlarge the Army of Peru. They came already instructed in modern tactics with which we were unfamiliar, so that they served as a model to the rest of the infantry and cavalry."[50] Generals Rondeau, Viana, Miller, and Guido are also on record as lavishing special praise on Afro-Argentine troops.[51]

The devotion with which thousands of Afro-Argentines fought for their country is a puzzling phenomenon, when one considers the meager rewards they received in return. Perhaps they actually believed the appeals to defend God and country with which their officers fired them before battle, but it is more likely that their bravery and even ferocity in battle sprang from two sources. The first source included the resentments and frustrations they suffered due to their position in Buenos Aires's society. The discontent and rage that they had to repress in the city could be released on the battlefield without fear of punishment, and the occasional testimonials to the "bloodthirstiness" and "savagery" of the Afro-Argentine soldiers suggest that they did not hesitate to take advantage of this opportunity. The fury they displayed on the battlefield was truly above and beyond the call of duty and hints at some deeper motive than mere love of country. The second source was the hope for promotion: upward mobility in the army and perhaps even in the greater society.

THE OFFICERS

Historians writing on the Afro-Argentines have traditionally maintained that it was virtually unheard-of for black men to attain officer rank. José Ingenieros stated unequivocally that the soldiers of the independence wars were always mestizos or blacks, their officers always white.[52] Emiliano Endrek concurred, saying that a few Afro-Argentines may have reached officer level during the post-1820 civil wars, but that black units of the colonial and independence periods were commanded entirely by white officers.[53] José Ramos Mejía maintained that even during the Rosas period, when the government made a policy of courting Afro-Argentine support, it was almost impossible for black men to rise above the rank of sergeant or lieutenant.[54] José Luis Lanuza echoed this statement, and even the normally well-informed Leslie Rout flatly states that "no acknowledged Negroid" held officer rank in the Argentine or Uruguayan colonial militias, and that no black Argentine rose above the rank of captain until after 1820.[55]

The very authors who make these assertions include incidental information which strongly suggests, and in some cases conclusively demonstrates, that black men did in fact reach command positions. In the same essay in which Endrek claims that no blacks served as colonial or independence-period officers, he includes the quotation in which General Belgrano excoriated his black troops as cowardly rabble, a quotation which terminates: "My only consolation is that white officers are coming [to command them], under whom perhaps they can be made of some use."[56] The implication is that at that point they were under the

The only known surviving portrait of Colonel Lorenzo Barcala (1795–1835). Date and artist unknown. Photograph courtesy Archivo General de la Nación.

command of black officers. Later Endrek refers specifically to the black officers of Córdoba's Afro-Argentine militia, who were displaced by white officers when the unit was sent off to fight in Bolivia.[57] Another case in point is a thesis written at the University of Córdoba in 1972, whose author asserts that blacks never became officers and then quotes an 1830 decree by General Paz that all liberto prisoners-of-war were to

Colonel José María Morales (1818–94). Date and artist unknown, but the drawing was probably done sometime during the 1860s, after Morales assumed command of the Second Battalion of the Third National Guard Regiment. Photograph courtesy Archivo General de la Nación.

be returned to their owners, with the exception of "those slaves who have served as officers in the invading army"![58] And there is little question that the above-mentioned authors are familiar with Vicente Fidel López's *Manual de la historia argentina*, one of the most frequently

Colonel Domingo Sosa (1788–1866). This portrait probably dates from the late 1850s or early 1860s. Sosa was a founder and the most prominent member of the Artisans Club, an Afro-Argentine social organization active from the 1860s through the 1880s. The club printed and sold copies of his portrait to members and other interested parties. Photograph courtesy Archivo General de la Nación.

quoted Argentine histories from the nineteenth century. Lanuza, for example, cites it frequently but inexplicably omits López's statement that every officer in Rosas's elite Fourth Battalion was black, with the sole exception of the colonel.[59]

Not only did black men serve as officers in Buenos Aires's army, but some rose to high levels of command. It seems to have been an unwritten rule that no Afro-Argentine could be allowed to reach the rank of general, but at least eleven rose to be full or lieutenant colonels (for brief biographies of these men, see Appendix C); doubtless more such cases lie concealed in the documentation of the period, waiting to be discovered. Furthermore, Afro-Argentine colonels could hardly have existed in isolation from an even larger number of Afro-Argentines at lower levels in the hierarchy. In order to identify these men and arrive at a coherent representation of the evolution of the black officer corps, I examined the officer staffs of seven all-black battalions in existence between 1800 and 1860.[60] White and integrated units were not included in this study because black officers in those units appear to have been too few in number to justify the expenditure of time and energy involved in searching for them. All seven battalions were infantry; four were regular line units, two were militia, and one, the Restorer Battalion, was a mixed unit of militia and line companies, a common form of military organization under the Rosas administration.

In order to insure comparability between militia and regular officers (who, as will be seen shortly, occupied very different positions in the military establishment), I relied wherever possible on the individual's regular line rank rather than his militia rank. Since almost all of the men in this study held line commissions at one or more points during their lives, it proved possible to compare careers over time using reasonably consistent data.

The names of every officer mentioned in the battalion rolls produced a universe of 186 men. Since roll calls never indicated an individual's race, it was necessary to verify race using other sources. These included military service records and evaluations, which occasionally mention race; enlistment records, which always do; censuses; birth, death, and marriage records; and newspaper articles. Using these data it was possible to establish the race of 104 of the 186 men, somewhat over half.

I tend to suspect that, due to a documentary bias in the data available, the majority of the unknown officers were black. The men for whom it was easiest to get information were those who had the most successful careers and were most prominent in the army and in the society as a whole. For obvious reasons, they tended strongly to be whites. Another complicating factor is the demonstrable tendency on the part of record keepers to cover up evidences of the black officers' African ancestry. Several instances may serve to illustrate this phenomenon. Sublieutenant Bernardo Pintos of the colonial Corps of Indians, Pardos, and Morenos was a successful musician and a rather well-known figure in the city. Histories of colonial Buenos Aires single him out as a renowned black organist, but in the municipal census of 1810 he was counted as white. When he married in 1828, his marriage certificate was filed in the book reserved for whites, despite the fact that the document specifically labeled him as a pardo.[61] Captain Gregorio Sanfines's 1761 baptism certificate described him as the son of a moreno father and a parda mother. By the time his son José María Sanfines married in 1813, however, the young Sanfines was eligible to be described in the marriage certificate as an *español*, a white. When Sanfines's other son, José Gregorio, married in 1816, no mention was made of his race, but when this son and his wife had a daughter in 1824 (the original captain's

Table 7.2. Racial Composition of Officer Corps in Selected Battalions from Buenos Aires Province, 1800–1860

Unit	Indian	Black	White	Unknown	Total	Percent black[a]
Corps of Indians, Pardos, and Morenos (1808)[b]	4	17	2	7	30	74
Battalion of Pardos and Morenos of Upper Peru (1813)	0	3	5	8	16	38
Seventh Infantry Battalion of Libertos (1814–15)	0	0	25	14	39	0
Second Battalion of Cazadores (1817–20)	0	1	11	7	19	8
Fourth Battalion of Cazadores (1829)	0	0	15	14	29	0
Restorer Battalion (1834–35)	0	6	4	8	18	60
Restorer Battalion (1852)	0	4	0	13	17	100
Fourth Battalion of the National Guard (1853)	0	10	2	12	24	83
Total[c]	4	41	64	83	192	38

Source: Data on the race of individual officers were taken from a variety of sources, including enlistment and service records; parish birth, death, and marriage registers; censuses; and newspaper articles. For citations of sources on each individual, see George Reid Andrews, "Forgotten but Not Gone: The Afro-Argentines of Buenos Aires, 1800–1900" (Ph.D. diss., University of Wisconsin, Madison, 1978), pp. 396–410.

    [a] Column calculated excluding unknowns from total.

    [b] Dates in parentheses indicate years from which roll call records were taken.

    [c] Totals exceed sample totals because several officers served in more than one unit.

grandchild), her baptism record was inscribed in the book reserved for *españoles*.[62] Thus an Afro-Argentine militia captain produced a white Spanish son and granddaughter. Lieutenant Colonel Cabrera's entire family was labeled as pardo in the 1827 census, but by the time his daughter Agueda died in 1881 she had been transformed into a white woman, at least according to her death certificate.[63] Lieutenant Lorenzo Castro of the Restorer Batallion was labeled a pardo in the 1827 census, but the priest who officiated at his 1818 wedding made no mention of his race on the marriage certificate. Castro is described simply as a native of Caracas and a lieutenant in the regular army, though his porteña wife is described as a parda.[64]

One can hardly blame the Afro-Argentine officers, who had attained some measure of social standing in the city, for wishing to conceal documentary evidences of their blackness, a guarantee of inferior social status in nineteenth-century Buenos Aires. But coupled with the other documentary bias, this results in its being very difficult to reconstruct the genuine racial composition of the officer corps. This is undoubtedly another contributing factor behind the misconceptions concerning Buenos Aires's black officers.

Table 7.2 describes the distribution of the sample by race and unit. Of the 104 officers whose race was verifiable, 39, over a third, were black, 61 were white, and 4 were Indian.[65] (The totals in Table 7.2 exceed these figures due to the fact that several officers in the sample served in more than one unit.) If one is willing to assume that the percentage of black officers among the unknowns was much higher than among the knowns, as seems reasonable, it is probable that black men made up at least half of the officer corps of the Afro-Argentine battalions.

The role of the black officers in Buenos Aires's army changed markedly between 1800 and 1860. The first unit considered, the colonial militia Corps of Indians, Pardos, and Morenos, was officered almost entirely by blacks and Indians, in complete contradiction of traditional claims that no black men achieved officer rank in the colony. Of 23 officers whose race is known, 17 were black, 4 were Indian, and only 2 were white. These free black officers went on to serve in two line units in the revolutionary army, the Sixth Infantry Regiment of Pardos and Morenos, and the Battalion of Pardos and Morenos of Upper Peru. Only the latter was included in this study, and very little information could be obtained on its officers, half of whom remain of unknown race. Of the 8 officers whose race could be verified, 5 were white and 3 black. More useful for the purposes of this study would have been the Sixth Infantry, whose roll calls were unfortunately not discovered until after this research project had been completed, at which time it was not possible to subject each name on the rolls to the careful cross-checking in a variety of sources undergone by officers in other units. However, of 39 officers in its 1814–15 rolls, 9 were immediately recognizable as black men who had served at lower ranks in the colonial militia.[66]

Free black troops in the revolutionary army were therefore commanded in large part by black men. This was not the case in the liberto units, represented in this study by the Seventh Infantry Battalion and the Second Cazadores. Only one officer in these two units was verifiable as Afro-Argentine. There are several possible explanations for this dichotomy between the free black batallions and the liberto batallions. First, the government was under no political necessity to make black men the officers of these units. Since the free blacks were accustomed from their colonial experience to serving under black officers, and members of the free black militia had been led to expect that a certain percentage of their number would eventually acquire officer status, the revolutionary government would instantly have alienated free black support by failing to continue this practice. Among the slaves, on the other hand, no such precedent existed. The mere promise of freedom was sufficient to insure their support for the new regime. Since there had never been slave officers, there was no need to elevate libertos into command positions.

Second, and perhaps more important, keeping the liberto regiments officered by whites prevented alliance of any sort between free black officers and the slaves, which the liberto troops in essence still were. In 1806 the town council had described the job of commandant of the Slave Corps (formed during the emergency of the English invasions and disbanded shortly thereafter) as "one of the most delicate positions imaginable."[67] The last thing the upper echelons of the military and the government wanted was to put recently freed black troops under the command of free black officers, producing a potentially explosive convergence of interests between the two.

The destruction of the free black battalions at the Battle of Sipe-Sipe therefore marked the end of a brief five-year period in which many Afro-Argentines enjoyed officerships in the regular army. As free black troops were displaced by libertos, the black officer corps in the regular army withered away and, by 1820, had disappeared almost completely. Regular army Afro-Argentine units from 1815 to 1830 were officered almost entirely by whites, as may be seen in the cases of the Second and Fourth Cazadores. Of 29 officers in the latter unit, 15 are of known race, and every one of them was white.

The color bar preventing Afro-Argentines from reaching officer status was dropped by the Rosas administration. Roll calls of the Restorer

Battalion at the beginning and end of its existence (1834–35 and 1852) produce a list of 35 officers, of whom 14 are of known race. Four are white and 10 black. This pattern of black dominance was continued in the post-Rosas Fourth Battalion of the National Guard. Of 24 officers in the unit's 1853 roll calls, 12 are of known race. 2 are white and 10 black, including the commander, Colonel Domingo Sosa.

How does one explain the resurrection of the Afro-Argentine officer corps in the 1830–60 period, after its apparent demise between 1815 and 1830? One explanation must be Rosas's policy of courting Afro-Argentine support for his administration, a policy which did not allow the continued relegation of black men to the lowest ranks of the army. Just as the revolutionary government of 1810 bartered officerships for black political support, so Rosas did the same in the 1830s and 1840s.

Another reason for the return of the black officers may be found in the changing legal status of the black population. As mentioned in Chapter 4, the municipal census of 1810 showed that 22.6 percent of the city's black population was free; by 1827 that proportion had risen to 54.8 percent. Following the policy adopted by the revolutionary government in 1810, the Rosas administration recognized that free black men could be impressed into service, but they would not fight well unless there were genuine opportunities for advancement. Since the need for manpower to fight the Indian and civil wars of the 1830s and 1840s was as great as it had been to fight the Spanish in 1810, the government was forced to cede black men the right to rise through the ranks.

When Governor Rosas came to power, he found a readily available supply of potential Afro-Argentine officers in the form of the militia officers. The dearth of black officers in the regular units from 1815 to 1830 can be deceiving, since it hides the fact that black men continued to exercise command in the city's militia units throughout that period. A cursory glance at the 1815 officer list of the Civic Regiment of Men of Color reveals a number of black men from the earlier colonial militia.[68] These officers, later joined by regulars returning from the campaigns in the northwest, continued in the unit well into the 1820s. Black officers who were later to achieve high rank in Buenos Aires's army all served in the black militia during this period in which their access to the regular army was barred. Young Domingo Sosa, after returning from service in the Sixth Infantry, was assigned to duty as a drill instructor in the slave militia, the Argentine Auxiliaries, and in 1828 was called up to serve in the all-black Fourth Militia Battalion.[69] Feliciano Mauriño, later to rise to major, served from 1826 to 1833 as an officer in the various black militia units of the city. He then made the unfortunate decision to be an anti-Rosista in the 1833 uprising, for which he was broken to common

soldier in the Restorer Battalion.[70] Even the extraordinarily talented
Lorenzo Barcala, Argentina's best-known black officer, saw service in
the War with Brazil not in a regular unit but in the Fourth Militia Battalion.[71]

Being restricted to the militia set the Afro-Argentines several ranks
lower in the military hierarchy than the white regulars. For one, regular
officers assigned to mobilized militia units were always elevated one or
two ranks above their customary rank. Thus, a regular lieutenant
assigned to the militia became an acting captain or even major, with
authority over all those officers below him. Black militia officers always
came out on the short end of this arrangement. Also, periods of active
service in the militia counted toward retirement and pension rights, but
periods of inactivity did not. Such slack time did count for regular army
officers, enabling them to collect the pensions that often eluded the Afro-
Argentines. Finally, regular officers were subject at all times to the
fuero, military legal jurisdiction, while militia officers were subject to
such jurisdiction only when they were on active duty. Being subject to
the fuero was considered to be one of the great privileges of military
service, since it made one immune to the civilian courts and the police;
officers found that their military peers tended to be more lenient in
punishing civil offenses than were the civilian courts.[72]

Although the Afro-Argentine militia officers do not appear to have
been disadvantaged in relation to white militia officers, their inability to
acquire line commissions during the 1820s was clearly the result of a
policy of racial exclusion. While not every white man could win a
position in the regular officer corps, no black man could. It was
therefore of concrete benefit to them that Governor Rosas allowed the
Afro-Argentines back into the ranks of the regulars.

Table 7.3. Highest Known Rank Achieved by Individuals of Known Race in
Selected Buenos Aires Battalions, 1800–1860

	Indian	Black	White	Total
General	0	0	6	6
Colonel	0	2	16	18
Lieutenant colonel	0	5	12	17
Major	1	5	7	13
Captain	1	13	10	24
Lieutenant	0	9	7	16
Sublieutenant	2	5	3	10
Total	4	39	61	104

Source: See Table 7.2.

Once having entered the regular army, however, the Afro-Argentines' race continued to have an adverse effect on their possibilities for advancement. A tabulation of the highest known rank reached by each individual in the sample (Table 7.3) shows that the average black officer in service between 1800 and 1860 was most likely to end his career as a captain, while the average white officer was most likely to end his as a colonel. No black man achieved the rank of general, whereas 10 percent of the whites did. And the increasing difficulty that black men experienced in winning promotion past the rank of captain can be seen in the fact that there are fewer black majors and lieutenant colonels than captains, and fewer black colonels than lieutenant colonels. Among the whites, there were more lieutenant colonels than majors, and even more colonels than lieutenant colonels.

Military service could and did serve as an avenue of upward mobility for those men skilled and determined enough to make their way to the top. An Afro-Argentine male looking to rise as high in the society as possible was probably best advised to join the army and bend such talents as he had toward acquiring a colonelcy. But such a man would have been a fool not to realize that the odds against his reaching that goal were extremely long, that access to the topmost levels of the hierarchy would be forever closed to him because of his race, and that even if he were lucky enough to rise as high as a black man could go, his influence and prestige could be cut short at any moment by political reversals or violent death (see the cases of Nicolás Cabrera and Lorenzo Barcala in Appendix C). Men seeking less spectacular but more secure advancement were better advised to master a more reliable and less hazardous trade than that of arms.

The twentieth-century reader may level the charge that the black soldiers and officers prostituted themselves to fight white men's wars. The charge is anachronistic, since it presupposes a political consciousness that simply did not exist in nineteenth-century Buenos Aires, nor in the United States. Many Afro-Argentines sincerely believed in love of country and the principles of heroism, loyalty, and valor, just as thousands of North Americans went to their deaths under similar banners in colonial wars in Mexico and Cuba. Others capitalized on their military service to win the upward mobility denied them by the society at large. The Afro-Argentines lived in a white man's society; the alternatives were either to fight his wars or to suffer the consequences of refusing to do so. While fighting those wars they served not only as followers but also as leaders, and as soldiers and officers they compiled a record of achievement that has been too easily relegated to history's back drawers. Let the record stand corrected.[73]

8

Community Organizations
The Quest for Autonomy

"In union there is strength." Buenos Aires's black community learned this lesson early in its history and mobilized its members into collective organizations as soon as circumstances would allow. Cut off from the city's whites and mestizos by racial strictures and prejudice, the Afro-Argentines established a tradition of community organizing which may be divided into a three-stage progression reaching from the 1770s to well past 1900.

THE COFRADIAS

The first type of organization to be established by and for the Afro-Argentines was the *cofradía*, the religious lay brotherhood. A common feature of Spanish American religious life to the present day, the lay brotherhood is an association responsible for contributing to the welfare of the church to which it belongs. The members collect alms, pay for masses and the upkeep of the building, are responsible for the maintenance of the altar of their patron saint, and perform various other duties for the benefit of the church and its priest. During the colonial period, membership in cofradías tended to follow fairly strict lines of racial segregation. While mestizos were occasionally admitted to membership in white brotherhoods, blacks remained a group apart and as such were usually required to establish separate organizations, which they did throughout Spanish and Portuguese America.[1]

The first black cofradía to appear in the city of Buenos Aires did so in

138

1772, when the Archbishop of Buenos Aires authorized the establishment of such an organization in the church of La Piedad.[2] The group chose as its patron saint the black King Balthazar (Baltasar, in Spanish), one of the three wise men who brought gifts to the baby Jesus. It was soon joined by three other black cofradías in the city, all established during the 1780s. The Convents of San Francisco and Santo Domingo (both of them large slaveholders: a slave census in 1813 showed that between them they owned 67 adult male slaves eligible to bear arms[3]) each had a black brotherhood. One was dedicated to San Benito, the sixteenth-century Ethiopian saint who died in Sicily, and the other to the black Virgin of the Rosary. A fourth cofradía, which has left only shadowy traces of its existence, was the Cofradía de Santa María del Corvellón in the church of La Merced.[4]

Membership in these groups was open to slave and free blacks alike. Judging from the frequent mention of slave members in documents concerning the brotherhoods, and the large slave holdings of two of the four sponsoring churches, it seems likely that most of the members were slaves. Women and men were equally welcome as members, though the female officers were subordinate to the males. The constitution of the Cofradía de San Baltasar is the only one of the four to have survived, but it serves to give an idea of what the brotherhoods demanded of their members.[5] First, they demanded money. The brothers were required to contribute regular dues, which were used to sponsor a weekly mass, a weekly class on instruction in Christian doctrine, and three special masses during the course of the year. Second, their presence was required at all these functions, as well as at four communions to be celebrated on selected holy days. Third, they were enjoined to live a Christian life in general, and in particular to pray twice a day and recite a portion of the rosary.

The benefits that the brothers received from membership in these bodies seem rather insignificant to modern eyes, and, in economic terms, were certainly inferior to those received by the church. The only benefit specifically mentioned in the constitution, besides the general uplifing of the brothers' souls, was that of a guaranteed funeral, with a set number of masses to be celebrated in memory of the deceased. Some of the brothers' most bitter complaints concerned their priests' alleged failure to comply with the proper procedure for burying members. In 1779 they petitioned the Vicar General of Buenos Aires to reprimand their chaplain for holding the masses for deceased members on work days rather than holidays. They protested that since the majority of the brothers were slaves, it was impossible for them to take time off to come to these masses. They therefore requested that the priest be ordered to hold memorial services only on feast days and Sundays.[6] Another funereal issue that provoked protests was the priests' insistence that black brothers be buried in walled-off, segregated areas of the church graveyard. The Cofradía de San Baltasar and the treasurer of the Cofradía de Nuestra Señora del Rosario both petitioned the authorities to redress this grievance, but their petitions were denied.[7]

The cofradías' concern with the proper execution of their members' funeral and memorial masses is not difficult to understand. Both Catholic doctrine and African religious tradition emphasized the importance of the manner in which the soul passes from this life to the next and the influence that ceremonies and observances by the living could have on its fate after death.[8] Those who led lives afflicted by slavery and poverty looked to salvation as one of the few avenues of upward mobility open to them; anything that could contribute to that salvation bulked correspondingly large in their list of earthly priorities.

The cofradías also provided other less tangible benefits which do not appear in the constitution. First, it would not do to neglect the very real spiritual rewards the members of the cofradía received, especially when they got along well with their priest. The brothers clearly derived comfort from being not only the recipients but also the sponsors of special masses and classes in religious instruction. Their being designated worthy of special ministration by the church did much for their self-esteem as a group and as individuals, though one should not forget that this benefit had a subtly insidious side. By making the members more content with their lives, by making them feel that they were living as God and the church wished them to and were storing up good deeds which would be taken into account at Judgment, the cofradía served as an instrument of social control through which the church (serving as an arm of the Spanish colonial regime) reconciled the blacks, both slave and free, to their unhappy plight. Thus, in the spiritual realm, as in the economic, the church certainly received as much in benefits as it gave.

The second benefit was entirely unintended, at least from the church's point of view. An 1879 article in one of the city's black newspapers recalled how the colonial cofradías had served to "inculcate and stimulate the spirit of association among the unfortunate blacks; a thing that up until that time was completely unknown."[9] The brotherhoods provided a vehicle for the development of group consciousness, a feeling of corporate pride and identity unavailable to the Afro-Argentines through any other means, except possibly through service in the militia. Evidence of this corporate solidarity in the cofradías is abundant. One of the complaints lodged by the brothers of San Baltasar against their priest was that he held the classes of religious instruction at two o'clock on Sunday afternoons, when the slaves were still busy serving their masters lunch. The brothers requested that those classes be rescheduled to four so that they would be able to attend "integramente," as a group.[10] On occasions when the cofradías achieved any kind of solid accomplishment, their pride was readily visible. The annual procession held in honor of the black Virgin in the interior city of Córdoba, a procession led by the city's black cofradía, was a high point of the year for Córdoba's Afro-Argentines.[11] In 1790 the Cofradía de San Benito succeeded in winning an apostolic communication direct from the Vatican.[12] Receiving such a document from Rome was no small achievement, for either a white or a black cofradía, and the brothers of San Baltasar wondered how it was that this younger organization should have scored such a coup while their brotherhood remained immobilized, bogged down in acrimonious exchanges with their roundly disliked chaplain: "[the Cofradía of San Benito] has plenty of property, they observe their constitution without difficulty, and when any controversy arises their priest listens freely to the opinions of the officers; only in our brotherhood do we collide in our humble pleas with the harsh personality of our priest."[13]

The brothers' lament revealed the fundamental tension underlying the cofradías: while they supposedly existed to serve the spiritual needs of the brothers, and while there was a superstructure of black officers which nominally ran the organization, in fact all power was lodged with the priest, the cofradía's chaplain. His power over the body was virtually absolute. Members could not speak in the meetings without first asking permission from the priest. The cofradía could not spend any money without his approval. The officer empowered to hold the money was not the treasurer but the syndic, an officer who had always to be from outside the cofradía, white, and appointed by the priest (all other officers were elected).[14] When there was little friction between a cofradía and its priest, things could go along reasonably well, as in the case of the Cofradía de San Benito. But when a priest and his lay brothers clashed, the basic reality of the members' lack of control over their own brotherhood rapidly became apparent. Indeed, one reason that so much documentation survives on the Cofradía de San Baltasar is the frequency of its petitions to higher authority to rid it of its priest. Both parties were equally ill disposed toward the other: the brothers charged their chaplain with cupidity, laziness, lack of Christian virtues, and a particular lack of sensitivity to their position as blacks and slaves. The priest retaliated by denouncing the brothers as liars, drunkards, and "of no use whatsoever to this parish."[15] In 1784 the brothers attempted to escape his control by asking the viceroy's permission to build a small chapel for their own use, which request was denied.[16] In 1804 they petitioned again, this time for permission to leave the church of La Piedad for good and transfer to the Convent of the Fathers of Bethlehem; again their request was denied.[17]

The priests' control over the cofradías meant that the brotherhoods could never grow into the kind of autonomous social organization that the city's blacks were seeking. It also explains why the institutions of religion and church never came to form the core of Afro-Argentine community life in the way that they did for the Afro-Americans of the United States. The determining factor working against such a development in Argentina was the differing role of the church in the two countries. Throughout colonial Latin America the church formed part of the state's governing apparatus; church and state traditionally worked in tandem to administer society. Even though the church's power was eclipsed in Argentina following independence, it remained very much a semiofficial institution, a flying wing of the state. This situation combined with the universal Catholicism of the country to render the very concept of a separate black church unthinkable. The church would never surrender administrative power to the Afro-Argentines in the same way that the North American Protestant churches did in allowing Afro-Americans to set up their own congregations and religious organizations.[18] Thus, even though the Cofradía de San Baltasar was not disbanded until 1856, and the Cofradía de Nuestra Señora del Rosario continued to be a reasonably prosperous and active organization until at least the 1880s, the Argentine church failed to provide the shelter for the city's blacks that the African churches of the United States did for the Afro-Americans. The cofradías therefore gave way to a new stage in community organization.[19]

THE NATIONS

Mention of loosely organized African ethnic associations appears in colonial documents as early as the 1770s; these forerunners of the later national societies coexisted in an uneasy and ill-defined relationship with the cofradías. In 1785 the brothers of San Baltasar petitioned the viceroy to forbid the various nations to collect alms at the large public dances held regularly by the black community (discussed in the next chapter). Describing how each nation set up a table and collected money for itself, the brothers protested that this practice deprived their cofradía of the alms it needed to continue its good works.[20] Other members of the brotherhoods were not above responding to the calls of their compatriots, however. In 1787 a number of the brothers of San Baltasar dressed in the Cambundá national costume to celebrate San Baltasar's Day.[21] And a 1791 petition from the brothers to the viceroy described their cofradía as the Brotherhood of Guinean Blacks.[22]

By the end of the colonial period the nations had become a visible element in Afro-Argentine community life. The Cambundá and Congo nations both petitioned the viceroy several times in the 1780s and 1790s for permission to sponsor regular public dances.[23] In 1809, twenty-eight members of the Congo nation bought themselves a house with money collected at their dances or earned at their jobs, thus becoming the first nation to have a headquarters.[24] During the following decade the other nations strove similarly to incorporate themselves, which led the government to issue a formal decree in 1821 outlining the procedure for establishing an African society.[25] Slightly revised in 1823 and 1834, this legislation was ominously reminiscent of the paternalism of the cofradía constitutions. All societies were to employ the same constitution, supplied by the government. This constitution set forth the goals of the societies, the procedure for elections, admission of new members, and financial dealings, and postulated a major participatory role for the police, who now replaced the church as the instrument for controlling the black organizations. Police officers were to be present at all elections to collect and count ballots and to announce the winners; the attending policeman could conceivably name any officers that he cared to. Also, society officers were required to inform the police of any criminal activity engaged in by members.[26]

Despite its shortcomings, this constitution still displayed a number of improvements over the cofradía system. For one, the nations had almost full power over their finances. Police permission was required before selling society property, but for the most part the societies were free to collect and spend their funds as they wished. Also, the constitution established several goals that could benefit members in very concrete ways. The primary function of the nation was declared to be the collecting of money with which to buy members out of slavery, which money would then be repaid to the society by the freedman at 5 percent interest, the society holding his freedom papers until the loan was repaid. The societies were to establish schools for the members' children; the president had the particular responsibility to make sure that students attended regularly and that, when males reached the age of sixteen, they were placed with an artisan master—no specific provision was made for female offspring. The societies were also empowered to make loans to members needing capital for farms and businesses, or who were temporarily prevented from working.

Still, the conservative aspects of these goals are clear enough. The realization of any of them, with the possible exception of the first, would directly benefit the government and elite of the city. Suffering from a perennial shortage of labor, particularly skilled labor, the elite of Buenos Aires hoped to use the nations as a means to create a sober, responsible, stable work force to supply the economic necessities of the city.[27] Urging the officers to promote the moral well-being of members and to inform on them when they committed crimes would aid the police in reducing crime and disturbances in the city. And asking the societies to support a separate school system would enable the city's schools to remain segregated while guaranteeing that black children would receive an education far inferior to that of the whites. This in turn would definitively consign future generations of Afro-Argentines to low-status jobs and keep them out of competition with whites for better economic position in the city's society.

As it turned out, the government's hopes for the societies never materialized; the nations instead discovered a number of ways to maintain their autonomy and to frustrate the authorities' intentions. The police soon found that their numbers and energy were simply not equal to the task of trying to control the societies. Despite several decrees seeking to limit the number of societies in existence at any given time, the nations proliferated at a rapid rate. The five major organizations—the Cambundá, Benguela, Lubolo, Angola, and Congo—were all officially incorporated in the 1820s, along with a number of smaller ones such as the Mina, Quisamá, Tacuá, Mozambique, and others.[28] Conflicts among the members soon produced splinter groups that established themselves as separate nations. The Lubolo nation split in two in 1828. One group retained the Lubolo name and headquarters, while the other established itself as the Huombé nation and bought itself a new building.[29] Then in 1839 the Lubolo split again, the Quipará seceding to form a separate nation, from which fragment the Zeda nation seceded sometime in the 1850s.[30]

The Congo nation was particularly plagued with these problems. In 1834 the two halves of the nation split peacefully into the Congo Augunga and the Loango.[31] The following year, the leader of the Momboma faction of the Congo Augunga petitioned the police for permission to secede and form his own society.[32] Though the officer responsible for supervising the nations at first tried to ignore this request, continued reports of strife among the Congo Augunga led him to investigate and file a report to the chief of police in 1837 on "the state of discord which affects some of those Societies but most particularly the very large one known as Congo."[33] Two years later the conflict reached such a pass that the Congo Augunga was redivided into two new societies, the Augunga and the Mayombé, the assets of the old nation being split between them.[34] Meanwhile, the Loango, the other half of the original Congo nation, was also having its problems, which eventually led to a decade-long court battle in the 1850s over control of the society's property and an attempt on the part of half of the Loango to secede and join the Goyo, yet another society.[35]

The case of the Congo nation is an extreme one, but the continuing divisions within the societies, plus the establishment of entirely new nations as time went on, led to a proliferation of organizations that rendered the job of police control ever more difficult. By 1842 there were over forty societies in the city, and by the 1850s there were more than fifty.[36] (See Appendix D for a list of the societies.) The commander of Ward Four, where most of the societies were located, was the officer specially charged with policing the societies, and the succession of policemen who occupied that position found it a taxing one. In 1836 Commander Pedro Romero informed his chief that the societies were in an extraordinary state of tumult and disorder, and he recommended radical reform of their structure.[37] There are occasional references in police records to a projected study and report on the societies to be conducted in 1836 or 1837,[38] but the report was either never made or never acted on, for the commanders of Ward Four continued to complain bitterly about the impossibility of supervising the societies. In 1850 Commander Torres complained that having to watch over the nations was robbing him of time that he badly needed for other police work.[39] In 1860 the police attempted a crackdown on the nations, closing down all those which did not have their incorporation papers in order, but on the whole they appear to have been fighting a losing battle throughout the 1830–60 period.[40] The societies were allowed to function more or less as they wished, the police intervening only when members demanded that they do so.

The nations took advantage of this lack of supervision to jettison some of the more obviously impractical or undesirable goals imposed on them by the government. No evidence survives of the nations' having established the schools that they were supposed to provide for their members. The societies also tended to disregard the constitution's injunctions to turn over criminal members to the police. Only one case of this is known to have occurred, an incident in 1836 in which the president of the Casanche nation turned over a free Casanche who had murdered a slave. The culprit was executed at a special ceremony which delegates from all the nations attended.[41] As a rule the presidents seem to have preferred not to turn wrongdoers over to the police. In fact, cases of presidents themselves engaging in illegal activity to aid members are considerably more common. One such instance occurred in 1847, when the president of the Mozambique nation was arrested for sheltering the runaway slave of a Brazilian resident.[42] Also, society presidents frequently aided members who had themselves been the victims of wrongdoing, as in the Casanche case mentioned above. In several instances society presidents brought libertos to police headquarters to claim their freedom from masters who wished to retain their services illegally after they had reached majority.[43] Or when slaves or libertos suffered injuries from their masters or other people, the presidents occasionally escorted them to police headquarters to make sure that the case was looked into. In 1831 the president of the Mondongo nation brought in the black woman Joaquina, who had been beaten severely about the head; the police called in her mistress to testify.[44]

It is somewhat more difficult to evaluate the economic benefits that the societies were supposed to provide for their members. A major difficulty in studying the nations is the documentary bias from which they suffer: virtually all of the surviving primary material on them is from the police archives, and therefore principally concerns instances in which things were going wrong in the societies. The societies' own records concerning themselves have either disappeared or remain in the hands of unknown private owners, so the nations must be viewed through the fairly negative eyes of the police. Even in this biased body of documentation, however, evidence exists of the tangible benefits that the societies brought their members. One of the most basic was housing. It was a rare society that did not own its own house, and those few that did not do so bought vacant lots upon which they erected makeshift buildings to serve as a meeting place and headquarters. Rooms in these houses were rented to society members, the income going into the treasury.[45] This system thus benefited both the nation and its tenant-members. The municipal census of 1827 shows more than ten buildings inhabited by two or three families of blacks; all the adults were Africans, the children Argentines. Independent sources confirm that two of these (the Cambundá house at 333 Chile Street, and the Loango house on Córdoba Street, between Montevideo and Uruguay streets[46], were definitely society headquarters, which suggests that the others probably were too.

The houses also served another need for the members, which was that of social center and hall for their dances, the candombes, the most important of the nations' social activities. As previously noted, the earliest corporate acts of the African nations were to petition the viceroy for permission to hold candombes. Official opposition to the dances continued into the national period, and it was not until Governor Rosas's administration that the Afro-Argentines were allowed to conduct their festivities without let or hindrance. One of the most striking works of art produced in nineteenth-century Argentina is Martín Boneo's painting of Governor Rosas attending a candombe at the Congo Augunga house, the society president seated on Rosas's left while the dictator intently watches the dancers.[47]

The full importance of the dances in the life of the black community will be examined in the following chapter. For the moment, suffice it to say that by providing both a locus for the dances and the political clout that forced Governor Rosas to concede them the right to dance when they wanted, the societies brought undeniable and profound social benefits to their members. In a 1902 feature article in which the magazine *Caras y Caretas* interviewed two of the last surviving members of the Benguela nation, their most vivid memory of society life was of the nation marching and dancing through the streets of the city: "even the cobblestones danced!"[48]

The extent to which the societies complied with their projected function as a loan institution to members and as a purchasing agent to buy members out of slavery must remain an open question. There is no solid 'evidence of such activity in the police archives, but then there is really no reason why there should be, since this would have been a routine business matter that did not require police attention. A hint of such activity appears in an 1836 case in which the secretary of the Hambuero nation denied charges that the president had illegally used society funds to buy his children out of slavery. The society had not even been established until 1825, noted the secretary, while the president freed his children in 1811, so the alleged favoritism in the use of society funds cannot be proven.[49] This at least suggests that society funds were used to buy slaves' freedom, though it is impossible to say with what regularity.

The fall of Governor Rosas in 1852 closely coincided with the beginning of the nations' decline. The final elimination of the slave trade in 1840 had already resulted in a marked decrease in the city's African population (see Chapter 5). Documents of the 1850s and 1860s frequently mention the nations' dwindling and aging memberships. Reports of presidents who died of old age appear regularly, and many presidents were forced to retire from office by general decrepitude. Antonio Vega, who had been present at the buying of the original Congo headquarters in 1809 and had served as president of the Congo Augunga from 1830 to 1858, finally retired because of old age. Joaquín Arriola stepped down as president of the Benguela in 1864 for the same reason, having served as chief executive since 1836. A police report from the

1850s on the Maquaqua described them as "composed for the most part of very old and chronically ill individuals," and an 1861 petition from the Congo Augunga presents the melancholy picture of a nation whose "number of Members was once considerable, [but] which has been scattered, some in the continuous wars of this Capital, as defenders of it; and others of natural illnesses." Thus by the 1860s the societies had declined from their former numbers to pathetic aggregations of ten or twenty members.[50] The 1870 constitution of the Mozambique nation recognized this process of decline by establishing in Article 21 a procedure for dissolving the nation. When the membership dropped to four members, stipulated the constitution, the property of the nation was to be divided among those four and the Mozambique nation was to be officially ended.[51]

As suggested by the Congo Augunga petition cited above, conscription of Africans into Governor Rosas's armies had levied a heavy toll on the nations. The government's drafts also had the incidental effect of temporarily unbalancing the sexual composition of the societies, leaving them in the hands of the female members during the lengthy periods while the men were away campaigning. As in the cofradías, women occupied a distinctly inferior position to men in the nations, but during the 1840s they took advantage of the men's absence to take control. The Mayombé nation, for instance, lost virtually all of its males in 1840 to Rosas's army, leaving one lone man and all the women to keep up the nation's headquarters. When the men returned in 1852, they attempted to sell the building, which had been much improved by the women in the meantime. The women refused to allow them to do so and went to court rather than see their headquarters sold. Eventually the Mayombé were split in two by court order, the men retaining the house but having to pay the women a large indemnity.[52] Similar events transpired in the Carabarí and Malavé nations, in which the women and a few male supporters refused to hand over control of the nation's property to the returned soldiers.[53]

The only hope for the nations' continued survival was the participation of the younger Afro-Argentines, but it appears that the old Africans actively resisted the entry of a new generation. After the 1863 elections in the Mina Mají nation, several young members came to the police to complain that they were being tyrannized by the old members and stood no chance of electing any of their candidates.[54] The 1870 constitution of the Mozambique nation allowed non-Africans to join the society but specifically denied them the right to vote or hold office.[55]

Even had the Africans been more receptive to new members, few young Afro-Argentines seem to have been interested in preserving the

African societies. Following a pattern common in immigrant societies, most second- and third-generation Afro-Argentines preferred to forget their foreign origins and their ethnic separateness. These young people turned their backs on reminders of their African heritage, of which the nations were one of the most obvious. They sought to cast aside their separateness and become part of the greater Argentine society, an ambition which the unitarians warmly encouraged. The post-Rosas government feared the nations as a possible source of support for a Rosista resurgence, and it made every effort to discourage their continuation. A representative expression of unitarian sentiment concerning the nations appeared in 1858 in the newspaper *La Nueva Generación* (The New Generation) in response to the appearance of Buenos Aires's first black newspaper, *La Raza Africana* (The African Race).[56] The editor objected strenuously to the new publication's title: why call yourselves Africans, he asked, when you are really Argentines? Accusing the paper of seeking to undermine the foundations of the liberal government by resurrecting the political spirit of the tyrant Rosas, the article urged the city's black population to forget the divisions of the past and join with the whites in rebuilding the city under a new, enlightened government. Most young Afro-Argentines were more than willing to accept this invitation, and in the process the nations were shunted aside as an anachronistic relic of a shameful past.

Later in the century, Afro-Argentine youths sought to rehabilitate the memory of their ancestors' social organizations, naming some of their Carnival marching bands, the comparsas, after the nations, e.g., Los Negros Lubolos, Los Benguelas, and Los Negros Munyolos. Also, the 1880s saw several court cases in which descendants of society members sued to recover control of the old society headquarters, then fallen into disrepair and occupied by outsiders, often white. An editorial in the black newspaper *La Broma* applauded a successful suit by descendants of the Quisamá nation to recover their headquarters, saying that the loss of this property had been an affront to the entire community.[57] Encouraged by the outcome of the case, descendants of the Auzá nation launched a similar suit the following year and also won.[58] But during the 1860s and 1870s, most Afro-Argentines wanted only to forget the Rosas years and the heritage of the nations. Indeed, it was in large part the wish to escape the incriminating associations of Africanism and to adopt the forms of white society that led to the next stage in the development of the black organizations, the socialist- and anarchist-inspired mutual aid societies.

A postmortem on the African nations must be a mixed judgment, and also a tentative one because of the documentary bias mentioned earlier.

In the police records the nations are seen at their worst: members appealing to the police to arrest their president for embezzlement, factions going to court over control of the nation's property, the police arresting members for fighting at the dances, and so on. Still, the incidence of police intervention is fairly low when one considers the large number of nations in existence at any given time. Approximately half of them never had cause to appeal to the police to intervene in their affairs, and it was a rare nation that suffered intervention more than once a decade. A number of the benefits that the nations brought to their members, such as housing and a site for social functions, aid in dealing with the government, a sort of collective bargaining power, are undeniable; others, such as the loans and projected manumissions, must remain matters of speculation.

As a form of community organization, the nations did possess one major shortcoming, which may or may not have been foreseen by the government when it instituted the nation system. If it was foreseen, that government must be credited with a Machiavellian subtlety in controlling and manipulating social groups. The shortcoming consisted of the cleavages that the nations created within the city's black community. The divisive effects of these cleavages are readily apparent in a survey of police records, in which petitions concerning ethnic conflicts and attempts by smaller groups to secede make up approximately a third of all the cases involving the nations.

This splintering tendency was one of the greatest weaknesses of the nation system. As long as the concept of the African nation existed, the secession of smaller groups on ethnic or national grounds had a legitimacy that it would not otherwise have enjoyed. There are several cases in which individuals and groups employed ethnic pretexts to cover disputes which were essentially political or personal in nature. For instance, an African named Tiburcio Quirno served as president of three societies in the 1840–60 period, exercising control over the Villamoani, Muñambani, and Maquaqua nations at different times. The Maquaqua was a splinter group of the Muñambani that came into existence only after Quirno had lost his position as president of the latter. This suggests that the Maquaqua was a nation created by Quirno mainly as a reaction to his having lost power in the Villamoani and Muñambani.[59] A similar case occurred in 1856, when a member of the Huombé nation complained to the police that his organization had been infiltrated by outsiders who had taken control of the society. "The Huombé nation does not exist," he explained to the police, and "the group represented by Freytas [the president of the nation, a non-Huombé] is nothing more than a miscellaneous collection of people. Our nation, sir, does not exist!

What exists is a genuine orgy, an aggregation that only produces scandals and outrages of all sorts."[60] Upon investigation, the police found this to be the case. A large foreign segment had invaded the Huombé and established themselves as the dominant faction of the society, using an assumed national identity to win a power base in the Afro-Argentine community. Similar complaints referring to the Congo and Malavé nations show that this type of occurrence was not rare.[61]

It seems, then, that while the nations provided their members with benefits both tangible and intangible, they also served to introduce disunity and at times discord into the city's black community. Still, this disunity was an inevitable stage in the history of the Afro-Argentines, since it reflected genuine ethnic differences and divisions transported from Africa which manifested themselves in slaveholding societies throughout the Americas.[62] With the decline of the African population in the city, these divisions could fade somewhat and the Afro-Argentines were able to join together and move on to the final stage in the development of their social organizations.

THE MUTUAL AID SOCIETIES

The activities of the African nations had included many mutualist aspects—providing housing and loans, buying members out of slavery, and paying funeral expenses, among others. It remained for the next generation of social organizations to jettison the cultural activities of the nations—the dances and other African survivals—and concentrate exclusively on the economic concerns of their members. The 1855 constitution of the first black mutualist society, the 134-member Sociedad de la Unión y de Socorros Mutuos, marked a number of advances over the constitution of the nations. The most important change was that the organization's constitution was actually written by the members themselves, unlike that of the cofradías, which had been supplied by the church, or that of the nations, which had been supplied by the provincial government. Perhaps as a result of the change in authorship, the mutualist activities of the society, and the mechanisms for financing them, are much more clearly and fully described than was the case in the nations' charter. Indeed, one of the most striking differences between the society's constitution and that of the nations is its purely economic emphasis. Misbehavior on the part of members and officers would be punished not by turning them over to the police or depriving them of membership (except in extreme cases) but by fines, which would serve to fill the society's treasury. The benefits supported by this system were substantial. Sick members would receive a daily stipend until they could work again, and every member was eligible to receive free medical treatment from the society's doctor. Echoing a traditonal concern of the cofradías and the nations, the constitution also provided for a delegation to attend members' funerals as mourners, though no financial benefits were offered in case of death.[63]

At least two other societies of this type were established during the 1850s, one the Sociedad del Carmen y de Socorros Mutuos, and the other a society of Brazilian blacks, the Sociedad Protectora Brasilera. These societies were roughly contemporaneous with the first white mutual aid societies to be established in Buenos Aires, those being two societies established in 1857 by Spanish immigrants, with goals and benefits very similar to those of the blacks.[64] The Sociedad Protectora Brasilera attempted to provide even greater benefits than the Sociedad de la Unión, offering free medical care and drugs in addition to a daily relief payment for sick members, and a free funeral in case the free medical care proved ineffective.[65] Subsequent documents suggest, though, that both these societies had difficulty delivering the promised benefits. Less than five months after its establishment in 1859, the Sociedad del Carmen was embroiled in a conflict reminiscent of the nations. The president of the "Corporation of Women," Basilia Azcuénaga, charged the society president, Roberto Smith, with unlawful conduct and with flouting majority rule. The society was apparently split along sexual lines, and the outcome of the dispute remains unclear. Then in 1860 the Sociedad Protectora Brasilera was abruptly deserted by its president, whose administration had left the headquarters (and presumably the finances) "in a state of complete destruction." New elections were held and the society limped along as best it could.[66]

The most successful of the black societies of the 1860–1900 period were La Fraternal and La Protectora. La Fraternal was the earlier of the two. Founded sometime in the 1850s by the musician and military officer Casildo Thompson, La Fraternal received warm and hopeful support from the black community. The first number of the black newspaper *El Proletario* reported on the existence of La Fraternal and urged all of Buenos Aires's blacks to join it. The article hints that Thompson was inspired by foreign models (one immediately thinks of the mutual aid societies of Europe), since the editor noted that such societies "in other countries have produced the most splendid and beneficial results." "*In union there is strength*," thundered the paper, and urged its readers to join together in mutual associations to rebuild the black community.[67]

La Fraternal realized one of the goals of the African nations, the establishment of a school for black children. Concluding that opportunities for blacks in the public schools were unacceptably limited, Thompson established an academy which functioned for fourteen years, expiring along with La Fraternal in the early 1870s.[68] The society has left no record of its benefit activities, so it is unclear to what extent it served as an economic cushion for its members in the way that mutual aid societies are designed to. It seems unlikely that the society could have generated sufficient revenues to support both a school and a large structure of relief benefits.

Still, the experience of La Fraternal had been sufficiently encouraging to lead the black community to embark on a second and much more successful experiment. In 1876 the black paper *La Juventud* (The Youth) launched a campaign on behalf of establishing another mutualist society, proclaiming that "our true religion is Mutual Aid."[69] *La Juventud*'s appeals found a response among the black stevedores and port workers, many of whom, curiously enough, were immigrants from the United States.[70] In July of 1877 they established La Protectora, an organization destined to outlive every one of its founders. Exceptionally well managed, the society increased both its membership and its assets steadily from 1877 to 1882 (the last year for which figures are available), growing from 30 to 150 members in that period.[71] In 1903 it purchased a house to serve as headquarters, which was expanded in subsequent decades to provide more space for activities. In 1936, the last date for which there is information on the society, it was still functioning as an active and autonomous organization.[72]

The benefits offered by La Protectora were typical mutual aid society features. The bulk of expenditures was for aid to sick members, the original motive for the society's founding. Members received free medical care, supplies, and a small stipend while they were prevented from working. Those who contracted chronic or incurable diseases, however, were declared ineligible for further benefits, since this would have been an excessive drain on the treasury.[73] In 1882 the society's new constitution called for death benefits to be provided also, all members to receive free funerals and burial in the mausoleum that the society built in the Recoleta cemetery in 1883.[74] Another service that La Protectora furnished its members was a library, opened in 1881 and added to by contributions of books and magazines from its members.[75] These benefits were financed through regularly collected dues and a series of benefit bazaars and dances.

La Protectora was a fitting end to the progression of nineteenth-century Afro-Argentine social organizations. Solidly successful, it won the unqualified approval of almost all sectors of black opinion. The fiercely antagonistic black newspapers *La Broma* and *La Juventud* agreed on very few issues, but they both backed La Protectora, frequently urging their readers to join the organization's swelling ranks. The stability of La Protectora and the quiet competence with which its affairs were managed was an undeniable refutation of the Afro-Argentines' alleged inability to do anything successfully on their own. The community took care to ensure that the society's accomplishments were brought to the attention of the city's whites. The society published a newspaper, *La Protectora*, off and on during the 1880–1910 period, and at one of its annual dinners and installation of officers it awarded a gold medal of appreciation to an editor of the prestigious Buenos Aires daily *La Nación* for his series of very favorable articles on the society.[76] Thus La Protectora met the double prerequisite for a truly successful Afro-Argentine social organization: not only did it promptly and regularly supply economic aid to its members, but it also served as a source of pride and self-respect to the community.

It is not clear when La Protectora ceased to exist. Though it was still alive in the late 1930s, there is some evidence to suggest that it might have taken the same road as the Cofradía del Rosario, which eventually evolved into the white brotherhood that it is today. The 1882 presidential report noted that several whites belonged to the society even at that early date, and a 1936 publication discussing the society made no mention of its being black.[77]

The three-stage progression of Afro-Argentine community organizations corresponds to the evolving relationship between the city's black population and the greater society. The cofradías represented the first tentative efforts of a repressed, subordinate community to create organizations capable of satisfying the spiritual and, occasionally, the material needs of its members. Constrained from creating their own forms of social organization, the slaves and free Afro-Argentines had no recourse but to organize through the cofradías, institutions originally created by and for white Spaniards and subsequently adapted to New World realities. Tensions and conflicts inevitably resulted between the traditional role of the brotherhood, an organization well integrated into Spanish society, and the marginal social status of the Afro-Argentines.

The nations resolved these conflicts by offering a form of organization based on the cultural and historical inheritance of the city's Africans and Afro-Argentines. But the existence of the nations presupposed a substantial African population in the city, and as that population died off, the creole black community abandoned the nations and embraced the mutual aid society. In so doing the Afro-Afrgentines quieted the uneasiness provoked in the greater society by the nations' alien and vaguely threatening character. It is significant that the 1936 book which includes the last notice of La Protectora's continued existence notes that the organization was founded by a group of men (the author did not specify their race, though he listed their names) who wanted to form a mutual aid society that would be "genuinely Argentine."[78] It was precisely this genuine Argentineness, plus very capable management, that enabled La Protectora to survive through a sixty-year period in which the black population virtually disappeared beneath a flood of European immigration.

And therein lies the irony of the black societies. The history of the Afro-Argentine social organizations is the history of the conflict between the black community's quest for corporate autonomy and the greater society's efforts to thwart that quest. Through the medium of the cofradías, and later through the nations, the government carefully monitored the community's efforts toward mobilization, using first the church and later the police as the instrument of control. Over time, the Afro-Argentines developed increasingly effective tactics for resisting these controls, and by the time the mutual aid societies were established the community had escaped the direct, overt domination represented by the cofradías and the nations. However, the community escaped these controls by removing the need for them: in so successfully adopting the mutual aid society, the Afro-Argentines turned their backs on black cultural and social separatism. The community achieved the autonomy it had sought for so long at the price of divesting itself first of its cultural identity and then of its racial identity, as it eventually was assimilated into the white population around it. In the end, does this not constitute the most effective control of all?

9

Afro-Argentines
in the Arts

Throughout the Western Hemisphere, Afro-Americans have distinguished themselves through their achievements in the arts. So irresistible have their talents proven that the societies of the New World long ago decided that they could not afford to waste the resource of black creativity, and it has become an unwritten law of the Americas that the arts are the field in which black people are freest to rise as high as their abilities will take them. No history of the Afro-Argentines of Buenos Aires would be complete, therefore, without a survey of their participation in the cultural life of the city.

FROM CANDOMBE TO TANGO

Such a survey should begin with dance, the area in which Buenos Aires has made its most widely diffused contribution to Western popular culture. It would be impossible to exaggerate the importance of dance in the life of the Afro-Argentines. Their public dances were cultural events in the fullest, broadest sense of the term. They brought the community together on a regular basis, strengthening the ties of friendship and community identity. They provided a source of recreation and rejuvenation and a means of self and group affirmation to a people denied this all-important right. Furthermore, their political significance was unmistakable, as may be seen in the continuing conflict between the community and the government over whether or not the dances were to be allowed to take place.

156

It is not clear exactly when the Afro-Argentines started holding their public dances, the candombes, though surviving documents show that by the 1760s they had caught the unfavorable attention of the authorities. The viceroy banned the blacks' dances twice in 1766, again in 1770, and again in 1790.[1] But these bannings referred only to gatherings held without official supervision—the viceroy specifically allowed the Africans and Afro-Argentines to hold public dances under the eye of properly delegated authority.[2] The viceroys also proved amenable to petitions from groups of Africans applying for permission to hold special dances for their own nations. In 1795 permission was granted the Congo blacks to dance on Sundays and holidays, and in 1799 a similar permit was granted to the Cambundá blacks.[3] The viceroys were careful to stipulate one absolute prohibition, however: these affairs could only be held as long as no black man was crowned or recognized as king of one of the African nations.[4] As the Crown's representative in the colony, the viceroy's primary responsibility was to maintain royal authority and power intact and unchallenged, and the crowning of African royalty at the dances would have been a direct, even if purely symbolic, threat to the Spanish monarch's hegemony. The royal administration had reacted quite strongly to a 1787 case in which a young slave had been crowned King of the Congo at one of the dances. An investigation of the incident revealed that the African Pedro Duarte had been invested with an umbrella and crown at the dance, after which many of the Congo made him obeisance. The case was dropped only after Duarte swore that the ceremony had meant that he was "greater, but not a king."[5]

On the whole, however, the royal administration was fairly lenient in the matter of the dances, perhaps recognizing their value as a release for the community's frustrations and dissatisfactions. The municipal authorities were not so permissive. The town council issued at least three reports to the viceroy in the 1780s and 1790s urging him to impose a ban on the dances. A 1788 report was the most lengthy and detailed, and its description of the candombes and arguments in favor of their prohibition sounded many of the themes that were to recur in nineteenth-century denunciations of the phenomenon.[6]

The council's complaints concerning the dances may be divided into three categories: moral, economic, and political. Of the dances' un-redeemed moral nature the councilmen had no doubt. Describing the lewd and lascivious movements performed at the candombes, the councilmen raged against the multiple offenses to God and man committed at these weekly gatherings and expressed special fear concerning "the little girls and innocent people" in attendance, who could only be corrupted by the spectacle. Economically the dances were dangerous for two reasons. First, the black nations and cofradías took up collections to sponsor the festivities and other social activities—where could this money come from, asked the councilmen, except from the slaves robbing their owners? Furthermore, the report maintained that the slaves became so vice-ridden and irresponsible as a result of these dances that they became utterly useless to their owners: they shirk their duties and "think of no other thing but of the time when they can go to dance." And in political terms, the councilmen viewed the dances with considerable misgivings. As a result of the bad influences to which they were subject at these celebrations, the blacks were now

in a continual state of agitation. . . . With members so perverted and corrupted, the State and the Public must necessarily experience grave and irreparable damage . . . since the number of Blacks in the City is so very great, much attention and care is required in watching over them, guarding their conduct, never losing them from sight, and never pardoning their slightest excesses; since they are by character inclined and disposed toward every evil, one must treat them with the greatest watchfulness.

The councilmen could not have made it clearer: they realized that as the elite of a slaveholding society they were living on the summit of a volcano that could erupt at any moment, and they feared the dances as a potential source of discord and agitation, a catalyst that might trigger the explosion.

Their fears are understandable. These large gatherings of Africans and Afro-Argentines (the 1788 report claimed that the dances were regularly attended by up to two thousand people) must have looked extremely ominous, especially when one takes into account the alien character of the dancers, their music, and their dances (of which more shortly). And occasionally the candombes did erupt into violence aimed at the authorities. In 1791 a policeman happened upon an unsupervised gathering of some two hundred people holding a dance at a free black person's home. When he tried to break it up, those present set upon him with swords and sticks and, after scaring him off, continued with their dance.[7] But for the most part the candombes were peaceful affairs, and the viceroy, who took a more detached view than did the councilmen, allowed them to continue through the end of the colonial period.

When royal control was terminated by the revolution and the local elites were free to rule as they pleased, they took the opportunity to ban black street dancing in 1822, and public black dancing of any kind in 1825.[8] Although these prohibitions were only fitfully enforced, they served to put a damper on the candombes which was not lifted until

A Carnival comparsa, c. 1900. Photograph courtesy Archivo General de la Nación.

Governor Rosas came to power. Under his aegis the candombes enjoyed their Golden Age, much to the horror of the porteño upper class (see Chapter 6). Following Rosas's fall in 1852 the unitarian government adopted a policy of enforcing selective curfews against African societies sponsoring dances.[9] With the decline of the nations and the rise of new styles of dancing among younger Afro-Argentines, the candombes gradually faded away during the second half of the century. Certainly they never regained the popularity and splendor they had enjoyed during the Rosas years, when the governor and his family would personally attend the festivities.

The vitality of African and Afro-Argentine dance could not be repressed by porteño society. It formed the basis of all social and cultural activities and even found its way into formal religious celebrations, usually to the church's chagrin. In 1779 one local priest complained to his superiors that blacks dancing outside his church to celebrate Easter had made so much noise that he had been unable to conduct services.[10] When the black Cofradía de San Baltasar petitioned in 1784 for permission to build its own chapel, the brothers specifically mentioned as one of their reasons for doing so their desire to have a place where they could hold their celebratory dances.[11]

The biggest black dances of the year were held on the Day of Kings (January 6), St. John's Day, Christmas, Easter, and especially Carnival, the week-long holiday in February before the abstinence period of Lent. The Carnival celebrations of Brazil, particularly in Rio de Janeiro, are justly famed for the Afro-Brazilian dances performed there—they are the throbbing heart of the week's festivities. The same was once true of Buenos Aires. Comparsas, marching and dancing bands, were first permitted in Buenos Aires during the Carnival of 1836. All the African nations fielded ensembles to parade through the streets in brilliant costumes, each with its own drum corps and dancers. These black comparsas dominated the Carnival festivities each year (except between 1844 and 1852, when Governor Rosas banned Carnival because of its excessive violence) well into the 1870s, when the white comparsas began to take over. Even as late as 1900, ten to fifteen Afro-Argentine groups participated in the merriment each year, sporting such names as Star of the South, Flower of Cuba, Don Juans of the Plata, Inhabitants of the Moon, and the names of the old nations, such as the Benguela Blacks, the Monyolo Blacks, and so on. But as the community sank to a tiny percentage of the city's population, the Carnival celebrations did not long survive it. By the 1930s the parades and street festivities of Carnival were no more.[12]

A curious footnote concerning the comparsas is the frequent efforts by white porteños to imitate the Afro-Argentine ensembles. Beginning in the 1860s and 1870s, and continuing into the present century, young whites paraded annually in blackface and sought to duplicate the black comparsas' music, dance steps, and marching routines.[13] The best known of these blackface comparsas was Los Negros, an organization of several hundred young men belonging to the city's most prominent families.[14] As befitted such a prestigious organization, news of Los Negros' meetings, elections of officers, and general doings appeared regularly in the porteño press during the 1860s and 1870s.[15] The group was one of the most popular attractions of the post-1860 Carnival, and its theme song was widely known and sung:

> The comparsa of Los Negros,
> The most faithful and loyal,
> Salutes all the little ladies
> In this brand new Carnival.
> To all the sweet young girls
> We offer ourselves as slaves,
> We'll be slaves body and soul,
> And faithful until death.
>
> Oh white girls!
> Have mercy!
> Hear the black men's sad lament.
> Though our faces
> Are colored,
> We're made of fire within.[16]

But to return to the role of dance in the black community: exactly what kinds of dances did the Afro-Argentines perform? In the 1750–1850 period they were obviously African in origin, with very few if any Argentine additions. Each African nation had its own particular dances—white observers and black petitioners concur on this point. When the brothers of San Baltasar appealed for the right to build their chapel, they began their plea by recalling, with a certain amount of exaggeration, that "from time almost immemorial, the brothers have been accustomed, with the prior consent of the various Governors, to hold their functions in the manner of their respective Nations."[17] The Congo nation's 1795 petition to the viceroy repeats that "each Nation performs its Dances according to its style, and with all due propriety."[18]

The whites were aware that the candombes were occasions at which the Africans performed their national dances, calling up memories of their homeland and recreating, even if only for an afternoon, a simulacrum of African society in the New World. Indeed, the town council singled out this element as one of the most threatening features of the dances.

It has been observed that in these dances the Blacks perform Gentile Rites of the places in which they were born, with certain ceremonies and speeches that they perform in their Languages. . . . they put on the various Dances by which each Nation distinguishes itself, and it can truthfully be said that in these dances they forget the sentiments of the most Holy Catholic Religion that they accepted, that they renew the rites of the gentiles, that they pervert the good customs that their Owners have taught them, that they learn nothing but vices, . . . and that the Republic is very badly served.[19]

"The Republic is very badly served"—the councilmen saw that in rejecting Catholicism and keeping alive African religion and cultural practices, the slaves were resisting one of Spain's most basic and potent controls of non-elite populations. Through the candombes the Afro-Argentines kept a part of their lives free of the absolute control that a slave-owning society sought to exercise over them. It was a small act of resistance, but it was one of the few open to them, and they refused to abandon it.

Even Europeans who spent brief periods of time in the city were struck by the way in which the Africans conserved and relived memories of their homeland. A previously quoted memoir written by an Englishman who lived in the city during the 1820s described the community's wedding ceremonies.

A wedding or other happy occasion is celebrated with African magnificence. They form pavilions of white clothing and the bride passes beneath them; they carry batons with red rags, which do for flags; they make noise with drums, pots, and pans; they dance solos as in Guinea or Mozambique, I presume; the music consists of singing and handclapping, after which come torrents of applause. . . . It is odd the way in which they preserve their African customs.[20]

The French naturalist Alcides d'Orbigny has left a stirring description of a candombe that he witnessed in Montevideo in 1827, a dance celebrating the Day of Kings. The Frenchman clearly recognized the importance of the dance as a way for the Africans to "regain for a moment their nationality" and escape, at least temporarily, the rigors of slavery.

All the blacks born on the coasts of Africa gathered together in tribes, each one of which elected a king and a queen. Dressed in the most striking manner, with the most brilliant outfits that one can imagine, and preceded by all the subjects of their respective tribes, these monarchs-for-a-day made their way to mass, then paraded through the city, and, gathered at last in the small square near the market, every one performed, each in his own way, a dance characteristic of his nation. I saw in rapid succession war dances, representations of agricultural work, and steps of the most lascivious type. There more than six hundred blacks seemed to have regained for a moment their nationality, in the heart of that imaginary country, whose memory alone, . . . in the midst of that noisy saturnalia of another world, made them forget, for one single day of pleasure, the pains and sufferings of long years of slavery.[21]

With the passage of time the original purity of the various national dance steps was lost, and a process of melding occurred. Africans from the different nations living in close contact with each other gradually developed a sort of composite dance, the candombe, which borrowed elements from a number of African dances. (Thus the word *candombe* has two meanings: a particular dance step [e.g., "he is doing the candombe"], and the public dances as a social event ["she is at the candombe"].[22])

The choreography of the candombe is divided into four stages. In the first, men and women form two lines facing each other, singing, chanting, and swaying to a slow and steady beat. Occasionally the lines come together for the *ombligada*, in which males and females strike stomachs together. At the end of this section, the "broomsman" performs a solo using a broom as a baton, twirling, throwing it, and performing various feats of skill as a sort of intermission. Following this, the rhythm picks up slightly and couples dance one at a time while the rest of the dancers form a clapping and singing circle around them. Couples succeed each other in the center until everyone has danced. In the third stage, men and women make a ring together and dance a sort of cakewalk step, bodies alternately thrown back and forward, the wheel moving to the beat of the drums. Then with an abrupt shout the lead drummer hurls himself into a wild and driving rhythm, in which he is immediately joined by the other musicians. The wheel dissolves and the whole crowd dances madly; each person improvises his or her own steps and dances however he or she pleases. The rhythm picks up speed and intensity over roughly half an hour. The dancers dance to exhaustion. Then as suddenly as it began, it is over: the lead drummer shouts out a command, his companions stop precisely on cue, and the dance has ended.[23]

Though such other African and Afro-American dances as the bamboula, the chica, and the calenda were also done in Buenos Aires (an obvious borrowing by the candombe was the stomach-bumping of the calenda), the candombe may be considered the representative Afro-Argentine dance of the first half of the nineteenth century. After a long afternoon and night of dancing, it always formed the climax of the festivities, regardless of the nation.

The dance's popularity, and indeed the institution of the public African dances, faded significantly after 1850.[24] Though the nations continued to hold candombes during the 1850s and 1860s, they became more and more lightly attended as young Afro-Argentines sought to integrate themselves into porteño society by taking up the waltzes, polkas, and mazurkas popular among the whites, and leaving behind the dances so closely associated with their African descent. One has only to read the social columns of the black newspapers of the period to see how the European steps had taken over. Dances continued to be the major social events of the community, but now the columinists reported on which young lady danced a polka with which young man, which couple sat out the mazurka, and so on. And if some older members of the community still cherished fond memories of the old dances, they caught the prevailing mood of the society well enough to know that the African dances were a shameful thing, to be kept under cover, hidden from the mocking eyes of the whites. An article from 1882 in a black newspaper complained about the young black drummers who continued to play and perform the candombe publicly, especially at Carnival. Protesting that these young people would serve the community much better if they learned how to play "musical instruments" instead of "the old pathetic drums that now serve only as the one reminder of the venerable but corrupted customs of long ago," the paper argued that the candombe had its place but that that place was not a public one.

There are an unlimited number of these youths, who, if one of our "aunties" [old women of the community] graciously asks them to play the drums in one of the few society headquarters that our grandfathers left as a reminder that they had a much better idea of what sociability meant than many of our young people, they refuse and instead go out to behave in a shameful way, showing off for the girls; . . . with no sense of shame, they smear their faces with soot and expose themselves to the general hilarity in the Calle Florida and in front of the Confitería del Gas, which we have had the disgrace of having to endure this year.[25]

Shame and disgrace: the feelings of this segment of the black community, trying so hard to achieve respectability and acceptance among the whites, could not be clearer. The candombe, like all other reminders of the black community's earlier history, should not be forgotten, but neither should it be exhibited.

The change in dancing styles in the black community did not pass unnoticed by the whites. A 1905 article titled "The People of Color" congratulated the Afro-Argentines on their "aristocratic salons, where instead of the grotesque candombe or semba—lewd as a monkey's grimace—they dance in modern clothes in the manner of Louis XV."[26] The porteño press had granted the black elite the ultimate accolade: the Afro-Argentines had finally succeeded in producing as good an imitation of European arts and forms as the Euro-Argentines.

But the candombe did not pass without leaving its imprint on Argentine culture. In fact, Afro-Argentine dance formed one of the major ingredients of Argentina's most exportable cultural commodity, the tango. As early as the first decade of the nineteenth century, documents referred to the "tangos de los negros," meaning their dances. Historian Ricardo Rodríguez Molas has unearthed a series of sales documents for a "house and tango site" owned by blacks during the first two decades of the nineteenth century. An 1818 will in which the property is mentioned refers to "the said lot situated in the neighborhood of the Parish of Concepción tango of the Blacks by which name it is known."[27] An ordinance considered by the Montevideo town council in 1807 proposed to prohibit "the tangos of the blacks," their weekly dances.[28] The composer of "El Entrerriano," accepted by many musicologists as the first tango of known authorship, was an Afro-Argentine, Rosendo Mendizábal, a tango accordionist who wrote the piece in 1896.[29] Though most scholars of the tango tend to place its beginnings in the 1880s, black newspapers of the 1870s contain occasional references to it, such as *La Broma*'s announcement in 1879 of Emilio Alvarez's having just written "a *terrible* Tango, that is to say, a lovely Tango."[30]

The very etymology of the world tango is strongly rooted in Afro-Argentine culture. The Brazilian anthropologist Artur Ramos is of the opinion that the word comes from a corruption of *tambor*, the Spanish word for drum. "Tocar tambor" means "to play the drum," and thus "vamos tocar tambor" (let's go play the drums) became "vamos tocá tambó" and eventually "vamos tocá tango" (let's play a tango).[31] Néstor Ortiz Oderigo argues for a more direct African descent, from such words as Shangó (the Yoruba god of thunder and storms), or from various African words for drum and dance, among which he mentions tanga, tamtamngo, tangana, and tangú. Ortiz Oderigo supports his case by observing how frequently the word tango is used to refer to Afro-American music throughout the hemisphere. A Cuban dance called the habanera was also known as the "tango americano"; black dances in

Veracruz, Mexico, were known as tangos; the jazz districts in New Orleans were called the Tango Belt; and so on.[32]

Anyone who has ever seen a couple dancing a genuine tango might well ask what that sinister, controlled, and highly stylized dance, with its unpredictable pauses following by sweeping, almost frantic runs across the dance floor, could possibly have in common with the intensely rhythmic, almost monotonous candombe, which starts out in gentle, relaxed swaying and gradually builds in intensity to the wild release that is almost the polar opposite of the tango. The question is a perfectly reasonable one, and better yet, a convenient one, for in the evolution from candombe to tango one has yet another object lesson in the role played by the Afro-Argentines in porteño society and culture. The links between the candombe and the tango were the dance halls, the *academias de baile*, and a dance called the *milonga*.

The academias de baile were analogous to the dance halls and saloons of nineteenth-century North American cities. Usually located in lower-class, outlying areas of the city, the academias formed the locus for Buenos Aires's low life. Though occasional parties of well-to-do young men might drop by looking for a night's amusement, the clientele of the academias were mainly the *orilleros* and *compadritos*, the inhabitants of Buenos Aires's demimonde.[33] Here the city's poor whites and poor blacks met to drink and gamble, to fight and dance. Out of this cross-racial contact was born the milonga, a dance created by the young white toughs in mocking imitation of the candombe. One of the first descriptions of the dance, written in 1883, specifically described it as an outgrowth of the candombe: "the milonga is only danced by the compadritos of the city, who created it to make fun of the dances that the blacks do. It has the same rhythm and movement as the drums of the candombe."[34] That statement is corroborated by another contemporary observer, an old black woman who recalled in 1902 how "the compadritos invited us to dance the milonga, based on our music."[35] Historian Vicente Rossi also gives the Afro-Argentines credit for developing the milonga: "All the creative and evolutionary process of the Milonga was the work of the blacks."[36]

A step which came into existence to burlesque the candombe served at the same time to preserve the Afro-Argentine dance, even if in altered form. And when the milonga evolved into the tango (a very direct evolution, since the milonga has been described as basically a slow tango), the candombe was preserved for decades to come. When the couple locks bodies tightly together and sways back and forth, we are seeing the lineal descendant of the first stage of the candombe, in which the swaying is interrupted by the bringing together of bodies for the ombligada. Or when the partners move rapidly across the floor, first the male leaning back at a sharp angle, then the female, it clearly derives from the third stage of the Afro-Argentine dance. The steps of the tango form a kinetic memory of the candombe, a dance that has died but in dying gave birth to the dance that identifies Buenos Aires, a dance exported around the world.

MUSIC

It was not only through dance, however, that the Afro-Argentines enriched the culture of their city and contrary. Closely allied to dance is of course music, and the black porteños won a deserved fame for their talents as composers and performers. The music that accompanied the candombes was almost entirely percussive, performed on drums and other percussion instruments, often accompanied by clapping, singing, and chanting. Melodic instruments did not stand much of a chance against the steady pounding rhythm of the drums. Those drums were among the community's proudest possessions—in 1902, when a popular Buenos Aires magazine ran an article on the last survivors of the Benguela nation, its photographs of the society's headquarters showed the nation's drums displayed prominently alongside its flag and presidential table.[37] Just as each nation had its own dances, so each nation had its own rhythms, so that there were Benguela beats, Mozambique beats, Cambundá beats, and so on.[38] One of the most exciting events of the nineteenth-century Carnivals was the legendary *tapada*, the drum battles joined among the various nations, in which each drum corps would try to overwhelm the others with a torrent of rhythm played for hours on end.[39] It was for good reason that the heavily black neighborhood of Monserrat was known as the Barrio del Tambor, Neighborhood of the Drum.

Such music was seldom agreeable to European and white Argentine ears. The traveler Concolorcorvo, upon witnessing a black dance in Argentina in the 1770s, complained that the music was so "annoying and disagreeable as to provoke one to stop up his ears and to cause the mules to stampede, and they are the most stolid and least flighty of animals."[40] In his history of the Rosas years, José María Ramos Mejía recalled it as "not a music, but rather a noise of the most disastrous effect, that resounded melancholically in the ears and the hearts of its listeners."[41] Black musicians who hoped to be rewarded by the society for their talents had to take up different styles and instruments, which

Composer Zenón Rolón (1857–1902). Date and circumstances of photograph unknown. Photograph courtesy Archivo General de la Nación.

they did most successfully. Many black keyboard players worked as church organists, while others earned high salaries as party and theater pianists, playing at fashionable entertainments and giving lessons. Among the more well known *maestritos*, as they were called, were Alejandro Vilela, Remigio Navarro, Federico Espinosa, Remigio Rivarola, Roque Rivero, and Tiburcio Silvarrios. Several of these men were also composers of some note. Roque Rivero had his short pieces published in the fashionable Buenos Aires magazine *La Moda*, while Remigio Navarro served as conductor of the Teatro Argentino orchestra and composed several songs in collaboration with the Argentine poet Esteban Echeverría.[42]

Rivero was also the father of the first notable Argentine violinist, Demetrio Rivero. Several other black men won reputations as excellent violinists, including Manuel G. Posadas and his son Manuel Junior, who studied at the national conservatory in Brussels.[43]

Black vocalists enjoyed their followings in the city's theaters and salons. One of the most prominent was Casildo Thompson, already introduced in Chapters 7 and 8 as a military officer and as founder of the mutual aid society La Fraternal. In addition to performing, Thompson composed several of the most popular songs of mid-century Buenos Aires. His son Casildo Gervasio Thompson continued in his father's footsteps, winning admission to the province's musical conservatory and, later, several national prizes for his religious compositions.[44]

The Thompsons are representative of a pattern that the reader will already have noted: the tendency of some Afro-Argentine families to produce two or more generations of musicians, the sons and even grandsons continuing in the same profession as their forebears. A black man who launched himself into music without the benefit of such family history was Zenón Rolón, who nevertheless managed to win a scholarship to study composition in Italy. He returned to Buenos Aires in 1880 to begin his career. As might be expected, his works revealed heavy European influences. He composed a number of pieces dedicated to Italian social clubs in the city, as well as two operettas written in Italian and another in French. His only black-oriented work was the symphonic march "Falucho," performed at the dedication of the statue of the black soldier Falucho in 1897. Rolón appeared occasionally as a conductor and pianist at the Teatro Rivadavia and the Teatro Colón, where his performances were well received but his compositions were not. Earning his living mainly by teaching piano and composition, he died in 1902 as a public school teacher in a small town in Buenos Aires province, a sad case of a musician who never realized his promise.[45]

Having never heard any of Rolón's works performed, I cannot form any judgment concerning their quality. But it is entirely possible that he and his fellow black musicians of the second half of the century were victims of the cultural snobbery of the porteño elite. As a white playwright who knew him recalled years later, "Rolón was a great musician and had one of the finest artistic temperaments I have ever encountered. . . . The extremely poor artistic circles in which it was his lot to travel when he returned from Italy never permitted him to extend his wings."[46] The black musicians had served well enough when Buenos Aires was an economic backwater, but as the city boomed and generated the wealth necessary to attract top talent from Europe, the Afro-Argentines were displaced from their positions as the fashionable musicians of the city. Only the rare black men who could acquire European training, such as Rolón or the young Posadas, were able to compete against the newcomers. An Afro-Argentine writing in the 1890s reflected bitterly on the changes in musical styles brought to the city by European musicians,

more greedy for money than for glory, the renowned musicians required by civilization, those who arrived with the patrimony of a document issued by the conservatories of Italy and Germany accrediting them as legitimate citizens of the capital of talent, and therefore the most qualified, the most authorized to flatter the ear and impress the soul by means of harmonic cadences drawn according to the most superior rules of art.[47]

The black musicians, unable to present such documents, were ignored by a society intent on adorning itself with the most certifiably European accoutrements available. So gradually the new arrivals wrested control of the music world from the Afro-Argentines, ejecting them from the salons and theaters of the city and reducing them to playing in the sleazy academias and bars of the lower-class neighborhoods, where they put their energies into creating the new music of the milonga and the tango.

There was one area of musical endeavor, however, in which the Afro-Argentines remained firmly in control throughout the nineteenth century and well into the twentieth. That is only to be expected, considering that the art form was almost purely African in its derivation. This was the *payada*, a sort of poetic duel in which two guitarist-singers spontaneously compose verses on a given theme or in response to each other's challenges. A vocal variation on the tapadas, the drum duels, the payada was the lineal descendant of the African tradition of musical contests of skill, a tradition which has produced similar phenomena in every American country where there is a large black population. In Brazil there is the *canto de desafio* or *canto de porfia*; in the United States there is the answer-back song; and in Argentina there is the payada.[48] The art form was immortalized in both of the two Argentine epic poems of the nineteenth century, *Santos Vega* and *Martín Fierro*. In the first, the hero engages in a payada with the Devil and loses his soul. The climax of *Martín Fierro* is a contest between Martín and an old black *payador* which touches at times on the question of race. The old man objects to Martín's having insulted him with a racial slur:

> They say God shaped the black man first
> When He planned man's shape and figure,
> Yet there's some white folks so mighty proud
> Though they ask him to sing to amuse the crowd,
> They don't remember he's got a name
> But only that he's a nigger.
>
> The white man paints the Devil black
> And the black man paints him white;
> But a man by his colour is not influenced.
> It don't hold for, nor yet against;
> The Almighty made only one kind of man,
> Though their faces are dark or bright.

Martín Fierro replies:

> Black and white God made, but He never said
> Which one of the two was duller;
> He gave them all the same cross to bear,
> And equal woes, and the same despair,
> But He also made light, and He made it white,
> The better to show up colour.
>
> There isn't any call to get personal
> Where there's been no provocation;
> I don't see how anyone is to blame
> If they call a thing by its common name,
> And a present you got on your first birthday
> Can't damage your reputation.[49]

It was no coincidence that Martín's opponent should have been black. The best known payadores were almost all Afro-Argentines, among them Pancho Luna, Valentín Ferreyra, Pablo Jerez, Felipe Juárez, Higinio D. Cazón, and Luis García.[50] Without question the greatest of them all was Gabino Ezeiza. Born in Buenos Aires in 1858, the son of an ex-slave, young Ezeiza first aspired to become a writer, and while still in his teens he worked on the editorial board of the black paper *La Juventud*. As his formidable talents developed, however, he turned increasingly to guitar

Gabino Ezeiza (1858–1916), the celebrated payador. The precise date and circumstances of this photograph are unknown, but it was probably taken just several years before his death. Photograph courtesy Archivo General de la Nación.

playing and his ability to concoct spontaneous verses to earn a living. During his prime, from roughly 1890 to 1915, Ezeiza toured throughout Argentina and Uruguay, fighting a memorable series of payadas and winning nationwide fame. He died in Buenos Aires in 1916; according to popular legend, he contracted terminal pneumonia as a result of having attended the presidential inauguration of Radical Party leader Hipólito Yrigoyen—Ezeiza was a long-time member and fervent supporter of the party.[51] There are only three statues of Afro-Argentines in all of Buenos Aires, a city that boasts some two hundred public monuments. Of those three, one is a memorial to the institution of slavery, another is a statue of the semimythical Falucho, and the third is a dilapidated bust of Gabino Ezeiza, its nameplate missing, set in a small playground in the outlying neighborhood of Mataderos, the Stockyards.

LITERATURE: THE ARTIST AS EXILE

The musical talents of the Afro-Argentines were undeniable and irresistible. They were, moreover, talents that the white Argentines were not able to develop in sufficient quantity and quality on their own, which meant that black dance and music occupied an important position in the city's cultural life throughout the nineteenth century. Not so with Afro-Argentine literature, whose practitioners were completely overshadowed by Euro-Argentine writers. The only black author of any note was the poet Horacio Mendizábal, a passionate and prolific writer whose career was cut tragically short when he died in the yellow fever epidemic of 1871 at the age of twenty-four. Born of an upper-class Afro-Argentine family (his father Rosendo Mendizábal, not to be confused with the previously mentioned musician of the same name, held a seat in the provincial legislature), he published *First Verses* at the age of nineteen, and *Hours of Meditation* two years later. Both volumes tend strongly toward the romantic: poem after poem invites various young women to contemplate the joys of nature and love with him. Nationalism, as exemplified in such poems as "Alerta" and "Arjentina," is a recurring theme. The second volume contains a number of poems in French and Italian, as well as translations of poems from those languages, Mendizábal obviously having been infected by the porteño worship of things European. The collection also includes sonnets in honor of Pope Pius IX, Garibaldi, Lincoln, and Benito Juárez, the Indian president of Mexico.

Mendizábal tended to avoid topics concerning race, though *First Verses* included poems dedicated to the black Colonels Domingo Sosa and José María Morales. *Hours of Meditation*, however, includes the impassioned "My Song," an indictment of Argentine racism.

> In the midst of my people I am alone.
> As my cradle was rocked
> It was pushed away from their side;
> A race of pariahs has remained
> And to that race I belong.
>
> We have no country—if it exists,
> It knew how to bar us from its heart;
> Let the burdens be for the sad man:
> We have but one right,
> Which must be the right to die.
>
> To die for the nation!
> You are a bastard, an irrational man:
> For a mulatto of tainted descent,
> For a vile black man, it is enough
> To don the halter and the chain.

Mendizábal has been quoted in another attack against race prejudice, though it is not known at what date this statement was made, or in what forum.

> Would you be horrified to see a black man occupying the highest position in the Republic? Why, if he were as enlightened as the best of you, as honest as the best of you, as wise and as dignified as the best of you? Just because the blood that ran in his veins had been darkened by the sun of Africa on his grandparents' brow? Would you be horrified to see sitting in the seats of Congress one of those men so insultingly called mulatto, only because his face is not the same color as yours? If so, I am ashamed of my country and despair of its ignorance.[52]

It was a tragic loss for the Afro-Argentine community when Mendizábal's voice was prematurely stilled, for no figure of comparable stature rose to replace him. A number of black journalist-poets worked in the city between 1860 and 1900, but none of them succeeded in having their work brought out in book form. Supporting themselves by working on both black and white newspapers, they published most of their artistic work in the black weeklies, and its quality is unexceptional. The most prominent of these figures were the elder Manuel Posadas; the payador Gabino Ezeiza; Froilán P. Bello, founder and editor of the black literary review *El Eco Artístico*; Santiago Elejalde, who managed to publish a collection of his inspirational essays; his son Mateo Elejalde; Dionisio García; Dionisio Malo; Ernesto Mendizábal, Horacio's brother; and Casildo G. Thompson, previously mentioned as a composer and musician.[53] Thompson was the only author who showed any sensitivity toward racial themes. His "Song of Africa," an evocation of the cruelties of the slave trade, employs a striking reversal of traditional porteño racial stereotypes. Here the white man is the savage, "a slavering wild beast" who destroys black families and lives in his relentless greed for profits. Black people are pariahs, as in "My Song," but they are also members of a noble and distinguished race:

> Of a race that is the martyr of history,
> A race worthy of glory
> Because it is noble and proud,
> Like the lion that lives in the jungle.[54]

Thus Thompson sounded the trumpet of black pride, a call seldom heard in Buenos Aires.

Though Afro-Argentines produced only limited contributions to the plastic arts in the nineteenth century, two members of their community, Juan Blanco de Aguirre and Bernardino Posadas, deserve mention. Blanco de Aguirre studied painting in Europe for five years and, doubtless for that reason, was able to support himself through his art.[55] Bernardino Posadas was not so privileged, but despite his lack of European training was appointed the first instructor of drawing in the Colegio Nacional.[56]

The black musicians, writers, painters, and other artists were marginal practitioners of the arts in Buenos Aires. Most artists prefer even scathing criticism of their work to utter indifference, which was the reaction accorded the creations of the Afro-Argentines. My year of research produced no indication whatsoever that the greater porteño society took any notice of the activities of the black artists, save for some of the musicians and the payadores. If articles concerning the artists, or critical reactions to their work, appeared in any of the Buenos Aires newspapers or magazines, they were so few as to be unfindable. Left alone with their muses, the Afro-Argentines struggled to create amid the neglect and indifference of the society around them. The community's intellectuals were aware of the deadly effect that this isolation had on their artists, particularly the younger ones in the process of experimenting and searching for their styles, and therefore so much in need of critical reaction. In an 1881 editorial titled "Things that are born and die unknown," the editors of the black newspaper *La Broma* lamented the white population's indifference to the efforts of the black artists. Young writers such as Casildo G. Thompson and Mateo Elejalde, and the painters Blanco de Aguirre and Bernardino Posadas, it stated, were known only in the black community—they were unheard of in the greater society of the city. (The editorial also commented on white ignorance of Afro-Argentine history—how many Argentines, it asked, have heard of the black warriors Lorenzo Barcala, Domingo Sosa, and Felipe Mansilla?) This limited audience, it continued, was completely inadequate to provide the necessary stimulus and encouragement, financial support, and most important, critical reaction to enable the young artists to develop and progress. The black community tended to be unreservedly positive concerning anything produced by black artists, complained the editors. What was needed was genuine criticism— without it, the Afro-Argentine arts would never progress beyond their present level and make themselves worthy of notice by white society.[57]

Another way in which the black artists' isolation took its toll was in the intrigues and jealousies that raged among them. A small circle of talented, sensitive people, removed from the rest of the city's artistic community almost as effectively as if they had been political exiles in another country, the black artists of the 1880s fell prey to exactly the same sort of debilitating disputes that so often tear communities of exiles apart. Though La Broma lamented a lack of constructive criticism to help the community's artists mature and progress, there was certainly no shortage of unconstructive criticism among the artists themselves. They dismissed each other's work as hopelessly second-rate and subjected each other to blistering mockery and contempt. In 1884 Casildo G. Thompson's review of Zenón Rolón's work, written "with all due frankness," attacked Rolón's compositions as aimless and erratic, poorly orchestrated, unoriginal, lacking in powers of musical conception, and displaying a slavish obedience to European forms, which Thompson denounced as decadent, tired, outdated, and a dead weight on native Argentine composition.[58] Thompson in turn took his lumps not only from the editors of La Juventud but from the journalist-musician Manuel G. Posadas: "We do not think that the young Thompson is a luminous constellation that has appeared among us to show us the path of redemption, nor an outstanding figure eligible to occupy the first seat among those who through their intellect and their compositions have demonstrated their profound literary knowledge."[59] Posadas himself was dismissed several years later by the young writer Jorge Miguel Ford, who admitted the quality of some of the journalist's work and his honored place in the community but whose final judgment was that "he did not stand out, he did not have the brilliance nor the position of the most active."[60] Ford's collection of biographies of prominent Afro-Argentines consigns all of the artists among them to a graceless mediocrity. Federico Espinosa is described as an enjoyable but crude composer; Horacio Mendizábal was an unpolished poet whose "lyre does not have brilliant tones"; and as part of Zenón Rolón's biography Ford included several extremely critical reviews of the composer's works.[61]

The lives of artists are not always happy ones, but those of the Afro-Argentines must have been especially bitter. Denied a hearing in the greater society around them, their works limited to a small and marginal audience either extravagantly enthusiastic or jealously vindictive and petty in its judgments, they were offered virtually no economic or social incentive to continue in their labors. But continue they did, producing a body of work that stands as a memorial to a persistence and creativity that could not be extinguished. While the community's literature went unread and unheard at the time of its creation and is today scattered and lost, its spirit survives in the music and dance which are the living symbol of the city of Buenos Aires. The tango could not have been created without the Afro-Argentines, and whenever the violins and concertinas of Buenos Aires sing their song, the drums of the candombe play on.

10

1850–1900
The Irreversible Decline

In Chapter 5 it was argued that the disappearance of the black community was a disappearance only in the sense that the Afro-Argentines became almost invisible in the city's ethnic mix. Black people continued to exist as an active and identifiable ethnic entity in the city, but one whose numbers shrank into insignificance in comparison to the waves of Italians, Spaniards, Jews, and other Europeans who poured into the city. Between 1880 and 1900 alone, almost a million Europeans settled in Argentina, the bulk of them in the capital. The rate of immigration actually accelerated after 1890, accounting for the phenomenal doubling of the national population (from 4.0 million in 1895 to 7.9 million in 1914) in a mere nineteen years. In 1855, less than half of Buenos Aires's adult population was foreign born; by 1895 that proportion had risen to three-quarters.[1]

As discussed in Chapter 2, the arrival of the immigrants wrought profound changes in the life of the city, transforming it from the "big village" of 1870 into the bustling, cosmopolitan metropolis that it was by 1914. One of the most significant of those changes was the freeing of Buenos Aires from its long-standing and multifaceted dependence on its black population: its dependence on black labor, its dependence on black men to fight in the army, its dependence on the black population not to rise up and put another Rosas in power. As the immigrants flooded into the city the whites were at last free to consign the Afro-Argentines to social oblivion, shunting them completely aside in the city's society, economy, and political system. This chapter traces the increasing isolation of the Afro-Argentines, their withdrawal in the face of the immigrants' advances, their crippling self-doubts and internal divisions, their efforts to become assimilated into white Argentine society, and the consistent rebuffs they suffered at the hands of their compatriots.

The existence of an active Afro-Argentine press during the 1850–1900 period affords us a rare opportunity to survey this process through Afro-Argentine eyes. Starting in 1858 with *La Raza Africana* (The African Race), the Afro-Argentines produced at least fifteen weekly and biweekly newspapers, a figure which clearly contradicts claims that the community had disappeared. Some of them published only a handful of issues; others lasted for periods of up to seven or eight years. *La Raza Africana*, for instance, ran for a mere eight issues, as did its successor *El Proletario* (The Proletarian).[2] A six-year gap separated these initial experiments from the next black publication, *La Igualdad* (Equality), which put out an unknown number of issues in 1864.[3] Though *La Igualdad* went under sometime that year, it was reincarnated in 1873 and published regularly for over a year before disappearing again.[4] Contemporaneous with this second incarnation was *El Artesano* (The Artisan), also titled *El Tambor* (The Drum), and another paper of which no trace survives, *El Candombero*.[5] Two other papers published between 1870 and 1873 were *La Crónica* (The Chronicle) and *El Porvenir* (The Future).[6] The late 1870s witnessed a flourishing of the black press, the most important and longest lived of its members being founded between 1876 and 1880. These included *La Perla* (The Pearl), *El Unionista* (The Unionist), *El Aspirante* (The Aspirer), *La Aurora del Plata* (Dawn of the Plata), *La Idea* (The Idea), *La Juventud* (Youth), *La Broma* (The Jest), *La Protectora* (The Protectress), and *El Látigo* (The Whip).[7] All of these papers except *El Látigo* continued into the 1880s, some of them going through several incarnations—*La Broma* set the record with six separate *épocas*, as they were called, between 1876 and 1885. The 1880s saw the birth of several additional papers, such as *La Razón* (Reason) and *El Obrero* (The Worker).[8] When added to the literary reviews *El Eco Artístico* (Echo of the Arts) and *La Ortiga* (The Nettle), these various publications stand as obvious evidence of the continued existence and vitality of the city's black community.

What makes these papers uniquely valuable as source material is the fact that they served as a forum for the presentation of almost every viewpoint held by members of the community. They regularly printed letters from private individuals, as well as poems, social notices, and guest editorials. Also, competition among the papers was fierce. *La Juventud* ran savage attacks against *La Perla*, *El Unionista*, and *La Broma*, even featuring a regular column entitled "La Broma," in which its opponent's issue of the previous week was ridiculed at length; *La Igualdad* was the declared mortal enemy of *El Artesano*. These disagreements were generally over political issues, but not infrequently they degenerated into personal vendettas between the editors, at which times the attacks and accusations became frankly insulting. The editors of *La Igualdad* dubbed their counterparts at *El Artesano* "Raw Meat" and "The Organ Grinder's Monkey," appellations which have somewhat more bite in Spanish than in English.[9] *La Juventud* described *La Broma* as a libelous rag run by a madman, and accused both its editors and those of *La Perla* of being public drunkards.[10] This competition, not to say outright antipathy, among the black papers insured an airing of all currents of opinion in the community, and through the divergences and agreements that emerge in these weeklies one gets a very good idea of the issues and problems on the community's collective mind.

THE AFRO-ARGENTINES FACE THE IMMIGRANTS

The black population of Buenos Aires entered the second half of the century under less than ideal circumstances. In the end the community had been badly served by its special relationship with Governor Rosas, and following his fall the black journalists and writers were unanimous in their condemnation of him. The second issue of *El Proletario* carried an editorial recalling "that barbarous and savage tyranny of twenty years" which ruined the whole city but especially the black community, which was kept "in a state of barbarism, or absolute ignorance . . . , shut up in the encampments and made the principal and unwitting instrument of his power and domination."[11] In 1882 *La Broma* ran an editorial very similar in tone, blaming the community's "upbringing" in the barracks and army camps for its continuing low socioeconomic status.[12] In 1874 *La Igualdad* denounced Rosas as a despot, a tyrant, and a bloody executioner.[13] *La Juventud* echoed charges of his being "the bloodiest tyrant ever known."[14]

In surveying these expressions of anti-Rosas sentiment, it should not be forgotten that it was highly expedient for the black editors to pledge strong allegiance to the principle of anti-Rosismo, a current which ran fast and strong in post-Rosas Buenos Aires. Hatred of Rosas was a constant and basic component of the city's political activity during the second half of the century. Since the Afro-Argentines had been very visibly associated with the dictator, it was in their interest to put as much distance as possible between themselves and the ex-governor.

But it is also undeniable that the Rosas years had done tremendous damage to the Afro-Argentines. Subsequent administrations made some effort to remedy the black community's plight, perhaps recognizing the truth in *El Proletario*'s warnings that unless the community received aid to rebuild itself, it might naïvely fall prey to another demagogue adept at exploiting its misery.[15] The public schools for boys were opened to black students, segregation was ended in the army, and the national and provincial constitutions of 1853 and 1854, respectively, declared all Argentine citizens officially equal before the law. But the colonial heritage of caste consciousness and racially discriminatory attitudes and practices proved too durable to be so easily overcome. In the area of education, for example, teacher and student hostility toward black pupils rendered the desegregation of the schools a largely empty gesture. Protests concerning the lack of educational opportunities for black children in the public schools appeared regularly in the Afro-Argentine papers. While some blacks wrote in to defend the government's policies, the editor of *El Aspirante* posed the question in 1882, "If in the state schools the white student is taught in the same way as the black, why is it that one out of every thousand black students comes out moderately well instructed, while among the whites the proportion is one in fifty?"[16] *El Proletario* attracted the unfavorable attention of the white press with its attacks on discrimination in the public schools. In response to charges that in criticizing the schools it had insulted Governor Alsina and his administration, the paper issued the following carefully worded apology, which suggests the delicate compromise the editors of the black papers had to make between arguing the community's cause and not offending the powers that were:

For many years we have been the first to acknowledge the beautiful principles and openly liberal ideas that have always distinguished and commended the present Chief of State; and we agree wholeheartedly that to him are owed in large part the benefits which we theoretically enjoy today; but it is also undeniable that social concerns and other circumstances no less powerful, which we shall have occasion in the future to point out, form practical obstacles, and frequently make the law illusory.[17]

It was in this weakened and disadvantaged condition that the Afro-Argentines had to face the arrival of the Europeans. Conflict was immediate. In a phenomenon paralleling similar developments in nineteenth-century Brazilian and United States cities, immigrants succeeded in pushing Afro-Argentines out of many of the occupational categories they had previously filled.[18] Black and European artisans had

One of the last of the Afro-Argentine street vendors, c. 1900. This individual attracted a city-wide following for his *mazamorra*, a kind of corn chowder. Copies of this photograph were printed and sold at the time as souvenirs. Photograph courtesy Archivo General de la Nación.

already clashed in the colonial period, when the arriving immigrants sought to evict the blacks and castas from the trades and make them an exclusively white concern. This conflict continued, and as massive immigration began in the second half of the century, it was compounded by immigrant efforts to push Afro-Argentines out of even such low-status jobs as street vending. The desperately poor Italians entering the city proved willing to perform this work for even lower remuneration than the Afro-Argentines, so that by 1876 a song sung at the Carnival of that year ran:

> Now there are no black bottle dealers,
> Nor carriers of loads,
> Nor black fruit vendors,
> Nor fisherman any more;
> Because of all those Neapolitans
> We can't even sell our pastries,
> And now they even want to rob us
> Of our jobs as housepainters.[19]

Listing all these previously black-dominated professions, the song went on to denounce the "Neapolitan usurpers" who were robbing the blacks of their livelihood. Other contemporary sources lend credence to this plaint. As late as 1873 a photo of washerwomen on the riverbank showed one of them to be black and one white; by 1899 a magazine article could describe the disappearance of the black washerwomen, who had surrendered their jobs to the "hearty Italian women."[20] An article in 1898 observed that the city's fruit and vegetable dealers were almost entirely Neapolitans.[21] An article in 1899 on the changadores, the free-lance street porters, included photographs of white porters only, and made no mention of any Afro-Argentine presence in the profession.[22] Compare that to the 1850s, when every ship arriving at Buenos Aires was met by swarms of black porters competing for work.[23] José Wilde's memoirs included mention that the broom-making trade, another black specialty, had been completely taken over by foreigners.[24] Immigrant replacement of black labor was such a widespread phenomenon that it even spread to the army: when the Eighth Infantry Battalion—which as a liberto unit had won laurels for itself in its seven-year campaign through Chile, Peru, and Ecuador before being disbanded in the 1820s— was reconstituted in 1871, it was formed of companies from the Italian Legion, a unit of immigrant soldiers.[25]

On the whole, black resistance to the immigrant invasion appears to have been less pronounced in Argentina than it was in the United States.[26] Having absorbed the traditional Argentine disdain for mechanical and manual labor, the Afro-Argentines were not unwilling to surrender their position in these fields.[27] Withdrawing fairly ungrudgingly in the face of the European advance, they entered the service sector, an area in which they had always predominated, in ever-increasing numbers. More and more of them became domestic servants, musicians, entertainment workers (e.g., dancers in the academias de baile), and low-level government employees.

Government service seems at first glance a surprising occupation for the Afro-Argentines to have entered, since it implies a certain degree of access to political patronage and influential figures. Nevertheless, black orderlies and secretaries were commonplace in Congress, in the presidential residence, and in the various ministries. An article of 1883 reported that black men "form the bottom class of employees, or, better said, they work as servants in public offices, very well dressed and shod."[28] In 1902 an illustrated magazine article on Congress included two photographs of five or six orderlies, every one of whom was black.[29] The black orderly was a frequent figure in turn-of-the-century cartoons. A typical one entitled "Realizable Hope" showed an orderly relaxing and counting on his fingers: "The president away on a trip, the vice-president also, and the president of the Senate sick in bed. Who knows—at this rate they may run through all the substitutes and I'll have to take over as acting president!"[30]

A prerequisite to performing a service job satisfactorily is a perfect understanding on the part of the employee of the relationship between him and his employer. The immigrants, as yet unattuned to the organizing principles of porteño society, operated at a disadvantage in relation to the Afro-Argentines, whose long history of service (both coerced and free) gave them an almost instinctive knowledge of the behavior expected of them by their employers. An extremely interesting document of the period is the memoirs of Mamerto Fidel Quinteros, a black man who served as a congressional orderly for some thirty years. He makes it abundantly clear that knowledge of and submission to the unwritten and unspoken rules of porteño class relationships was essential in his work—in fact, he devoted an entire chapter to a discussion of the etiquette between orderlies and congressmen. Congressmen never commanded, but rather requested—nevertheless, the orderlies were expected to react to the request as to an order.[31] Quinteros himself was well fitted for this work, having been brought up as a retainer in an elite household in which all members were expected to act as became their station in life. "Today it is said that that was something to be ashamed of, because it represented caste privilege. I don't know, it could be, but what I do know is that in those families morality and good manners were maintained like a religion. The ladies were ladies in reality as well as in appearance, and the gentlemen were truly gentlemen." Quinteros himself was well aware of his own place in this system: when he entered service in Congress, "I was a respectful and well brought up little black."[32]

Another advantage that the Afro-Argentines had in competing with immigrants for government positions was the fact that they, after all, were citizens, and the immigrants were not. The Argentine constitution granted foreigners most of the constitutional rights of citizens, so there was little incentive for immigrants to naturalize themselves. In the occasional cases in which they attempted to do so, they encountered formidable red tape and bureaucratic resistance. By 1895, out of 206,000 foreign-born men in the city, only 715 had become citizens.[33] Black citizens thus possessed an automatic advantage over white foreigners, namely the right of suffrage, and the black vote was actively sought by the municipal party machines. The Afro-Argentine newspapers *La Igualdad* and *El Artesano* were heavily subsidized by the Avellaneda and Mitre political interests, respectively, in order to win black support in the presidential election of 1874.[34] Black participation in that election and others won the community the right to patronage, which came in the form of positions as secretaries or orderlies.

The community occasionally expressed resentment over its automatic consignment to the lowest levels of government service. In 1879 *La Broma* attacked "the leaders of the parties, those who try to take the juiciest morsels from the pot for themselves, without leaving even the crumbs for our humble fellows."[35] But for the most part the Afro-Argentines settled for what they could get. Government service, even at the orderly level, was especially attractive to black men because of its relative prestige, a quality that most Afro-Argentine occupations singularly lacked. The orderlies tended to identify themselves closely with the government body or ministry for which they worked, deriving status from that source. Quinteros recalled one incident in which a party held jointly by the black orderlies of the presidential residence and of the Congress erupted into a fight after one of the presidential orderlies made insulting remarks concerning the Congress. "These attacks on parliamentary privilege could not be tolerated by us without our becoming accomplices to a flagrant violation of the Constitution."[36]

There were also concrete benefits to be gained by government service. The orderlies' proximity to the congressmen gave them a certain amount of influence in extracting small favors from their superiors, especially when they succeeded in establishing patron-client ties with given legislators. This reality was commented on in a semihumorous essay in the popular magazine *Caras y Caretas,* in which an Afro-Argentine approaches a friend of his who is a congressional orderly. The first man knows a woman who is willing to pay two hundred pesos to anyone who can guide a petition of hers through the bureaucratic maze of Congress. The friend asks the orderly if he can do it and proposes a fifty-fifty split of the money. The orderly agrees, assuring his friend there will be no problem since the orderlies always take care to cultivate the friendship of those congressmen who look as though they will have a long and successful career in politics.[37] Between the accumulated prestige and occasional influence-peddling that was a perquisite of government service, the black orderlies enjoyed considerable status within the community: though I did not make an exact count, I would estimate that over half of the front-page obituaries that appeared in the black papers were of orderlies or other government employees.

But it was a lucky Afro-Argentine who was able to win his way into government service. Most remained in the much less illustrious position of domestic servant, a low-status job with little opportunity for advancement either for the worker or for his or her children. The national census of 1895, though it provided no statistical information concerning race, noted in one of its chapters that the great majority of blacks in the capital continued to work as domestic servants, concentrated in the service of the wealthy families, who liked to show off their liveried butlers and coachmen.[38] Because of the large numbers of the community in domestic service, the black press tended to take notice of labor issues concerning that area of work. In 1881, for instance, *La Broma* ran an editorial attacking a proposed ordinance requiring domestics to give ten days' notice before leaving a job.[39]

But if domestic service offered little opportunity for betterment, it at least offered relative security and, especially in the wealthy families, paternalistic protection against the vocational competition introduced by the Europeans. Steadily bid out of the trades by European immigrants willing to work long hours for low pay, the blacks retreated to the shelter of service occupations.

Black-versus-immigrant competition extended to the area of housing. The new arrivals tended to settle initially in the poorest neighborhoods of the city, which naturally happened to be those in which the Afro-Argentines were concentrated. By the 1870s the black neighborhoods of the center city were breaking up and dissolving under the white onslaught, driven out by rising rents and animosity between the two groups. The Afro-Argentines retreated toward the outlying areas of the city. In the papers of the 1870s and 1880s one reads frequently of black social events in Flores, then a suburb of the capital and to this day the location of a small black neighborhood. They also moved into the Barracas area along the Riachuelo, the stream marking Buenos Aires's southern boundary. Even here the immigrants pursued them, and one Argentine historian recalls that their "mutual antipathy erupted more than once into impressive brawls among blacks, creole whites, and Italians."[40]

Black resentment of the immigrants emerges frequently in writings from the period. In 1874 an editorial in *La Igualdad* complained that immigrants enjoyed all the rights of citizenship without having to shoulder any of the duties, that they had been disloyal in not going to fight in the civil wars and in Paraguay against Buenos Aires's enemies, and that "that foreign element that enjoys all rights and privileges, that is received with open arms, that is more protected than any, as soon as it sets foot on our territory becomes an enemy of all the authorities created by national law."[41]

Especially vehement on the subject of the immigrants was the black congressional orderly Quinteros, who, of all the black writers, most passionately voiced the Afro-Argentines' anger at the way they had been shunted aside by the foreigners. Observing that black and white Argentines were themselves largely responsible for the immigrant domination of the skilled and mechanical trades because of the natives' disdain for such work, he argued for increased federal aid to vocational schools in order to enable Argentines to reenter the trades and compete with the Europeans. He attacked immigrant participation in politics and proposed that high government positions be barred by law to immigrants and their children. In a complete reversal of the ideas of Sarmiento and other Argentine thinkers who perceived European immigration as the country's salvation, Quinteros denounced Italo-Argentines as "the Argentine Calabria, descendants of immigrants inherently unadaptable to the culture of the civilized centers, and the representatives of the most brutish people produced by the peninsulas of the world."[42]

The anger of the Afro-Argentine musicians displaced by the newly arrived maestros of Europe was mentioned in Chapter 9. An especially delicate aspect of the conflict between immigrants and Afro-Argentines was touched on in 1880, when *La Broma* printed a short piece on the phenomenon of marriages of black women to Italian men. With considerable sarcasm, the editor congratulated such brides on their good fortune and said that he looked forward to seeing them selling spaghetti in the street soon. The author's bitterness is unmistakable, though he consoles his readers with a brief reflection on the sexual imbalance in the community that forces black women to seek husbands elsewhere, concluding with the witticism that when you can't get bread, you must settle for pasta.[43] (The males of the community had their revenge several weeks later when it was announced that one of their number would soon be marrying a Basque woman.[44])

Interestingly enough, that little article is the sole reference in all the black press to the Afro-Argentines' declining demographic position. Though a *Caras y Caretas* article in 1905 reported that the community was very upset each time one of its young people married a white, there is no indication of this in the black papers.[45] The social columns never comment on the race of engaged couples, and it is only from their mention of European birthplaces that the researcher can conclude that black-immigrant marriages were not uncommon. The black writers of the period seem to have been relatively unconcerned by the long-term implications of widespread intermarriage.

SELF-CRITICISM

Anti-immigrant feeling ran high among porteños of both races.[46] Black and white *criollos*, as native Argentines called themselves, joined in heaping abuse on the newcomers. But while some blacks expressed rage, others gave way to a sort of resigned defeatism in the face of immigrant successes and black retreats, an occasionally voiced feeling that the blame for the decadent state of Afro-Argentine society rested not on the immigrants but on the Afro-Argentines themselves. An 1878 editorial in *La Juventud* reflected on the community's sad situation and compared it to that of the Europeans resident in the city:

> It causes pain, it inspires tedium; and above all, it inspires shame to consider and look at the fact that all the foreign Colonies resident here in South America, even those in small number, are forming Beneficent Societies, Schools, Social Clubs, etc., while we are the only ones that remain isolated, sunk in chaos, magnificently playing the role of pariahs in our own house.[47]

A similar editorial in 1876 attributed the immigrants' successes to their "way of being" (*manera de ser*), describing how they saved every peso they earned until they had accumulated stocks of capital either to start new businesses or to return to Europe in style, whereas the Afro-Argentines were too ready to squander their wages on idle amusements.[48] The mulatto editor Froilán Bello analyzed the community's failings in racial terms adopted from the greater society, blaming them on "the semibarbarous vices and habits that come to us by racial tradition, that up until now we have not been able to restrain completely."[49]

Other black thinkers and spokesmen sought a more constructive approach aimed at identifying the community's failings and correcting them. The questions consistently asked were: what are we doing wrong, why are we falling so far behind the immigrants, and what can be done to remedy the situation? Despite frequent and rancorous differences of opinion,[50] a consensus of sorts did emerge by the end of the century. The shortcomings of the community were ascribed to four causes: a tendency to waste time, money, and energy on idle amusements and entertainment; an aversion, common to black and white Argentines alike, to manual labor; a crippling lack of educational opportunities; and a profusion of jealousies, rivalries, and internal divisions within the community that rendered its members incapable of uniting and working cooperatively toward their collective betterment.

As early as 1858 the black press had sought to rouse its readers against the community's alleged tendency to spend money and energy on amusements rather than on constructive projects such as education or mutual aid societies.[51] This message was repeated frequently in the black papers, and indulgences such as liquor, expensive clothes, and the frequent dances held in the community formed a favorite target for the black editors. Santiago Elejalde's campaign on behalf of founding an Afro-Argentine mutual aid society made much of how black porteños preferred to invest themselves in organizing Carnival comparsas rather than institutions which could provide concrete long-term economic benefits in place of a fleeting night's entertainment.[52] Tiburcio Puentes Gallardo, the most fiery of the Afro-Argentine journalists, specifically blamed the collapse of the mutual aid society La Fraternal on its members' weakness for holding dances. "So what has happened in the end to all the societies established among us? We repeat: a dance here, a banquet there, a meeting here, a ceremony there, and everything goes to the Devil." Puentes Gallardo added that he had no objections to a yearly dance held as a fund-raising event, but the mutual aid societies tended to give them every two weeks—"at this rate not even the capital of the Bank of London would last six weeks in our hands."[53]

This excessive fondness for amusement and diversion was closely linked to the Afro-Argentines' dislike for manual labor, according to several black editors and writers, though Puentes Gallardo was astute enough to see that working-class blacks sought positions as government workers or domestic servants because at least in those jobs they could dress well and escape to a certain extent from the low prestige of the mechanical trades. "The blacksmith, the carpenter, they cannot go about all day in frock coat and top hat" like the orderlies and servants of the wealthy families. The trades are regarded by everyone as *empleos bajos*, low-status jobs, observed Puentes, "and one must add that, concerning these jobs, whites and blacks alike have the same weakness" of considering them unfit to be performed.[54]

The black papers printed and reprinted appeals to the working-class population to leave the demeaning occupation of domestic service, with its paternalistic ties and personal dependence so reminiscent of the slave regime, and win their independence as free skilled laborers. A guest editorialist of *La Broma* sounded the call: "Come on, to the workshops, our sons; to the workshops, our successors!"[55] When Jorge Miguel Ford published his collection of Afro-Argentine biographies in 1899, he devoted a chapter to berating the community for its failure to enter the mechanical trades, for being "more devoted to setting up recordplayers than to love of hard work, more disposed toward pleasure than toward vicissitudes, more dedicated to seeking soft jobs than to breaking the earth with a plow, more toward hearing a bit of *La Traviata*, *Falstaff*, or *Rigoletto* than the harsh sound of the hammer falling on the anvil."[56] In order to reverse this trend, Ford included in his book the biography of Eduardo Magee, a young black man who received a scholarship from the government to go to Great Britain and study mechanics and engine repair. After spending five years in England and Scotland, he returned to Argentina and was made a machinist's mate in the navy. Ford held up his example as an inspiration to Afro-Argentine youth to take up the mechanical trades.

But perhaps the most debilitating problem facing the community, the one that its leaders viewed with the greatest uneasiness, was posed by the never-ending feuds and divisions which wracked the collectivity, divisions created in large part by the leaders themselves. Politics formed one of the primary sources of discord. The hard-fought presidential campaign of 1874 resulted in particularly bad feeling. The rival factions went at each other hammer and tong, the conflict eventually culminating in a fistfight at a fashionable Afro-Argentine social gathering.[57] Seeking to remove this sort of disturbance from the life of the community, *La Broma* took a stand against working for any machine or candidate, arguing that the white politicians had consistently used the blacks in times of need and then forgotten them when it came time to divide the spoils. It attacked *La Igualdad* for having served as the mouthpiece of the Avellaneda interests, and in 1879 announced that it would endorse nobody in the coming elections because it was completely disillusioned with all parties. Urging the community to avoid partisan divisions, the paper proclaimed that "our motto is to unite, not divide, and on that we stand!"[58]

The editors of *La Juventud* also approached the question of party politics with frank and unvarying cynicism. Like *La Broma*, they argued that politics served only to divide the community and produced no benefit whatsoever. An article on the black legislators of the period described them as party hacks who slavishly followed the dictates of the machine bosses.[59] A later article accused the white press of exploiting the black community for political purposes. It charged that the white dailies only reported on the black community when it organized to support a candidate favored by the papers; when the community struggled to establish an apolitical mutual aid society or newspaper, its efforts went unreported by the major papers. The white press thus encouraged conflict and discord within the community and ignored efforts to mobilize it for constructive ends.[60]

Besides politics, the other major source of division within the community was class differences. Chapter 3 touched on the small number of black professionals and property owners documented in the 1827 census. This nascent middle class continued to grow during the second half of the century. The black newspapers were supported in part by regular advertisements from such black-owned businesses as Juan Pablo Balparda's cigarette factory and the dance halls owned and operated by members of the community. Successful musicians and journalists commanded incomes above the ordinary, as did such professionals as Tomás B. Platero (who in 1882 became the first Afro-Argentine notary public), or high-ranking military officers. This class was further expanded by blue-collar workers who through shrewd investment in the city's expanding economy amassed comfortable financial holdings. An early example of this phenomenon was a black musician and coachmaker of the 1830s who became sufficiently wealthy to open negotiations for the purchase of a Spanish title of nobility.[61] A later example was Eugenio Sar, a stevedore whose investments in real estate made him one of the most well-to-do members of the black community. His name appeared regularly, along with those of the rest of the black middle class, on subscription lists for the periodic fund drives held by the black papers.[62]

La Broma was the organ of this "black bourgeoisie," as E. Franklin Frazier labeled its counterpart in the United States.[63] From the very outset *La Broma* presented itself as the mouthpiece of Afro-Argentine high society. In its first issue it announced that it would scrupulously avoid all political questions and sources of possible conflict and instead would confine itself to news of dances, club meetings, get-togethers, and social events in general.[64]

This approach absolutely infuriated the working-class weekly *La Juventud*, which responded with an editorial mocking the newly founded

Members of the black porteño middle class. These matrons were photographed in 1902 at one of the *"really* big dances" decried by the working-class paper *La Juventud.* Photograph courtesy Archivo General de la Nación.

paper: "Nothing related to party politics and a great deal related to detailed chronicles of tea parties!!! coffee parties!!! hot chocolate parties!!! of big dances!!! of *really* big dances!!! of strolls!!! soirées!!! meetings!!! etc."[65]

La Juventud's editorial philosophy and policies were diametrically opposed to those of *La Broma*. Taking its vocabulary and ideology directly from Marxist thought, the journal called its readers' attention to certain "contradictory facts" in the city's situation: "contradictory, when thousands of arms lie idle, and a great number of families are sunk in the most complete misery. Discontent is widespread, and he who has work today cannot count on having any tomorrow."[66] The editors returned again and again to the theme of union as the only possible protection against the bourgeoisie. "The workers are those beings who more than any other require union to protect themselves"; the bourgeoisie are "those beings who wear frock coats the better to hide the leprosy of their souls."[67]

These appeals for union were often couched in purely racial terms. An 1876 editorial on "the society of color" argued that "our society's endeavors are great and solemn. Its principles are of the highest . . . and the number of its members is enormous. . . . It need only unite itself to achieve the triumph of its most precious rights and liberties."[68] The New Year's Day editorial in 1878 warned that unless the community could overcome its divisions and unite, the "devastation" in which it found itself could prove to be permanent. A later editorial celebrating Independence Day repeated the message, closing with the cry, "one for all, all for one!"[69]

La Juventud consistently explained these divisions in terms of class. Indeed, its angriest blasts were reserved for those middle-class Afro-Argentines who set themselves above the rest of the community. A representative example is a controversy that erupted in 1876 concerning a social club called The Argentine Hope. The club was founded by several of the more prosperous black families and charged dues too high for a manual laborer to pay. *La Juventud* attacked this exclusionism, accusing the club's founders of harboring social pretensions that would split the community. The editors urged the club's members to forget their class superiority and concentrate instead on uniting the city's black population.

Let us make no more propaganda against our own brothers. . . . Let these disastrous pretensions end, on the part of those who so evilly call themselves *men of circumstance* [*hombres de categoría*]. Let the great divisions that exist among us be ended; . . . Let us gather together about a single flag, and we will give the lie to those who have already consigned us to oblivion.[70]

But The Argentine Hope did not lower its fees, so several weeks later *La Juventud* announced the formation of a new club, The Sons of Order, "truly an association composed of humble workers, in which exist *union, progress, and friendship.*"[71]

La Broma's initial response to *La Juventud's* war cries was to feign indifference and even ignorance. In the same article in which it described the stylish social events of the community as its major interest, it absolved itself of responsibility for responding to *La Juventud's* analysis of the society's ills. "If occasionally we write a serious little article, it is not with the intention of enlightening anybody, because we can hardly pretend to teach others what we do not know ourselves and wish that others would teach us."[72] On the occasions on which it replied to *La Juventud*, *La Broma* angrily denied its opponent's charges of division within the community. "The society of color is united, it thinks as a single man, it longs for the realization of its hopes according to a single prediction, and it is animated with vitality like a heart that beats to a single rhythm."[73] But these reassuring statements were given the lie by the hostility with which the paper treated The Sons of Order and other working-class organizations in its pages. Its gingerly treatment of the conflicts within the mutual aid society La Protectora revealed its tendency to ignore division within the community. From May through July 1879 the organization was apparently shaken by an internal struggle on which *La Broma* commented cryptically from time to time. Only when the dispute had been resolved did the paper print an article frankly acknowledging the existence of discord within the society and then congratulating the members of La Protectora for having resolved their differences. Significantly, even this article was entitled "Rumors concerning La Protectora."[74]

In retrospect, *La Broma* and the class that it represented must be judged guilty of the charges brought against them by *La Juventud*, charges of promoting class division over racial unity. *La Broma* spoke for a black middle class intensely desirous of escaping the stigma of its racial status and being accepted as equals by the white middle class. This previously unthinkable concept looked as though it had become an actual possibility in post-1850 Buenos Aires. Not only did economic expansion provide opportunities for the growth of the black middle class, but white society itself seemed more amenable to the idea of accepting blacks as equal partners. The progressive legislation of the 1850s was discussed earlier in this chapter. These laws constituted part of the unitarian strategy to prevent any future Rosas-style populist from seizing power by exploiting the discontentments of disadvantaged groups. In passing this legislation, which had as its apparent goal the integration of

The whitening of an Afro-Argentine. This advertisement for collars and cuffs appeared in the picture magazine *Caras y Caretas* on several occasions during 1902. Photograph courtesy Archivo General de la Nación.

the black population into the greater society, the government seemed to be urging the Afro-Argentines to forget their past separateness and join in the task of building a new and united Argentina. This appeal was made explicit in the 1858 editorial "La Raza Africana," discussed in Chapter 8.

Ostensibly given the opportunity to escape the caste status they had endured for generations, the Afro-Argentines responded with a will. This response manifested itself most noticeably in a turning away from the community's black and African past and an embracing of the European culture and refinements favored by the white bourgeoisie. As has been seen, the African mutual aid societies faded away during the 1860s and 1870s as the young Afro-Argentines refused to join and maintain them. The community abandoned the candombe in favor of such imports as the waltz, schottische, and mazurka. Black and white Argentine artists studied the European masters equally faithfully—several black painters and musicians even won government scholarships to go to European conservatories and academies to study.[75]

The nationalist verities of the republic were scrupulously honored by the middle-class Afro-Argentines. The "glorious principles" of the revolution of 1810 were reaffirmed each Independence Day in *La Broma*; the poet Horacio Mendizábal wrote several verses to the glory of Buenos Aires and Argentina; and young Jorge Miguel Ford sang the praises of "that colossus of a capital, beacon of South America, standing like a Parthenon in a sea of progress."[76]

In short, nobody could accuse the middle-class Afro-Argentines of having failed to respond to the invitation to help form a new Argentine state and society. Not even *La Juventud* could completely resist the siren's song of assimilation: like *La Broma*, it too printed editorials promoting the principles of middle-class propriety, and at one point it even ran a serialized novella whose protagonist had "skin as white as snow, and golden curls falling in profusion to her shoulders."[77] Nevertheless, the expected rewards did not materialize. The black middle class's studied imitation of the norms and mores of white society did attract white notice and approval, but that approval tended to be of a markedly condescending sort, and it brought few if any concrete benefits. In 1880 the white editor Horacio Varela commented in his paper, *El Porteño*, on "the good upbringing and behavior of all those people of color," a remark which earned him accolades in *La Broma* as "the true defender of our rights and liberties" and "the nicest man in the Americas."[78] A 1905 magazine article titled "The People of Color" commented on the progress made by the black middle class. It mentioned their newspapers, literary reviews,

beneficent societies and aristocratic salons, where instead of the grotesque candombe or semba—lewd as a monkey's grimace—they dance in modern clothes in the manner of Louis XV . . . Those numerous corrals in which the people of color used to live all thrown together, in a depressing promiscuity, have now disappeared. Now there are black families that ride in coaches with liveried servants and fabulous jewels.[79]

But this praise was a token achievement at best, and it was heavily outweighed by the continuingly disadvantaged position of the Afro-Argentines within porteño society. During the second half of the century it was amply and consistently demonstrated that white porteños thought of their black countrymen as blacks before they thought of them as Argentines. One finds increasingly frequent letters in the black press of the 1870s and 1880s protesting continued discrimination in the city. A particularly ugly incident in the summer of 1879–80 formed a watershed of sorts, demonstrating to even the congenitally optimistic *La Broma* the realities of race relations in the city.

Segregation had been an on-again, off-again reality in Buenos Aires throughout the century, but during that summer opposition to black presence in places of entertainment solidified and manifested itself in a series of newspaper advertisements specifically prohibiting blacks from entering a number of theaters and dance halls. Black protest was immediate, editorials appearing in all the community's papers. Even the white press sided with the Afro-Argentines: editorials in *El Porteño*, *La Tribuna*, and *La Nación* all protested the exclusion of black people from any public facility. The editor of *El Porteño* offered to rent a room at one of the offending halls for an Afro-Argentine ball, thus forcing the owners to admit blacks, but the community's leaders politely declined and instead petitioned the mayor for a redress of the situation. The mayor recognized the gravity of the issues involved, and several days later the chief of police announced that he would not aid the dance hall owners in the enforcement of their discriminatory rules, though he did not say that he would aid the blacks in any efforts to defy those rules. In the face of so much negative opinion, however, the owners backed down and agreed to admit nonwhites. One hall, Variedades, even took out an ad in the black papers saying that it had never prohibited black people from attending its dances.[80]

The episode had ended happily, but it had been of sufficient ugliness to chill the hopes of even the most sanguine members of the community. A profound change in *La Broma*'s orientation dates very closely from this affair. The paper printed one of its earliest angry editorials at that time. Its author, Froilán Bello, described the multitude of whores and pimps who frequented the academias and expressed rage at the fact that "thieves, hoodlums, and cardsharps can enter, because they are white. A compadrito, a bum, one of these professional vagabonds can enter the theater . . . and the owner looks at him and instead of throwing him out, shows his pleasure with a happy smile: because after all, he is white!" Bello prophesied that this discriminatory step boded no good for the community in the future. "Today it is the theater that is closed to us, tomorrow it will be some other public place, and the day after it will be the church, where we all have the right to go to worship God, who is the kind father of all human beings, regardless of race or color."[81]

A COMMUNITY UNITED

Race prejudice had raised its ugly head in a way that not even the most blindly optimistic member of the black middle class could ignore, and once *La Broma* had been forced to recognize this prejudice, its editors began to face the permeating effect of racism on all relationships between white and black porteños. The image of the black race as the pariah of the city was a frequent one in Afro-Argentine writing of this period; it appears in the poetry of Mendizábal and Thompson, in the writing of Jorge Miguel Ford, in the pages of *La Juventud*. As of 1879 and 1880 the word "pariah" also began appearing in *La Broma*. The paper's editorials began echoing sentiments expressed several years earlier in *La Juventud.* For example, in 1878 *La Juventud* had printed an editorial protesting how whites and blacks alike had ignored and forgotten Afro-Argentine history. In 1882 *La Broma* printed an editorial on exactly the same theme, observing that "the history of our country has many blank pages."[82] An editorial discussed in the previous chapter complained about white indifference to black artists and the disastrous effects that this indifference had had on the writers, musicians, and painters of the community.

The angriest features of all, which may stand as incontrovertible evidence of *La Broma*'s awakening to the realities of race relations in the city, were printed late in 1879. One recalled how black soldiers had won Argentina's liberty and contrasted the race's glorious role in the independence struggle with its present situation, maintained in a permanently inferior position by the government's failure to enforce laws forbidding discrimination.

The men charged with enforcing the Constitution and making it respected are the first to violate it. They begin by withholding from us the right to hold any public office, forgetting that it was so that they could enjoy this right that we have always been the first to abandon our homes and families to fly to the defense of the fatherland when it has been invaded by enemies.

When some provincial strong man has risen against the established order, we have been the defenders of the duly constituted authorities.

And what has been our recompense?

Scorn and humilitation.

And when we have invoked the Constitution as the saving foundation of our rights, they have replied to us with a sarcastic laugh.

Equality in our country exists only in form.

This is the liberty before the law that our class enjoys.[83]

It was at this point that *La Broma* seems to have recognized the necessity of joining with the working class to form a truly unified black community. Besides printing editorials supporting ideas which had appeared several years earlier in the workers' press, *La Broma* took the highly significant step in 1880 of appending the motto "Organ of the Working Classes" to its masthead. This phrase had previously been part of *La Juventud*'s logo, but following the collapse of that paper and *El Unionista* early in the year, the editors of *La Broma* apparently felt it necessary to take up the cause of the black workers. The paper published several editorials opposing municipal ordinances controlling domestic service, and in 1881 it printed a memorial article to the vanished black washerwomen, honoring them as the respected mothers and matrons of the community.[84]

The publication that was going to report only on happy things, on the parties and dances of the comfortable black middle class, had been forced into joining the rest of the black press in bitter denunciations of a society that would not allow Afro-Argentines to rise and progress as the immigrants had done. The outpourings of black expression from this period repeat the themes of disillusionment and resentment over and over. Even the usually embarrassingly loyal Quinteros, the "good little black" who longed for the return of the golden days of the traditional aristocracy, when blacks and whites alike knew their place and kept to it, could not prevent a moment of anger in the final pages of his memoirs, in which he gave vent to the desire to avenge himself by bloodying his fists on "those who took advantage of my inferior position to inflict on me insults and injuries which I have forgiven but which it has not been granted me to forget."[85]

The invitation to the Afro-Argentines to join in the reconstruction of post-Rosas Buenos Aires had not been honored—it was retracted in the face of the community's obvious willingness to respond and join in the task. The arrival of the Europeans freed the city from its dependence on black economic and political cooperation, and once the community no longer had indispensable services to sell, it forfeited the right of entry into the society of the post-1850 city. The Afro-Argentines' hopes of participating in that society as equal partners were realized only as their skin color lightened. But while some trigueños with African ancestry probably did succeed in acquiring white racial status, it seems that most Afro-Argentines labeled as trigueños in official records tended to remain black in the minds of white porteños. In Chapter 5 we witnessed the liability of trigueños to being counted in official hospital records as black. There is additional evidence that as the century progressed the scheme of porteño race relations altered significantly from a three-tier racial hierarchy to one incorporating two tiers, or, to return to Carl Degler's study, from a Brazilian model of race relations to a North American one. In documents from the first half of the century the distinction between pardo and moreno was always made in describing black people; after 1850 that distinction disappeared, replaced by a tendency to lump "morenos," "negros," "mulatos," and "pardos" together under the general denomination of "people of color." This tendency is quite visible in the municipal censuses. Printed forms for the 1827 census specifically directed census takers to distinguish between pardos and morenos in their counts. The censuses of 1836 and 1838 also observed the distinction between pardos and morenos but tabulated the two together as a single total. The annual Statistical Registries of the 1854–80 period, and the municipal census of 1887, abandoned the use of pardo and moreno completely and instead simply published all demographic statistics in two columns: white and "de color."

Changing porteño attitudes toward race may also be seen in a comparison of previously quoted newspaper articles. The 1843 article defending Manuelita Rosas's occasional practice of dancing with black men carefully distinguished among the various gradations of blackness: "The pardos and mulattoes. . . . the honored pardos and morenos. . . . the mulattoes and morenos. . . . the honest and hard-working mulattoes, pardos, and morenos." After the fall of Rosas, however, articles such as *La Tribuna*'s appeals in 1853 to the government to impress black people into domestic service, or *La Nueva Generación*'s editorial in 1858 against *La Raza Africana*, referred to the Afro-Argentines generically as the "people of color." The *Caras y Caretas* article in 1905 on the Afro-Argentines used "The People of Color" as its title.

There are hints in *La Broma* of irritation at this aggregation of people with varying amounts of African ancestry under a single rubric: several articles refer to Afro-Argentines as "the so-called men of color" or "men of color, as some call us," implying that the editors were not altogether pleased with this label.[86] As a North American–style two-tier system of race relations replaced the former three-tier system, all people of visible African ancestry were increasingly confined to the "colored" social category. Even Afro-Argentines of sizable personal means tended to remain "people of color," separated from the whites by their African ancestry, diluted though it might be, and compelled to seek their social arena in the columns of the black newspapers rather than the white.

Thus while white Argentines recognized and indeed approved of the process of race mixture that was going on in the city, a process analogous to the Brazilian case, their vision of race and racial estates became more and more North American in nature. Those porteños who showed noticeable evidence of their African ancestry were prohibited entry into white society and therefore continued to form part of the community which entered the twentieth century diminished but by no means eliminated. The community survived because the greater society would not let it die, but rather maintained it as a group whose members could not be socially integrated until they were genetically integrated. The Afro-Argentines were lost to view, but they had disappeared only in the eye of the beholder. They were still visible to whoever wanted to see them, a small but continuing element in the city's ethnic mix.

11

Buenos Aires in Comparative Perspective

Caste, Class, and Race Relations in the Americas since Emancipation

To return to a point made in Chapter 1, the history of the Afro–Spanish Americans since emancipation remains to be written. Leslie Rout's efforts to produce a synthesis of existing secondary sources on black people and race relations in the Spanish American countries during the nineteenth and twentieth centuries amply demonstrated the almost complete absence of such studies. Although considerable work has been done on conditions of slavery in colonial Spanish America, neither Latin American nor foreign historians have devoted much attention to the role of black people in the societies and economies of the national period.

This situation may be contrasted with the significantly more advanced state of historical studies on Afro-Brazilian and Afro–North American populations since abolition. Numerous questions concerning national-period race relations in those countries remain to be addressed and answered, but researchers working on that time period have generated a substantial and steadily growing body of literature. Indeed, so relatively developed is the state of knowledge on Brazil and the United States that almost a decade ago the North American historian Carl Degler was able to use secondary sources to produce his seminal work *Neither Black nor White* (1971), a comparative study of slavery and postabolition race relations in the two countries.

The following effort to set the case of Buenos Aires into the comparative context defined by Degler's work, and by other more recent research, attempts to suggest some parallels among the historical experiences of English, Portuguese, and Spanish America. Historians have tended to focus on the divergences among systems of race relations present in the different regions of the hemisphere, but in a number of respects the similarities in those systems are more striking than the differences. Discussions of the relative benevolence or severity of slave regimes tend to obscure the fundamental fact that the slaveholding societies of the Americas threw fairly uniform sets of obstacles in the way of black people striving to alter their economic and social status. Legal mechanisms by which slaves could acquire freedom existed in all three empires, but it is the present consensus of scholars writing on the subject that the ability of bondspeople actually to take advantage of those mechanisms varied in direct relationship to the economic characteristics of the region in question.[1] Slaves working on isolated rural plantations were unlikely to be able to earn the income with which to purchase their liberty, as were slaves resident in economically stagnant areas. And black people lucky enough to buy, be granted, or be born into freedom acquired an ambiguous status in no way equal to that of their white compatriots. The Spanish, Portuguese, and English colonies enforced varying combinations of legal and social strictures on the rights of their free black populations, but those structures had the common goal of dividing the colonial societies into a clearly defined hierarchy of racial estates in which nonwhites were relegated to inferior status. The tendency of Brazilian colonial legislation to refer to free black people as "free slaves" is just one indication of the stigma which people of African descent carried with them from slavery into freedom.[2]

The revolutions of the 1775–1825 period offered as one of their possible outcomes the termination of restrictions on the rights of black people. Revolutionary rhetoric on both continents proclaimed the equality of all men (as is usually the case, women did not benefit from a change in regime) in the newly formed republics, and occasionally explicitly extended this equality to nonwhites. Black men fought enthusiastically for whichever side they perceived as more likely finally to remove the many constraints on their freedom. Afro-Argentine units distinguished themselves fighting against the Spanish; in Venezuela black men responded to the offers of both sides, rebel and royalist, to abolish slavery and the caste regime in return for black support of their cause; in the United States, the reluctance of the Continental Congress to enlist slave and free black soldiers persuaded thousands of Afro–North Americans to join the British forces in exchange for promises of freedom.

The postrevolutionary decades in the United States witnessed a deterioration in the economic and social condition of free black people, and only partial abolition of slavery (in the Northern states).[3] In Spanish America, on the other hand, the immediate abolition of slavery in Mexico, the Central American countries, and Chile, and the programs of gradual abolition enacted in the other countries, guaranteed the early termination of the "peculiar institution" which would persist in the United States until 1865 and in Brazil until 1888. Most Spanish American countries also enacted legislation or even constitutional articles between 1810 and 1860 intended to ensure the equality of all citizens before the law, regardless of race.[4] Two historians who have conducted research on Mexico and Uruguay argue that such legislation allowed the entry of black people into the newly forming class societies of those countries and that their integration into those societies is now complete.[5] This argument forms the basis on which many Spanish Americans claim that if black people suffer from discrimination in their countries it is the product of class prejudice rather than race prejudice.[6]

Students of postemancipation race relations in Brazil and the United States are well aware of the many and varied ways, some subtle and some not so subtle, in which elements inherited from the slave and caste regimes of the colonial period have survived into the present to condition contemporary patterns of race relations. Segregation and discrimination have long been recognized as the dark side of the American dream, and while Brazilians hold their country up to the rest of the world as the racial democracy of the Americas, a social paradise in which racism never rears its ugly head, objective observers find no great difficulty in identifying the manifestations of deeply ingrained racial inequities.[7]

One may greet with some skepticism, then, the argument that the Spanish American nations successfully integrated black people into their postcolonial societies. Certainly if such integration were to have taken place, Buenos Aires would have formed an exceptionally conducive setting for it. As described in Chapter 2, the city's spectacular growth between 1870 and 1914, both in economic and demographic terms, stimulated the early formation and development of a class-based society in the city. Assuming that the heritage of the caste regime had truly been banished with the ending of colonial rule, one would expect individual Afro-Argentines to be able to take their places in the new social and economic order just as white Argentines did. And given the steadily decreasing demographic representation of black people in the city's population, one might speculate that white porteños would feel little necessity to enforce racially discriminatory laws or customs against the Afro-Argentines, since black competition for jobs, housing, and other resources would pose little threat to the greater society in which they lived. Systematic discrimination might be expected in the Caribbean, the American South, or the Brazilian Northeast, where a white minority had to defend its predominance by locking black people out of the social and economic contest.[8] But in Buenos Aires, of all the settings in Latin America, one would expect a quiet attitude of live-and-let-live, a willingness to allow the members of the dwindling Afro-Argentine minority to find their place in the city's class structure, unfettered by the restrictions of the earlier caste system.

As we have seen, this was not the case. As black people acquired the objective prerequisites for working-class and middle-class status, they were denied admission to those classes by the Europeans and white Argentines, who declined to grant them the accorded status essential for class membership. Black office workers and professionals thought of themselves as members of Buenos Aires's white-collar class, but middle-class white porteños continued to consign them, along with working-class and impoverished Afro-Argentines, into the all-embracing category of *gente de color*, people of color. While Buenos Aires evolved into a society increasingly defined in terms of class, the Afro-Argentines remained literally a race apart, a caste divided into classes which paralleled those of the larger society but were almost completely marginal groups.

This impression of the black community as a group apart is reinforced by the Afro-Argentines' own way of collectively referring to themselves. To the present day, they call themselves *la clase de color* (the colored class) or *gente de clase* (people of the class). When asking each other whether a third party is black, they will say, "*¿es de clase?*" (are they of the class?). "Class" as used by the Afro-Argentines is thus not a socioeconomic term but rather a purely racial one, reflecting their own historical experience of having been shunted aside in the porteño class structure solely on the basis of their race.

In searching for the reason why the seemingly optimum conditions of Buenos Aires did not result in the integration of Afro-Argentines into porteño society, we might turn to Carl Degler's previously cited study. In seeking to explain the more relaxed and seemingly more amicable state of race relations in Brazil as compared to the United States, Degler focused on, among other factors, the relative stasis of the Brazilian economy and society during the colonial period and the nineteenth century. Divisions among social strata remained well defined and for the most part impermeable, due primarily to the character of Brazilian development prior to 1900, which left wealth concentrated in the hands of a small landholding class. Little opportunity existed for large-scale upward mobility, so what few challenges there were to traditional systems of class and race relations posed no real threat to the status quo. Social and racial controls could therefore be more subtle and less overt than in the United States, where a rapidly expanding economy and a class structure in the process of formation allowed for substantial upward and downward mobility. It was very much in the interest of lower- and middle-class North American whites to remove black people from the crowded competition for social and economic position. Thus racial discrimination in the United States became much more open and blatant than was the case in Brazil.[9]

The proof of Degler's proposition may be found in one of its apparent exceptions, the Brazilian city of São Paulo. São Paulo is comparable in many ways to Buenos Aires: both cities were the first in their countries to become integrated into the modern, industrialized world economy, and today they form the dominant financial, commercial, and industrial centers of Brazil and Argentina, respectively. Since 1900 race relations in São Paulo have become considerably more strained than in the economically stagnant Brazilian Northeast. In a remark that might well be applied to Buenos Aires and to a number of cities in the United States, Florestan Fernandes has observed that the arrival of nineteenth- and twentieth-century immigrants to the city in response to economic opportunities there "contributed clearly to worsen the appearance and the reality of racial inequality."[10] In the face of growing conflict among groups competing for limited resources, black people were increasingly barred from participating in the society on equal terms with whites. This is what occurred in the United States and it appears that, in the mobile society of the boom years between 1870 and 1914, the same thing happened in Buenos Aires. Competition for entry into the new porteño middle class was intense, as was competition for passage from the middle to the upper class. As in São Paulo and the United States, the black population was ruled out of the contest.

Further proof of the applicability of Degler's argument can be found in the transformation of porteño race consciousness documented in the previous chapter. The replacement of the spectrum of racial terms employed in the first half of the century by the "white/colored" dichotomy used increasingly after 1850 tended to sharpen the lines of racial exclusion and to introduce a style of race relations with distinctly North American overtones.

Of particular importance in comparing the case of Buenos Aires to São Paulo and to the United States is the fact that abolition occurred in Argentina considerably earlier than it did in either Brazil or the United States. In his analysis of race relations in São Paulo, Fernandes emphasized the inability of the Afro-Brazilians to compete effectively in the new social and economic order due to the crippling effects of their having previously participated in the regional society and economy as slaves. Abruptly cut loose from the paternalist protections of the slave regime and thrown into the hostile environment of the free labor market, the former slaves were ill fitted to make their way in the rapidly developing city. Similar arguments have been advanced concerning freedmen in the post–Civil War American South.[11]

Argentina's programs of gradual emancipation, freedom through military service, and individual manumission produced a population of black porteños that was over 50 percent free by 1827. By the time of final abolition, in 1861, it appears that only a small proportion of the city's black people were slaves. Furthermore, the labor which they had performed, and the conditions under which they performed it, were in no way comparable to the plantation labor carried out by the slaves who migrated to São Paulo city following abolition. Whether artisans, street vendors, or agricultural horsemen, the slaves of Buenos Aires enjoyed the opportunity to carve out a considerably larger breathing space than was available to laborers on Brazilian and North American plantations. Thus the Afro-Argentines left slavery earlier, and entered freedom better prepared, than did the newly emancipated slaves of Brazil or the United States.

Despite these relative advantages, the Afro-Argentines fell victim to patterns of discrimination remarkably similar, if somewhat milder in degree, to those which afflicted black people in English and Portuguese America. One begins to perceive a bleakly depressing historical cul-de-sac for Afro-Americans of all languages and cultures. The continuation of colonial or semicolonial socioeconomic structures in the less modernized areas of Latin America guarantees the relegation of non-whites to inferior social and economic status. Modernization and development, usually accompanied in the nineteenth century by philosophies of economic and social liberalism and a strong belief in the concept of progress, appear to hold out the hope of structural transformations that will allow black people to assume their place in class-based societies in which race is merely a physical characteristic neither more nor less significant than any other. Economic growth should not only increase the amount of wealth and resources which a society can divide among its members but should also break down traditional patterns of distribution to replace them with more progressive ones.

But far from improving or ameliorating systems of race relations inherited from the colonial period, modernization and growth have had the effect of altering but reinforcing the mechanisms by which black people are excluded from the social and economic competition. Growth is never sufficient to satisfy the demands of all members of the society, and in order to preserve a larger share for those members of the racial group traditionally dominant throughout the Americas, the lines of segregation and discrimination are drawn more clearly and enforced more rigidly.

We are here faced with a grim historical dialectic in which thesis, antithesis, and synthesis all produce much the same result. As one contemplates the future, it is quite clear that the long-standing patterns of racial inequality in the hemisphere will be overcome only through conscious decisions on the part of societies and governments that such inequality is deleterious to the well-being of their nations, and that the state must actively intervene to promote the social, economic, and political participation of its black citizens. The only multiracial countries in the hemisphere to have taken such a decision are, curiously enough, those at opposite ends of the ideological spectrum, namely Cuba and the United States. Combatting racism has been announced as one of the foremost goals of the Cuban revolution, while governmentally en-forced programs of equal opportunity and affirmative action constitute the North American response to the continuing dilemma of racism. It is too early to judge the effectiveness of these national efforts to eliminate racial inequities. What is perhaps most significant about each of them is that, for the present, it is inconceivable that similar experiments could be undertaken in any additional Latin American countries. Societies cannot decide actively to combat racism until they are willing to recognize the phenomenon, a preliminary condition that no Latin American country besides Cuba has yet fulfilled. Whereas racism forms a widely recognized and even publicized aspect of North American life, Latin American societies actively promote the myth that racism does not exist in their societies (the Argentine variant of this proposition is discussed in the following chapter). This myth is accepted by blacks as well as by whites, and effectively undermines any efforts by Afro–Latin Americans to mobilize and pressure their governments to redress racial inequities.[12]

In conclusion, the case of Buenos Aires cannot be used singlehandedly to disprove the assertions of writers and public figures who claim the integration of Afro–Spanish American populations into their nations' societies. It is clear, however, that Argentina acted similarly to the other Spanish American countries in enacting laws and constitutional articles seeking to eliminate the colonial heritage of slavery and caste. It is equally clear that, as in Brazil and the United States, that heritage nevertheless persisted into the national period and up to the present day, producing a system of race relations which preserves patterns of racial inequality that had their genesis in the slave societies of the eighteenth and nineteenth centuries. The case of Buenos Aires therefore serves to suggest that such claims of integration and racial harmony spring from an excessive attention to official laws and pronouncements dating from the independence period, and a concomitant failure critically to examine the historical evolution of race relations since abolition and the extent to which those laws and proclamations went unenforced. It is my hope that future research in this area will address itself to this and other controversies surrounding the postemancipation history of black people in the Americas.

12

Epilogue
The Afro-Argentines Today

The history of Buenos Aires's Afro-Argentines in the twentieth century has been one of slow and steady demographic decline. The census of 1887 set their numbers at eight thousand. Current estimates suggest that there are perhaps three or four thousand black people in the city, an infinitesimal fraction of Greater Buenos Aires's eight million people.[1] The decline would probably have been even greater had it not been for a small trickle of black immigration from Portuguese Africa, particularly the Cape Verde Islands. Those Africans who have entered the city during the course of this century, however, have not integrated themselves to any extent into the rest of the Afro-Argentine community. They remain a group apart, with their own mutual aid society and social club, the Asociación de Socorros Mutuos Caboverdeana, which presently counts some six hundred members.

Another wave of immigration that has probably helped sustain the city's black population is that of the so-called *cabecitas negras* (literally, "little black heads") from the interior. The rural-to-urban migration stream which Argentina shares in common with most developing countries has resulted in the arrival in Buenos Aires of over a million cabecitas from the interior. With their noticeable Indian and, occasionally, African ancestry, the new arrivals are an uncomfortable reminder to the porteños that not all of Argentina is the white preserve that it is widely thought to be.[2]

Not surprisingly the cabecitas tend to occupy the lowest rungs in porteño society, working at the worst-paid and lowest-status jobs (they

209

are strongly represented, for instance, in construction and domestic service) and living in the *villas miserias* that ring the capital. Their presence in the city poses puzzling racial issues for porteño society. Because they form a large and rapidly growing element in the city's population, it does not really do to label them as nonwhites, since this clashes with the myth of an all-white Argentina. On the other hand, these dark-skinned migrants are definitely not of the same ancestry as the European porteños, and most natives of the city take a condescending view of the recent arrivals. Many porteños refer to the migrants simply as "los negros," a shorthand reference which at times proves confusing. The Afro-Uruguayan actor Rey Charol recalls an incident when he was talking casually with some white friends in a Buenos Aires bar and one of them began complaining about "all those negros." Charol protested immediately, whereupon the friend hastened to reassure him: "But no, *morocho* [a colloquial term for a dark-skinned person], I wasn't saying it about you . . . I really like you *morochos*. What bothers me are those *negros*, the *cabecitas negras*."[3]

Charol's confusion was understandable, since "negro" now does double duty to refer both to in-migrants and Afro-Argentines. The racial dichotomization of Buenos Aires society described in Chapter 10 is now even more pronounced than it was in the late 1800s. The expression "people of color" is now used only by Afro-Argentines; white people tend to refer to all black people, whether they are mulattoes or pure blacks, as negros. Gone is the distinction between pardos and morenos—porteños tend to share the North American belief that visible African ancestry makes one a negro, a black. Thus the term "Afro-Argentine," which some Argentines protested to me as being a term of North American origin not applicable to Argentine social realities, is in fact entirely appropriate.

The tendency to label all black people "negros" is readily apparent in a survey of the titles of articles and books on the Afro-Argentines published in Buenos Aires during the last twenty years: León Benaros's "Negros en Buenos Aires" and "Oficios de negros en el antiguo Buenos Aires" (both 1970); Luis Grassino's "Buenos Aires de ébano [ebony]" (1971); Bernardo Kordon's "La raza negra en el Río de la Plata" (1969); Blas Matamoro's "Los negros han desaparecido del ámbito de Buenos Aires" (1976); José Luis Molinari's "Los indios y negros durante las invasiones inglesas al Río de la Plata, en 1806 y 1807" (1963); Ricardo Rodríguez Molas's *La música y danza de los negros en el Buenos Aires de los siglos XVIII y XIX* (1957), "Negros libres rioplatenses" (1961), and "El negro en el Río de la Plata (1970); and so on. There are exceptions, of course: Marta Goldberg's "La población negra y mulata de la ciudad de

Buenos Aires" (1976); Máximo Simpson's "Porteños de color" (1967); and Luis Soler Cañas's "Pardos y morenos en el año 80 . . ." (1973). But the bulk of relevant titles, and the overwhelming evidence of conversations with white porteños, suggests that those who were formerly "people of color" have now become "negros." We might hark back for a moment to Elena Padilla's explanation of the significance of trigueño in Puerto Rico: "Persons who are being talked about in their absence may be referred to as Negroes, but they will probably be described as *trigueños* in their presence." Exactly this system of etiquette seems to have applied on a corporate scale in Buenos Aires: while black people still formed a major portion of the city's population, they were referred to as trigueños. Now that they have dwindled to an insignificant portion of the total and, for all practical purposes, have virtually disappeared, the term "negro" has resurfaced. In their presence the Afro-Argentines were trigueños; in their absence they are negros.

Despite (or perhaps because of) the fact that Afro-Argentines are no longer very visible in Buenos Aires, many porteños share a fascination with things African and Afro-American. I happened to be strolling down the fashionable downtown street Calle Florida one afternoon in 1976 when I witnessed an extraordinary episode. I had read several days earlier of a basketball team from Senegal that would soon be arriving in the city to play a few exhibition games. That afternoon I saw a group of young black men who could only have been that team disembarking from a tour bus. The spectacle of ten or fifteen Africans, all of them over six feet tall and wearing colorful bellbottoms and tunics, had an absolutely galvanizing effect on passers-by. Spectators came trotting from as far as two blocks away to form a buzzing, expectant ring around the puzzled Africans. Within less than a minute the team was completely boxed in by several hundred porteños who had come to see this curiosity. The young men broke free and headed off down Florida, but their escort would not be shaken off. They continued to accompany the Africans, exchanging no words with their quarry, just watching intently.

The incident was representative of the strong porteño interest in black people and in blackness as a phenomenon. During the eighteen months that I was in Argentina, four newspaper and magazine articles on the disappearance of the Afro-Argentines were published in the Buenos Aires press; doubtless others appeared that I missed.[4] Other articles displayed an interest in and considerable knowledge of North American black history. One on the possible vice-presidential nomination of Senator Edward Brooke in 1976 touched on the history of Afro-American music, the Harlem Renaissance, Garveyism, and intellectuals such as W. E. B. Dubois, Langston Hughes, Eldridge Cleaver, and Martin Luther King.[5]

Afro-Argentine themes occasionally appear in porteño entertainments. The 1940 musical *Candombe de San Baltasar* was based explicitly on Afro-Argentine music and dance; at least three other reviews in the 1940s included black performers in candombe numbers. Rolando González Pacheco's *Cuando había reyes* (When There Were Kings), produced for the first time in 1947, was a drama of life in the black community during the Rosas period. The "kings" of the title refers to the presidents of the African nations. We may presume that the original cast of the play was white, since it was first staged in Yiddish, and Yiddish-speaking Afro-Argentines are a rare breed indeed. The play did sufficiently well to be produced in Spanish, however, and enjoyed a long run. And one of the most popular events at the parish of San Telmo's sesquicentennial celebration in 1956 and a subsequent festival in 1966 was candombes performed by black and white Argentines.[6]

Whenever I discussed my research with Argentines, there was an immediate response of interest and curiosity concerning my findings. The majority of people I talked with presented the traditional explanations—the wars, high death rates, and miscegenation—with unfailing regularity. Although a small minority were not aware that there had ever been black people in Argentina, the bulk of the population has heard of the disappearance and accepts the traditional explanations more or less uncritically. Somewhat disturbingly, my attempts to explain the directions my research was taking and the results it was producing met with fairly negative response. The majority of Argentines resisted what I was telling them, with various degrees of intensity. Some argued vehemently; others became irritated and fell back on the defense that, as a foreigner, I could not really understand the reality of their country's history; others simply changed the subject. A minority expressed interest and encouragement.

Yet it has been frequently recognized that the history of the Afro-Argentines is in need of substantial revision. As early as the 1870s the black community's writers were calling for the restoration of black people to their rightful place in Argentine history. The white historian M. F. Mantilla seconded this point in 1890, writing an essay on the forgotten black soldiers who helped free Argentina from Spanish rule.[7] José Luis Lanuza opened his 1946 book on the Afro-Argentines with a reflection on how Argentine historians have badly neglected black people's role in the country's history.[8] His book, *Morenada* (The Blacks), won a municipal prize for history the following year. But in 1961 Ricardo Rodríguez Molas, another Argentine historian, could with reason still complain of the sentimental romanticism surrounding the history of the Afro-Argentines, a romanticism which hides the racist realities of their history.[9]

The racist distortions introduced into Afro-Argentine history by such nineteenth-century writers as Sarmiento, Ingenieros, and others have been discussed in previous chapters. Such racism continues to deform works written in this century. It varies in intensity from fairly subtle to startlingly virulent. An example of the latter is *Cosas de negros* (Things of Blacks), by Vicente Rossi, a cultural history of black people in the Río de la Plata which was first published in 1926 and then re-published in 1958. The title itself is objectionable, since in Argentine slang a "cosa de negros" is something done ineptly or badly. Blacks were supposedly incapable of performing tasks without constant supervision; a "cosa de negro" therefore became synonymous with anything that had been badly botched. The book is full of useful information but is blighted by Rossi's ceaseless efforts to present Afro-Argentines and Afro-Uruguayans as childish, ignorant simpletons. The book opens with a claim that black people in the Río de la Plata had no idea that their ancestors were Africans, nor how those ancestors had arrived in the Americas. "Idiotized by their captivity," Rossi's blacks are a South American version of Stanley Elkins's Sambo. Their mentality is hopelessly infantile, so that they "talk like a child and obey like a dog. . . . as dim and dark of understanding as of skin, the black men ended by thinking natural and just their condition as domestic animals, and to the whim of the 'lord and master' they sacrificed even the secret right to think. The beast-man of the African jungles was transformed by suffering into the dog-man."[10] Rossi dismissed the ceremonies of the African nations as "a childish game" and persisted in treating Afro-Argentine culture and society as idiotic and perverse.[11] He failed utterly to understand the process of syncretism by which African and Argentine practices were combined to produce new social and cultural forms.

Despite the book's fatal and fundamental flaws, it and *Morenada* are regularly cited as the two basic works on black people in the Río de la Plata. Other books and articles betray similar biases. A 1961 essay cited frequently in previous chapters closes with the reflection that the Afro-Argentines "contributed labor, but they greatly lowered the moral and cultural level" of the country.[12] A 1965 book on the history of the tango described the Afro-Argentines as "the primitive children of rhythm" and recalled how the beat of the candombe rhythm "fanned the flames of their lust, alcoholism, and passion."[13] A series of short sketches on Afro-Argentine history that appered in 1970 in the widely circulated popular history magazine, *Todo Es Historia* (Everything Is History), lifted racist clichés directly from the nineteenth-century historians to describe the fat, jolly women and the stupid, shiftless men who allegedly formed the picturesque black community of the previous century. Aunt Jemima and Stepin Fetchit live on, though the author concluded his series with the ritual reflections on "the old traditional neighborhood that civilization and the progress of this great capital have erased, reclaiming those filthy lots with handsome houses and sumptuous palaces."[14]

This racist bias is accompanied and intensified by the Argentine belief that the country does not suffer from any type of racism at all. Some writers have recognized this myth for the delusion that it is,[15] but it remains the dominant strain in Argentine thought. Conversations with numerous Argentines amply demonstrated to me that they sincerely believe their country to be completely free of racism; they frequently contrasted their own country and the United States, where racism is a well-publicized fact of daily life. This contrast was made explicit by a group of one hundred Argentine women who wrote an open letter in October 1976 to Congressman Donald Fraser to protest the hearings he was chairing on human rights violations in Argentina. The women argued that the United States had no right to censure Argentina for alleged violations of human rights since it had itself performed so badly in the area of race relations. They claimed that slavery had been abolished in Argentina more than 150 years earlier (1813) and Argentina "never had racial discrimination in schools or public transport."[16] These statements are of course false. Slavery was in fact not abolished in Argentina until 1853, in Buenos Aires not until 1861, four years before it was abolished in the United States. And as we have seen, racial discrimination occurred in schools and places of public entertainment throughout the last century, and it continues to the present day.

The main reason why Argentines persist in believing that their country is free of racism is that they have a very different conception from North Americans of what racism is. After many discussions on this question with Argentines, I have concluded that to an Argentine racism means an automatic, immediate, and intensely hostile reaction to members of a race different from one's own. If a person does not experience that reaction, then he or she is not a racist, by Argentine standards. This is different from United States usage, where racism certainly includes that reaction but is also considered to embrace the belief that a person's intelligence, natural abilities, behavior, and other nonphysical qualities are irrevocably determined by his or her racial heritage and that environment will have little or no effect on altering the results of that heritage. Thus in the United States it is considered a racist attitude to believe that black people can be useful to society only in the manual trades. In Argentina that would not necessarily be considered racist. A type of remark that I heard repeatedly in Buenos Aires was one on the order of "but of course we're not racist. When I was young my parents had a black cleaning lady, and nobody thought anything of it!" Writing in 1927, Alfredo Taullard offered as proof that there is no racism in Argentina the fact that porteños never hesitated to do business with black street vendors.[17] The congressional orderlies, of whom several are still black, are frequently cited as evidence of Argentina's lack of racism. If the country were racist, goes the argument, would it allow black men to work in its government offices? The counterargument, that it is racist to restrict black workers to the lowest levels of government service, is dismissed as irrelevant.

There is a more sophisticated variation of the no-racism argument. Some Argentines admit that there is prejudice against Argentines of darker skin, but assert that this prejudice is of a class nature, not of a racial nature.[18] Certainly it is true that Latin American class lines are much less fluid than North American ones, that movement across them occurs rather infrequently, and that members of higher classes tend to treat the members of lower ones with considerable disdain. This argument finds further support in the historical confusion between race and class throughout Latin America. Well-do-do black people could win the right to describe themselves as white, and racial labels became as much social in nature as biological. But the awkward fact remains that there is an extremely strong correlation between skin color and social class, and that dark-skinned Argentines are exposed to racial epithets never directed toward their white compatriots.

This racism, which applies to other groups besides blacks, receives tacit recognition in Argentine press policies. A North American journalist resident in Buenos Aires from 1973 to 1977 told me that when he arrived in Argentina he was informed by an Argentine colleague that there were two taboos in the national press. First, no articles concerning anti-Semitism, which is a serious problem in the country, can be printed. Second, no articles concerning present-day problems with the Indian population can be printed. During eighteen months in Argentina I witnessed occasional exceptions to these taboos. The newspaper *La Opinión* (defunct since the arrest of its publisher Jacobo Timerman in 1977) was particularly forthright in exposing the anti-Semitism which plagues Argentina, and it once ran a report on the desperate condition of the Indians living around the mountain resort of Bariloche. But for the most part the Argentine newspaperman proved to be correct. The prejudice which afflicts these two Argentine minorities is studiously ignored. Indeed, the very existence of the country's Indian population is ignored, just as was the continued existence of the Afro-Argentines in the last century. Since the Jews are a white, European group, their presence in the country is compatible with its cultural mythology, and articles on their collective and individual activities appear frequently in the porteño press. As far as the black population is concerned, now that it is demographically insignificant, it is perfectly permissible to print articles on its "disappearance" and the remnants of the community that remain. Also, now that the blacks are more or less gone, it is unusual to find a porteño who will admit to being antiblack. In regard to Jews and Indians, however, public expressions of racist sentiment are not considered socially unacceptable, and one occasionally hears the most blood-curdling declarations imaginable, up to and including desires for the mass elimination of both groups from Argentine life. The autobiography of General Perón, after describing the Nuremberg trials of Nazi war criminals as "an infamy . . . a great outrage that history will never pardon," goes on to relate his reaction to proposals that his government liquidate the Argentine Jewish population. He rejected the idea on the grounds of practicality: "How do you figure," he replied to one adviser, "that I'm going to get involved in that morass of a Jewish problem when you know perfectly well that Hitler, with his one hundred million Germans, couldn't resolve it[;] what am I going to do with fifteen or twenty million Argentines?"[19] Perón instead proposed and implemented the solution of allowing the Jewish population to work and produce for the good of the fatherland. To this day, however, the right wing of the Peronist movement displays alarming anti-Semitic tendencies. Since blacks no longer form a visible element in Argentine national life, such intensity of feeling is no longer called for, though the anti-Brazilianism prevalent in Argentina is often expressed in terms of scorn for the racially mixed character of the Brazilian population.

Despite these consistently expressed sentiments, the myth of no racism in Argentina persists, promoted in part by the Afro-Argentines themselves. A Cape Verdean immigrant married to a white Argentine woman reports that "I never had any problems. You see that my child is white. If I were living in South Africa, do you think I could go to the movies with him?" Another Cape Verdean concurred. "Problems? Please! Here there isn't a single black man who hasn't had five or six white girl friends. They prefer blacks."[20] He may be right—it is a curious fact that at least a quarter of the male mannikins in Buenos Aires clothing store windows are gleaming black vinyl, especially striking in comparison to the bland plaster tones of the white mannikins. Invariably crowned with flamboyant Afro wigs, sometimes in blue or pink, these virile figures in the display cases are an eerie presence in a city from which black people have almost disappeared.

The Cape Verdeans singled out probably the most liberal area in Argentine race relations. In a reversal of North American mores, interracial dating and marriage are not greatly frowned upon in Buenos Aires. When my wife and I were invited to the annual Carnival dances of the Shimmy Club, a black social organization, we were surprised to find that the majority of the couples were biracial. All-black couples were actually rather uncommon, especially among young people. Black-Italian marriages, already common in the 1880s and 1890s, are run-of-the-mill today, with the result that the heavily Italian neighborhood of La Boca is one of the areas of the city where one most frequently sees Afro-Argentines. So common is intermarriage that in a 1971 magazine article in which the black government employee Carlos Boot was mentioned, the writer felt it either necessary or of interest to mention that Boot's wife was black.[21]

But in other areas Afro-Argentines have to endure painful and embarrassing discrimination. Black musicians find it difficult to enter white bands. Black television and movie actors complain that they are always relegated to playing butlers and maids and occasionally musicians—it is impossible for them to get a leading part in an Argentine production. The actor Rey Charol stated: "I don't want to appear resentful, because I owe a lot to Argentina. But there is a subtle, underhanded racism here."[22] An Afro-Argentine physician reported that some patients refused to believe that he was a doctor; they insisted instead that he must be an orderly. Blacks find it difficult to get jobs as salespeople. There have been incidents of black people being refused service in Buenos Aires's restaurants. And in a particularly unpleasant incident several years ago, after a black child was admitted to a nursery in the city all the other parents withdrew their children, the workers resigned en masse, and things were not set right until the child was withdrawn and the psychologist responsible for admitting him fired. The director of the school, who ironically was a Japanese-Argentine and thus a member of another group which suffers from race prejudice, made a public statement saying that "we don't want any kinky-haired blacks here."[23]

The readiest way to get in touch with what remains of the Afro-Argentine community is through the Shimmy Club, a group that has no activities other than sponsoring occasional dances. The ones we attended in 1976 were held in a large hall in a working-class area near Congress and were attended by three to four hundred people. Many of the people there were white, either the lightened offspring of mixed couples or simply people from the neighborhood who had dropped by for a good time (admission was seventy cents). Two bands alternated on the dance floor, one a traditional tango orchestra, the other an electric Brazilian-tropical band. Downstairs three young men played the candombe on conga drums and other percussion instruments; two of them were white.

The club's president, Alfredo Núñez, is a third-generation orderly at Congress. He recalls that the club was once more active than it is today, but that the population has declined and the young Afro-Argentines seem less interested in maintaining community organizations and traditions. Similar observations have been made by other people writing on the community.[24] Afflicted by their blackness, many young Afro-Argentines would just as soon leave that part of their heritage behind, just as their forebears of a century ago tried to do. This impulse is by no means universal: the Afro-Argentines take great pride in the achievements of such North American blacks as Richard Wright, Sidney Poitier, Duke Ellington, and Martin Luther King. But there is a distinct current of younger blacks who want to get out from under the burden of being black in a white society.

At least two young Afro-Argentine women have reacted against this tendency by actively researching their black roots and presenting their findings to the public, but they are exceptional in several ways. Carmen and Susana Platero are granddaughters of the notary public Tomás B. Platero, and as such they belong to one of the most distinguished Afro-Argentine families. Susana lived in Chicago for a year while studying Afro–North American music; their brother Tomás, Jr., traveled to Africa several times as a member of Argentine trade delegations. In 1976 my wife and I attended the sisters' show, *Calugan Andumba . . . y la Ñapa*, a sung and spoken review of Afro-Argentine history. Accompanied by two percussionists, a white Argentine and an Afro-Uruguayan, the two women dramatized slave sales and manumissions, recalled the role of black men in fighting Argentina's wars, presented a sketch demonstrating how racism operates in Buenos Aires, and traced the development of Afro-Argentine music. In interviews after the show, the sisters made clear their awareness of the inadequacies of Afro-Argentine history as it is presently written and their resentment of how the black role in national life has been covered up and forgotten. They saw their show, which they were hoping to present at the Black Arts Festival in Nigeria, as a step toward the revision of that history.

The sisters themselves are living documentation of the gradual fading away of the Afro-Argentines. Though Susana showed visible African ancestry, Carmen would be considered as white in both Argentina and the United States. They are children of a mulatto father and an Italian mother and, as one review of the show noted, the women "have whitened dangerously."[25] Their whiteness did not prevent an incident during the intermission, however. Apparently irritated by the sisters' taking a lengthy break during the show, one of the white organizers of the event was heard complaining loudly in the lobby about "these *negras* and their lack of discipline." Afro-Argentines can whiten considerably and still not escape their African heritage, especially when they display it to the world as a source of pride.

So the gradual process of disappearance goes on, the black Argentines lightening and entering the ranks of the whites. It has continued for so long, however, and its conclusion has been prematurely claimed so often, that one wonders whether the Afro-Argentines will every truly disappear from Buenos Aires. Perhaps one day there will indeed be no black people in Argentina. But in a greater and deeper sense, the Afro-Argentines will never disappear. They helped make Buenos Aires what it is, and they live on in the history of Argentina's armies, in the black saints and Virgins still to be seen in Buenos Aires's churches, in the milonga and the tango, in the paintings that evoke the city's past, in the porteño words derived from African origins. Their blood flows in the veins of Argentina, and the Afro-Argentines live on, forgotten, but not gone.

REFERENCE MATTER

Glossary

academia de baile: dance hall.
achuradora: scavenger and vendor of waste meat products.
aguatero: water seller.
altiplano: the Bolivian mesa, very high in altitude.
asiento: royal permit to engage in trade.
audiencia: royal tribunal.
barbero: barber-surgeon.
cabecita negra: migrant to Buenos Aires from the interior of the country.
candombe: Afro-Argentine dance.
casta: caste; person of racially mixed or nonwhite ancestry.
caudillo: personalist military leader.
changador: porter.
chinchulines: braided, grilled beef intestines; in the United States, chitlings.
cofradía: lay religious brotherhood.
compadrito: a tough, a hoodlum.
comparsa: Carnival marching band.
conventillo: type of housing inhabited by the lower class.
corsario: privateer.
criollo: creole; a native-born Argentine.
cuartel: ward; municipal administrative unit.
empanadas: meat pies.
estancia: large cattle ranch.
estanciero: rancher.
fábrica: workshop or factory.
fuero: special legal jurisdiction applied during the colonial and early national periods to members of the clergy, military, and other privileged groups.
gaucho: a cowboy.
gente de clase, gente de color: collective terms for Afro-Argentines.

223

gente decente: collective term for elite members of colonial society.

gente de pueblo: collective term for non-elite members of colonial society.

gracias al sacar: royal decree permitting nonwhites to purchase the legal status and rights of white people.

hacienda: large farm or ranch.

liberto: an Afro-Argentine theoretically free but still legally bound to serve a master or the state until the age of majority.

maestrito: pianist and singer popular in society circles as an entertainer and music instructor.

mestizaje: race mixture.

milonga: a dance popular in Argentina and Uruguay.

moreno: a person of pure African descent.

morocho: slang term for a dark-skinned person.

mulato: a person of racially mixed ancestry.

negro: in the last century, a person of pure African descent; in this century, an Afro-Argentine or a *cabecita negra*.

negro alzado: literally, a "risen black"; a runaway slave at large on the pampa.

negro descaminado: literally, a "black who has lost his way"; slaves brought into Buenos Aires under this guise could be sold without royal permits and free of import duties.

niño de bien: son of a well-to-do family.

orillero: inhabitant of a working-class neighborhood. The term derives from the word *orilla*, meaning riverbank, and was originally associated with the slums along the Riachuelo, the stream on the city's south side.

pampa: the grassy plain of Argentina and Uruguay.

pardo: person of racially mixed ancestry; a mulatto.

payada: spontaneous rhyming contest.

plebe: term used during the colonial period to denote non-elites.

porteño: a native of the city of Buenos Aires.

Régimen de castas: colonial legislation by which society was organized into racially defined estates or castes, arranged hierarchically.

rescate: program by which slaves were purchased by the state to become soldiers.

saladerista: owner of a meat-packing establishment.

saladero: meat-salting and -packing establishment.

soroche: illness caused by prolonged exposure to low temperatures and high winds.

tapada: drumming contest.

trigueño: a person of indeterminate racial ancestry, neither black nor white.

villa miseria: slum on the outskirts of Buenos Aires city.

zambo: a person of mixed African and Indian ancestry.

Appendix A
Occupational Categories Listed in Samples of the 1810 and the 1827 Municipal Censuses of Buenos Aires

The occupational categories employed in Tables 3.2 and 3.3. contain the following occupations listed in the censuses.*

PROPERTY OWNERS
    landlord
    owner of an *estancia*
    owner of an *hacienda*
    property owner

PROFESSIONALS
    accountant
    chemist
    doctor
    government official
    lawyer
    military officer
    notary
    pharmacist
    priest

PROFESSIONALS *(cont.)*
    schoolteacher
    surveyor
    university graduate

COMMERCE
    broker
    businessman
    cafe owner
    employee
    innkeeper
    retailer
    shopkeeper
    stallkeeper
    storekeeper

* I wish to acknowledge the assistance of Thomas Shick and Juan-Carlos Garavaglia in preparing these occupational categories. See also Mark D. Szuchman and Eugene F. Sofer, "The State of Occupational Stratification Studies in Argentina: A Classificatory Scheme," *Latin America Research Review* 11 (1976): 159–71.

SMALL FARMERS
farmer (*quintero, labrador, afincado*)

ARTISANS
baker
barber-surgeon
blacksmith
butcher
carpenter
cooper
dyer
engraver
gunsmith
harness maker
hatmaker
mason
miller
musician
pastry chef
potter
printer
shoemaker
silversmith
tailor
tinsmith
watchmaker

SEMISKILLED
barber
candle maker
caretaker, watchman
carter
caulker
chocolate maker
cigarette maker

SEMISKILLED (*cont.*)
coachman
cook
cordwainer
fan maker
fisherman
mattress maker
noodle maker
orderly
painter
policeman
sailor
seamstress
sexton
skinner
soldier
tanner
waiter
wineskin maker

UNSKILLED
day laborer
herdsman
laundry person
maid
porter
servant
warehouse worker
water seller
well digger
woodcutter

INACTIVE
retired
student

Appendix B
The Samples of the 1810 and the 1827 Municipal Censuses of Buenos Aires

In order to guarantee a sufficiently large sample of Afro-Argentines for statistically significant analysis, the population was stratified for sampling into two categories, black and nonblack. The latter category includes whites, Indians, and mestizos. The former include pardos, morenos, negros, and mulattoes. From the 1810 census, a one-in-seven sample was taken of the Afro-Argentines (14.3 percent) and a one-in-fourteen sample was taken of the nonblacks (7.1 percent). From the 1827 census, a one-in-eight sample was taken of the Afro-Argentines (12.5 percent) and a one-in-twenty sample was taken of the nonblacks (5.0 percent). The selection of the sample was made by taking every nth person encountered in the rolls. Data concerning the individual, the head of his or her family, number of children in the family, the head of the household, and number of people in the household were tabulated for each case.

Both censuses are incomplete. Of twenty cuarteles (wards), the 1810 census lacks six. Of the remaining fourteen, three include no information concerning race, leaving only eleven cuarteles containing 18,854 people, or 57.9 percent of the population in the fourteen cuarteles for which information survives.* By 1827 the city had expanded and had been reorganized into fifty-four cuarteles, of which one through sixteen form the central areas of densest population. Of the thirty-six cuarteles for which canvassing sheets survive, four and part of a fifth contained no information on race and therefore were not included in this sample.

* Marta B. Goldberg, "La población negra y mulata de la ciudad de Buenos Aires, 1810–1840," *Desarrollo Económico* 16 (Apr.-June 1976): 79.

As sampling proceeded, it became clear that the Afro-Argentine population in the suburban precincts was so sparse as to render them of little worth in analyzing trends among the black population. I therefore decided not to sample cuarteles 30, 31, 34, 50, and 52, letting cuarteles 21 through 29, 35, 46, 47, and 54 serve to represent the overwhelmingly white outlying regions of the city.

Appendix C
Afro-Argentine Colonels, 1800–1900

Barbarín, Manuel Macedonio (1781–1836). Barbarín was born on the Calabar coast of West Africa and brought to Buenos Aires as a slave. It is not clear at what date he obtained his freedom, but he first appears in military records serving as a sergeant of black militia during the English invasions of 1806. He eventually rose to become a lieutenant colonel of regulars and second-in-command of the Defenders of Buenos Aires. He was a stalwart of the Rosas regime, and his death was marked by several memorial articles in the *Gaceta Mercantil*, the official government newspaper.

Barcala, Lorenzo (1795–1835). Barcala was born in Mendoza province, the son of African slaves. He entered military service at the age of eighteen and spent the rest of his life in uniform. He served in the revolutionary wars, in the War with Brazil, in several anti-Indian campaigns, and on both sides of the ceaseless civil wars between unitarians and federalists. Attaining the rank of colonel in 1829, he served from 1831 to 1835 under the federalist caudillo Facundo Quiroga, governor of Córdoba and La Rioja provinces. When Quiroga was assassinated in 1835, Barcala returned to Mendoza, where he was accused by Governor Molina of plotting to overthrow the provincial government. He was executed by a firing squad.

Cabrera, Nicolás (1780–1832). Born in Córdoba province, Cabrera subsequently moved to Buenos Aires, where he rose to the rank of captain in the black militia by 1806. He served in the revolutionary army, was appointed commandant of Buenos Aires's free black militia in 1815, and was made a lieutenant colonel of regulars in 1819. He lost his commission for political reasons the following year and entered a premature retirement. Governor Rosas restored him to the rank of lieutenant colonel in 1830 and assigned him to service in the Defenders of Buenos Aires. Cabrera died two years later.

Irrazábal, Pablo (1819–69). A native of Buenos Aires province, Irrazábal was born in the town of Mercedes, some forty miles outside Buenos Aires city. He fought in the civil wars and spent the last decade of his life putting down the final federalist resistance to unitarian rule in the interior. He was personally responsible for the capture and execution of Angel "El Chacho" Peñaloza, one of Argentina's last and best-known federalist caudillos.

Maldones, Estanislao (1826–76). Born in Buenos Aires city, Maldones began his military career at the age of fourteen in Governor Rosas's Restorer Battalion. His outstanding record in the civil wars and the Paraguayan War resulted in his promotion to lieutenant colonel in 1868. His health broken by service in Paraguay, he died at the relatively young age of fifty, but not before arranging admission for his son, Estanislao Junior, to the Military College. The younger Maldones went on to become a major in the regular army.

Morales, José María (1818–94). Born in Buenos Aires city, Morales was originally in training to be a tinsmith, but in 1838 he left Buenos Aires for Montevideo to serve with the anti-Rosas forces in exile. Returning to Buenos Aires with the victorious unitarians in 1852, he went on to serve in a number of militia and regular units that fought in the Paraguayan War and in a series of civil disturbances. He served three terms as a provincial legislator, and late in his career his fellow legislators proposed that he be promoted to general. The idea was rejected, for reasons that remain unclear, and Morales died in 1894 as a colonel.

Narbona, José (?–1850). A shadowy figure of whom little is known, Narbona was a prominent supporter of Governor Rosas and an alleged leader of Rosas's secret police, the Mazorca. Narbona rose to be a lieutenant colonel and commander of the Restorer Battalion.

Pesoa, Inocencio (ca. 1775–?). Equally little material survives on Pesoa, who experienced a dizzying series of promotions between 1806 and 1813, rising from a lowly sergeant of black militia to become a lieutenant colonel in the Battalion of Pardos and Morenos of Upper Peru. He disappears from military records after that, perhaps being killed while on campaign.

Sosa, Agustín (1755– ca. 1820). An Afro-Brazilian who migrated to Buenos Aires by way of Córdoba, Sosa so distinguished himself during the English invasions of 1806–7 that he was recommended by royal officials for promotion to lieutenant colonel of militia, an unprecedented rank for a black man. The Crown approved the promotion in 1809. Sosa joined the revolutionary army in 1810 and was confirmed at the rank of lieutenant colonel of regulars the following year. It is unclear at what date he left military service.

Sosa, Domingo (1788–1866). The son of Agustín Sosa, Domingo entered service in the black militia in 1808 and remained in uniform until his death by natural causes in 1866. He was made a full colonel by Governor Rosas and granted command of the Provisional Battalion in 1845. His talents were such that he was allowed to retain his rank and command under the unitarian administration that succeeded Rosas, and he went on to serve in the provincial legislature from 1856 to 1862. Following his death a battalion of the provincial army was renamed the Sosa Battalion in his honor.

Thompson, Casildo (1826–73). A native porteño, Thompson served under Domingo Sosa in the Fourth Battalion of the National Guard. In 1868 he was made a lieutenant colonel and commander of the Second Battalion of the Third Regiment of the National Guard, succeeding José María Morales in the position. A man of many parts, he was a noted singer and composer, as well as founder of the black mutual aid society La Fraternal.

Note: Biographies of Barbarín, Barcala, Irrazábal, Maldones, Morales, and Domingo Sosa may be found in Jacinto R. Yaben, *Biografías argentinas y sudamericanas*, 5 vols. (Buenos Aires, 1938–40).

Appendix D
Origins and Names of the African Nations of Buenos Aires, 1770–1900

WEST AFRICA
Abayá
Auzá (Hausa)
Bornó
Carabarí (Kalabari)
Goyo
Main
Maquaqua
Mina
  Mina Mají
  Mina Nagó
Moros
Sabalú
Santé (Ashanti)
Tacuá
Yida

CONGO
Augunga

CONGO (*cont.*)
Basundi
Cambundá (Cabinda)
Congo
Loango
Lubolo
Lumboma
Luumbi
Mayombé
Momboma
Mondongo
Umbonia
Zeda
Zongo

ANGOLA
Angola
Benguela
Casanche (Kasanje)

I am indebted to Jan Vansina for assistance in locating African place names. Useful secondary sources included Philip D. Curtin, *The Atlantic Slave Trade: A Census* (Madison, 1969), pp. 291–98 et passim, and Gonzalo Aguirre Beltrán, *La población negra de México* (Mexico City, 1946; rpt. Mexico City, 1972), pp. 333–40, 351–66.

ANGOLA (*cont.*)
Ganguelá
Huombé
Lucango
Majumbi
Muñandá
Quipará (Kibala)
Quisamá (Kisama)
Umbala

EAST AFRICA
Malavé (Malawi)
Mancinga
Mauinga
Mozambique
Muchague

EAST AFRICA (*cont.*)
Mucherengue
Muñambani

AFRO-ARGENTINE
Argentina Federal

AFRO-BRAZILIAN
Brasileños Bahianos
Nación Brasileira

UNKNOWN
Bagungane
Hambuero
Monyolo
Villamoani

Notes

See the Bibliography for an explanation of the archival abbreviations and document citations that appear in these notes.

Chapter 1: The Riddle of the Disappearance

1 Ysabel Fisk Rennie, *The Argentine Republic* (New York, 1945), p. 43; and James Scobie, *Argentina: A City and a Nation* (New York, 1971), p. 32.
2 Era Bell Thompson, "Argentina: Land of the Vanishing Blacks," *Ebony*, Oct. 1974, pp. 74-84.
3 José Luis Moreno, "La estructura social y demográfica de la ciudad de Buenos Aires en el año 1778," *Anuario del Instituto de Investigaciones Históricas* (Rosario, 1965), 8:166.
4 Marta Goldberg, "La población negra y mulata de la ciudad de Buenos Aires, 1810-1840," *Desarrollo Económico* 16 (Apr.-June 1976): 79.
5 Ibid., p. 98.
6 *Censo general de la ciudad de Buenos Aires, 1887*, 2 vols. (Buenos Aires, 1889), 2:56-57.
7 For some expositions of this theory, see *Segundo censo de la República Argentina: Mayo 10 de 1895*, 3 vols. (Buenos Aires, 1898), 2:xlvii; José Ingenieros, *La locura en la Argentina* (Buenos Aires, 1937), p. 30; Domingo F. Sarmiento, *Conflicto y armonía de las razas en Américas.* 2 vols. (Buenos Aires, 1900), 1:72-73; Alvaro Yunque, *Calfucura, la conquista de las pampas* (Buenos Aires, 1956), pp. 187-88; and Andrés Avellaneda, "Prohibe la Junta el ingreso de esclavos," *La Opinión* (Buenos Aires), May 28, 1976, p. 8.
8 Juan José Soiza Reilly, "Gente de color," *Caras y Caretas*, Nov. 25, 1905; Máximo Simpson, "Porteños de color," *Panorama*, June 1967, p. 85;

Goldberg, "La población negra," p. 85; and Emiliano Endrek, *El mestizaje en Córdoba, siglo XVIII y principios del XIX* (Córdoba, 1966), pp. 18–19.

9 Ricardo Rodríguez Molas, "El negro en el Río de la Plata," *Polémica* 2 (May 1970): 55–56; Woodbine Parish, *Buenos Aires y las provincias del Río de la Plata*, trans. Justo Maeso (Buenos Aires, 1958), p. 179; and Nicolás Besio Moreno, *Buenos Aires: Estudio crítico de su población, 1536–1936* (Buenos Aires, 1939), pp. 24, 290, 380.

10 Leslie Rout, *The African Experience in Spanish America* (Cambridge, 1976), p. 194.

11 Magnus Morner, ed., *Race and Class in Latin America* (New York, 1970), pp. 214–15.

12 Rout, *The African Experience*, pp. 212, 244, 254, 282.

13 To cite some representative titles, one thinks of Miguel Acosta Saignes, *Vida de los esclavos negros en Venezuela* (Caracas, 1967); Gonzalo Aguirre Beltrán, *La población negra en México* (Mexico City, 1946; rpt. Mexico City, 1972), which covers only the colonial period; Frederick P. Bowser, *The African Slave in Colonial Peru, 1684–1750* (Stanford, 1974); David W. Cohen and Jack P. Greene, eds., *Neither Slave nor Free: The Freedman of African Descent in the Slave Societies of the New World* (Baltimore, 1972); Franklin W. Knight, *Slave Society in Cuba during the Nineteenth Century* (Madison, 1970); John V. Lombardi, *The Decline and Abolition of Negro Slavery in Venezuela, 1820–1854* (Westport, Conn., 1971); Rolando Mellafe, *Negro Slavery in Latin America* (Berkeley, 1975); Colin Palmer, *Slaves of the White God: Blacks in Mexico, 1570–1650* (Cambridge, Mass., 1976); Josefina Pla, *Hermano negro: La esclavitud en el Paraguay* (Madrid, 1972); Richard Price, ed., *Maroon Societies: Rebel Slave Communities in the Americas* (Garden City, N.Y., 1973); and William F. Sharp, *Slavery on the Spanish Frontier: The Colombian Chocó, 1680–1810* (Norman, Okla., 1976). The situation is not completely one-sided: publications such as Magnus Morner's and Leslie Rout's previously cited works, Carlos Rama's *Los afro-uruguayos* (Montevideo, 1967), several essays in Robert Brent Toplin's collection, *Slavery and Race Relations in Latin America* (Westport, Conn., 1974), and Norman Whitten's *Class, Kinship and Power in an Ecuadorean Town: The Negroes of San Lorenzo* (Stanford, 1965) and *Black Frontiersmen* (New York, 1974) delve into the history of Afro-Latin Americans in the nineteenth and twentieth centuries. But the trend is clear.

14 Gonzalo Aguirre Beltrán, "The Integration of the Negro into the National Society of Mexico," in Morner, *Race and Class*, pp. 11–27.

15 Magnus Morner, "Recent Research on Negro Slavery and Abolition in Latin America," *Latin American Research Review* 13 (1978): 274; see also Magnus Morner, "The History of Race Relations in Latin America: Some Comments on the State of Research," *Latin American Research Review* 1 (1966): 34.

16 According to some twentieth-century historians, "pardo" could be applied to any racially mixed person, regardless of whether the individual had African ancestry (Endrek, *El mestizaje*, p. 27). Most authors, however, argue that the

word applied only to people who had African ancestry, and not to Indians or mestizos (Aguirre Beltrán, *La población negra de México*, p. 173; Pla, *Hermano negro*, p. 31; and Rout, *The African Experience*, p. 133). As used in Argentina and Uruguay, the word clearly implied a person of African descent. In virtually every document in which it appears, it is modified by the words "free" or "slave." Since only people of African descent were legally liable to be slaves, "pardo" was therefore a euphemism for mulatto. See also Goldberg, "La población negra," pp. 81–82 n. 25.

CHAPTER 2: THE SETTING

1 This discussion will have only a few notes since, as a brief overview of the city's history, it consists almost entirely of generalizations arrived at after several years of secondary reading, archival research, and conversations with Argentine and other historians. A comprehensive history of nineteenth-century Buenos Aires remains to be written, though two books by James Scobie were extremely useful in preparing this chapter: *Argentina: A City and a Nation* (New York, 1971) and *Buenos Aires: Plaza to Suburb, 1870–1910* (New York, 1974). Reading the latter book in conjunction with Chaps. 1–8 of Miguel Angel Scenna's *Cuando murió Buenos Aires, 1871* (Buenos Aires, 1974) gives the reader a very nice sense of the physical and social ambience of the city. Colonial Buenos Aires is well described in José Torre Revello, *La sociedad colonial* (Buenos Aires, 1970), and Juan Agustín García's dated but still classic *La ciudad indiana* (Buenos Aires, 1900; rpt. Buenos Aires, 1955). Readers seeking further information on nineteenth-century Buenos Aires are referred to Tulio Halperín Donghi, *Revolución y guerra* (Buenos Aires, 1972) and its English translation, *Politics, Economics, and Society in Argentina in the Revolutionary Period* (London, 1975); Torcuato S. Di Tella et al., *Argentina, sociedad de masas* (Buenos Aires, 1965), Chaps. 2–5; Gino Germani, *Política y sociedad en una época de transición* (Buenos Aires, 1971), Chap. 7; David Tiffenberg, *Luchas sociales en Argentina* (Buenos Aires, 1970); and Vols. 3–5 of the Paidós publishing company's *Historia Argentina*: Tulio Halperín Donghi, *De la revolución de independencia a la confederación rosista* (Buenos Aires, 1972); Haydeé Gorostegui de Torres, *La organización nacional* (Buenos Aires, 1972); and Ezequiel Gallo and Roberto Cortés Conde, *La república conservadora* (Buenos Aires, 1972). Readers are also referred to the fine bibliographies in Scobie's two books.

2 For an introduction to the controversy still raging over Rosas in Argentine historiography, see Clifton B. Kroeber, "Rosas and the Revision of Argentine History, 1880–1955," *Inter-American Review of Bibliography* 10 (Jan.–Mar. 1960): 3–25.

3 For excellent treatments of these complexities, see the following works on other Spanish American countries: for Guatemala, Severo Martínez Peláez,

La patria del criollo (San José, 1975); for Mexico, Lyle McAlister, "Social Structure and Social Change in New Spain," *Hispanic American Historical Review* 43 (Aug. 1963): 349–70; for Peru, James Lockhart, *Spanish Peru, 1532–1560* (Madison, 1968); and for Uruguay, Lucía Sala de Tourón et al., *Estructura económico-social de la colonia* (Montevideo, 1967).

4 For a statistical study of the elite of a colonial city comparable in many respects to Buenos Aires, see Stephanie Bower Blank, "Social Integration and Social Stability in a Colonial Spanish American City, Caracas (1595–1627)" (Ph.D. diss., University of Wisconsin, Madison, 1971). Juan José Sebreli's *Apogeo y ocaso de los Anchorena* (Buenos Aires, 1974) is a history of one of the most durable of Buenos Aires's elite families.

5 Lyman L. Johnson, "The Artisans of Buenos Aires during the Viceroyalty, 1776–1810" (Ph.D. diss., University of Connecticut, 1974).

6 Scobie, *Argentina*, p. 119.

7 Figures taken from Gallo and Cortés Conde, *La república conservadora*, pp. 166, 168.

8 This figure from Scobie, *Buenos Aires*, pp. 216, 273.

Chapter 3: Slavery and the Slave Trade

1 Elena F. Scheuss de Studer, *La trata de negros en el Río de la Plata durante el siglo XVIII* (Buenos Aires, 1958), p. 87.

2 Nicolás Besio Moreno, *Buenos Aires: Estudio crítico de su población, 1536–1936* (Buenos Aires, 1939), p. 267.

3 José Torre Revello, *La sociedad colonial* (Buenos Aires, 1970), pp. 77–78.

4 Rolando Mellafe, *La introducción de la esclavitud negra en Chile* (Santiago, 1959), pp. 242–43.

5 José Luis Lanuza, *Morenada* (Buenos Aires, 1967), p. 17. The bishop was also involved in contraband slaving to Paraguay (Josefina Pla, *Hermano negro: La esclavitud en el Paraguay* [Madrid, 1972], p. 56).

6 Mellafe, *La introducción*, pp. 244–45.

7 Studer, *La trata de negros*, p. 102.

8 Torre Revello, *La sociedad colonial*, p. 79.

9 Ibid., p. 81.

10 Mellafe, *La introducción*, pp. 200, 252; Studer, *La trata de negros*, p. 237; William F. Sater, "The Black Experience in Chile," in Robert Brent Toplin, ed., *Slavery and Race Relations in Latin America* (Westport, Conn., 1974), pp. 21–22; Felix A. Torres, "El comercio de esclavos en Córdoba, 1700–1731" (thesis, Universidad Nacional de Córdoba, 1972), pp. 17–18; and Carlos Sempat Assadourian, *El tráfico de esclavos en Córdoba, de Angola a Potosí: Siglos XVI–XVII* (Córdoba, 1961).

11 Torre Revello, *La sociedad colonial*, p. 79.

12 Studer, *La trata de negros*, p. 236.

13 Ricardo Rodríguez Molas, "El negro en el Río de la Plata," *Polémica* 2 (May 1970): 41.

14 Studer, *La trata de negros*, Table 15, "Buques negreros llegados al Río de la Plata desde 1792 hasta 1806."

15 Rodríguez Molas, "El negro," p. 43; Studer, *La trata de negros*, graphs between pp. 256 and 257; see also Lucía Sala de Tourón et al., *Estructura económico-social de la colonia* (Montevideo, 1967), pp. 29–30.

16 Quoted in Rodríguez Molas, "El negro," p. 44; see Philip D. Curtin, *The Atlantic Slave Trade: A Census* (Madison, 1969), pp. 275–76, for a discussion of mortality rates among the crews and cargoes of slave ships.

17 Lanuza, *Morenada*, p. 55.

18 Ibid.

19 Ildefonso Pereda Valdés, *El negro en el Uruguay pasado y presente* (Montevideo, 1965), pp. 16–17; and Néstor Ortiz Oderigo, *Aspectos de la cultura africana en el Río de la Plata* (Buenos Aires, 1974), p. 173.

20 Emeric E. Vidal, *Picturesque Illustrations of Buenos Ayres and Montevideo* (London, 1820), p. 65.

21 *Acuerdos del Extinguido Cabildo de Buenos Aires*, 88 vols. (hereafter *Acuerdos*) (Buenos Aires, 1907–34), Ser. 3, Vol. 8, Bk. 48, p. 390.

22 José Luis Molinari, "Los indios y negros durante las invasiones inglesas al Río de la Plata, en 1806 y 1807," *Boletín de la Academia Nacional de la Historia* 34 (1963): 657–58.

23 Torre Revello, *La sociedad colonial*, pp. 89–90.

24 *Acuerdos*, Ser. 4, Vol. 3, Bk. 64, pp. 447–48.

25 *Acuerdos*, Ser. 3, Vol. 8, Bk. 48, p. 397.

26 On the large number of domestic slaves in colonial Lima, see Frederick P. Bowser, *The African Slave in Colonial Peru, 1684–1750* (Stanford, 1974), p. 100; for colonial Caracas, see Miguel Acosta Saignes, *Vida de los esclavos negros en Venezuela* (Caracas, 1967), p. 181.

27 J. Anthony King, *Veinticuatro años en la República Argentina* (Buenos Aires, 1921), p. 178.

28 These paintings may be viewed at the Museo de Bellas Artes, Buenos Aires.

29 *Telégrafo Mercantil*, July 11, 1802.

30 Lina Beck-Bernard, *Cinco años en la Confederación Argentina, 1857–1862* (Buenos Aires, 1935), p. 183.

31 Lyman L. Johnson, "The Artisans of Buenos Aires during the Viceroyalty, 1776–1810" (Ph.D. diss., University of Connecticut, 1974), pp. 9–10; and Domingo Sarmiento, *Conflicto y armonía de las razas en América*, 2 vols. (Buenos Aires, 1900), 1:74. On the importance of slave and free blacks as artisans in other North and South American cities, see Bowser, *The African Slave*, pp. 125–46; David W. Cohen and Jack P. Greene, eds., *Neither Slave nor Free: The Freedman of African Descent in the Slave Societies of the New World* (Baltimore, 1972), pp. 102–4; and Mary Catherine Karasch, "Slave Life in Rio de Janeiro, 1808–1850" (Ph.D. diss., University of Wisconsin, Madison, 1972), pp. 252, 412, 465–78.

32 Johnson, "Artisans of Buenos Aires," pp. 56–58.

33 Ibid., Chap. 5.

34 Rodríguez Molas, "El negro," p. 50; see also Tourón et al., *Estructura económico-social*, pp. 138–39.
35 Alexander Gillespie, *Buenos Aires y el interior* (Buenos Aires, 1921), p. 65.
36 Vidal, *Picturesque Illustrations*, pp. 13–14.
37 See, for example, the *Gaceta Mercantil* for the 1824–30 period, or Nelly Beatriz López's study of slave sales in the interior Argentine city of Córdoba, "La esclavitud en Córdoba, 1790–1853" (thesis, Universidad Nacional de Córdoba, 1972).
38 Richard C. Wade, *Slavery in the Cities* (London, 1964), pp. 38–47; Bowser, *The African Slave*, p. 103; and Karasch, "Slave Life in Rio de Janeiro," pp. 125–26, 134–36.
39 Rodríguez Molas, "El negro," p. 50; and see also Torre Revello, *La sociedad colonial*, pp. 87–88.
40 Johnson, "Artisans of Buenos Aires," p. 56.
41 *Telégrafo Mercantil*, July 11, 1802. For the case of an Angolan slave who fought back against such a master and won, see AGN, Register 7, 1804, folio 257v.
42 Lanuza, *Morenada*, p. 39.
43 AGN, 10 32–10–2, Bk. 5, folio 185.
44 See, for example, José Antonio Wilde, *Buenos Aires desde setenta años atrás* (Buenos Aires, 1908), pp. 165–75, 176; Victor Gálvez, "La raza africana en Buenos Aires," *Nueva Revista de Buenos Aires* 8 (1883): 252–53; and Ortiz Oderigo, *Aspectos de la cultura africana*, pp. 123–31.
45 W. H. Hudson, *Far Away and Long Ago* (London, 1951), pp. 97–98.
46 Woodbine Parish, *Buenos Aires y las provincias del Rió de la Plata*, trans. Justo Maeso (Buenos Aires, 1958), p. 195.
47 Wilde, *Buenos Aires*, p. 176.
48 Torre Revello, *La sociedad colonial*, pp. 87–88.
49 Beck-Bernard, *Cinco años en la Confederación Argentina*, p. 61.
50 Lanuza, *Morenada*, pp. 97–98; and Francisco L. Romay, *El barrio de Monserrat* (Buenos Aires, 1971), p. 64.
51 Tourón et al., *Estructura económico-social*, pp. 56–57, 65; and Johnson, "Artisans of Buenos Aires," p. 225.
52 Tourón et al., *Estructura económico-social*, p. 56; and AGN, 10 10–7–1.
53 Marta B. Goldberg de Flichman and Laura Beatriz Jany, "Algunos problemas referentes a la situación del esclavo en el Río de la Plata," in *IV Congreso Internacional de Historia de América*, 6 vols. (Buenos Aires, 1966), 4:65.
54 AGN, 10 23–5–5, 23–5–6; and Lanuza, *Morenada*, pp. 97–98.
55 *Gaceta Mercantil*, June 11, 1824; July 10, 1824.
56 Ricardo Rodríguez Molas, "O negro na história argentina (1852–1900)," *Alfa* 4 (Sept. 1963): 190.
57 See, for example, the colonial accounts of the Estancia de las Varas, AGN, 9 37–5–4; Rodríguez Molas, "El negro," pp. 50–51.
58 Rodríguez Molas, "El negro," p. 50; and Tourón et al., *Estructura*

económico-social, p. 143. For an 1831 case of a Buenos Aires woman winning a draft exemption for her slave foreman, see AGN, 10 15-9-4.

59 Tulio Halperín Donghi, *Politics, Economics, and Society in Argentina in the Revolutionary Period* (London, 1975), pp. 50–51.

60 See Ricardo Rodríguez Molas's excellent *Historia social del gaucho* (Buenos Aires, 1968) for a discussion of the phenomenon of the gaucho, whose way of life was immortalized in José Hernández's epic poem *Martín Fierro* (first edition published in Buenos Aires, 1872, English translations published in New York in 1936, 1948, 1960, and 1968).

61 Bernardo Kordon, "La raza negra en el Río de la Plata," *Todo Es Historia* 3 (1969), Supplement 7, pp. 7–9; and Ricardo Rodríguez Molas, *La música y danza de los negros en el Buenos Aires de los siglos XVIII y XIX* (Buenos Aires, 1957), pp. 4–6.

62 For a discussion of the low status of manual labor in Hispanic societies, see James Scobie, *Buenos Aires: Plaza to Suburb, 1870–1910* (New York, 1974), pp. 218–20. See also Emiliano Endrek, *El mestizaje en Córdoba, siglo XVIII y principios del XIX* (Córdoba, 1966), pp. 69–74.

CHAPTER 4: THE TRANSITION FROM SLAVERY TO FREEDOM, OF A SORT

1 Eugenio Petit Muñoz et al., *La condición jurídica, social, económica, y política de los negros durante el coloniaje en la Banda Oriental*, 2 vols. (Montevideo, 1948), 1:377–78.

2 Frederick P. Bowser, *The African Slave in Colonial Peru, 1684–1750* (Stanford, 1974), pp. 279–98; and Leslie B. Rout, *The African Experience in Spanish America* (Cambridge, 1976), p. 91. In the case of Bahia, in Brazil, 47.7 percent of slaves freed between 1684 and 1745 paid for their freedom, though that percentage varied considerably over the sixty-year period. In the 1680s, 37 percent of manumitted slaves paid for their freedom; by the 1740s, 57 percent did so, an increase which Schwartz associates with the rise in slave prices (Stuart Schwartz, "The Manumission of Slaves in Colonial Brazil: Bahia, 1658–1745," *Hispanic American Historical Review* 54 [Nov. 1974]: 623–24).

3 Lyman L. Johnson, "La manumisión en el Buenos Aires colonial: Un análisis ampliado," *Desarrollo Económico* 17 (Jan.–Mar. 1978): 639.

4 *Acuerdos del Extinguido Cabildo de Buenos Aires*, 88 vols. (Buenos Aires, 1907–34), Ser. 4, Vol. 2, Bk. 61, p. 476.

5 José Luis Lanuza, *Morenada* (Buenos Aires, 1967), pp. 65–66.

6 *Acuerdos*, Ser. 4, Vol. 2, Bk. 62, pp. 694–95.

7 Lanuza, *Morenada*, pp. 56–57; and *Acuerdos*, Ser. 4, Vol. 5, Bk. 69, pp. 592–94.

8 Johnson, "La manumisión en el Buenos Aires colonial," pp. 639–44.

9 David W. Cohen and Jack P. Greene, eds., *Neither Slave nor Free: The Freed Man of African Descent in the Slave Societies of the New World* (Baltimore, 1972), pp. 7–9.

10 Petit Muñoz et al., *La condición de los negros*, 1:313.
11 Miguel Acosta Saignes et al., "La vivienda de los pobres," in *Estudio de Caracas* (Caracas, 1967), Vol. 2, Bk. 2, p. 64.
12 Cohen and Greene, ed., *Neither Slave nor Free*, p. 97.
13 Ibid., p. 316.
14 Mary Catherine Karasch, "Slave Life in Rio de Janeiro, 1808–1850" (Ph.D. diss., University of Wisconsin, Madison, 1972), pp. 10–16.
15 Ira Berlin, *Slaves without Masters: The Free Negro in the Antebellum South* (New York, 1974), pp. 47, 137.
16 Karasch, "Slave Life," pp. 219–21; and Rout, *African Experience*, p. 88.
17 Cohen and Greene, eds., *Neither Slave nor Free*, pp. 97, 318–19; and Berlin, *Slaves without Masters*, pp. 177–78.
18 Lyman Johnson makes this point in his article "La manumisión de esclavos durante el Virreinato," *Desarrollo Económico* 16 (Oct.–Dec. 1976): 340.
19 See Rout, *African Experience*, pp. 126–60, for a discussion of the Régimen. See also Magnus Morner, *Race Mixture in the History of Latin America* (Boston, 1967), pp. 53–75.
20 Petit Muñoz et al., *La condición de los negros*, 1:63–64.
21 José Torre Revello, *La sociedad colonial* (Buenos Aires, 1970), p. 80; Bernardo Kordon, "La raza negra en el Río de la Plata," *Todo Es Historia* 3 (1969), Supplement 7, p. 7; and Ricardo Rodríguez Molas, *La música y danza de los negros en el Buenos Aires de los siglos XVIII y XIX* (Buenos Aires, 1957), pp. 6–7.
22 Petit Muñoz et al., *La condición de los negros*, 1:337; Lucía Sala de Tourón et al., *Estructura económico-social de la colonia* (Montevideo, 1967), pp. 90–91.
23 Elena F. Scheuss de Studer, *La trata de negros en el Río de la Plata durante el siglo XVIII* (Buenos Aires, 1958), p. 333; Torre Revello, *La sociedad colonial*, p. 98; and *Telégrafo Mercantil*, June 27, 1801, pp. 1–3.
24 Lyman L. Johnson, "The Artisans of Buenos Aires during the Viceroyalty, 1776–1810" (Ph.D. diss., University of Connecticut, 1974), pp. 79–80, 191–92.
25 See Chap. 9.
26 Emiliano Endrek, *El mestizaje en Córdoba, siglo XVIII y principios del XIX* (Córdoba, 1966), p. 86.
27 *Telégrafo Mercantil*, June 27, 1801, p. 3.
28 Alberto González Arzac, *Abolición de la esclavitud en el Río de la Plata* (Buenos Aires, 1974), p. 25.
29 From the *Grito del Sud*, Aug. 18, 1812, quoted in Marta B. Goldberg de Flichman and Laura Beatriz Jany, "Algunos problemas referentes a la situación del esclavo en el Río de la Plata," in *IV Congreso Internacional de Historia de América* (Buenos Aires, 1966), 6:61.
30 For the figures, see ibid., pp. 65–66.
31 For discussion of the Libertad de vientres, see González Arzac, *Abolición de*

la esclavitud, pp. 25–26, 73–74; José Luis Masini Calderón, "La esclavitud negra en la República Argentina—Época independiente," *Revista de la Junta de Estudios Históricos de Mendoza*, Ser. 2, 1 (1961): 150–52; and Orlando Carracedo, "El Régimen de castas, el trabajo, y la Revolución de Mayo," in *Anuario del Instituto de Investigaciones Históricas* (Rosario, 1960), 4:171–72. For a detailed study of how the Libertad de vientres fared in Venezuela, see John V. Lombardi, *The Decline and Abolition of Negro Slavery in Venezuela, 1820–1854* (Westport, Conn., 1971).

32 González Arzac, *Abolición de la esclavitud*, p. 26.

33 Masini Calderón, "La esclavitud negra en la República," p. 151.

34 AGN, 10 33–1–2, Bk. 47, folio 13.

35 Berlin, *Slaves without Masters*, pp. 86–103; and Leon F. Litwack, *North of Slavery: The Negro in the Free States, 1790–1860* (Chicago, 1961), pp. 6–14.

36 See for instance Lina Beck-Bernard, *Cinco años en la Confederación Argentina, 1857–1862*, trans. José Luis Busaniche (Buenos Aires, 1935), p. 184; and Emeric E. Vidal, *Picturesque Illustrations of Buenos Ayres and Montevideo* (London, 1820), p. 73.

37 Johnson, "The Artisans," p. 255.

38 Ricardo Rodríguez Molas, "El negro en el Río de la Plata," *Polémica* 2 (May 1970): 45.

39 González Arzac, *Abolición de la esclavitud*, pp. 26–27.

40 AGN, 10 32–10–7, Bk. 19, folio 189.

41 Carracedo, "El Régimen de castas," p. 174.

42 González Arzac, *Abolición de la esclavitud*, pp. 28–29.

43 AGN, 10 31–9–5.

44 See, for example, Don Juan Miller's acquisition of the young liberto Antonio directly from the owners of the *corsario Presidente* (AGN, 10 32–10–7, Bk. 19, folio 173); Don Jaime Couri's acquisition of the liberta Isabel from the same source (AGN, 10 31–9–5); and Federico Guittarde's acquisition of the liberta María from the captain of the *Triunfo Argentino* (AGN, 10 31–9–5). See also Masini Calderón, "La esclavitud negra en la República," p. 153.

45 AGN, 10 33–1–2, Bk. 46, folio 90.

46 Rodriguez Molas, "El negro," p. 45. Argentina's neighbor Uruguay employed an unusual legal device to continue the slave trade past its 1830 abolition. Legislation of 1832 established a program by which African "colonists" were brought to Uruguay by licensed entrepreneurs. These colonists were required to be under the age of sixteen, and their transporters had to produce lots divided equally between males and females. Upon arriving in Uruguay they were to be assigned to patrons, as in Argentina, who they would serve for a twelve-year period. The "colonists" were charged two hundred dollars for the trip, which was paid for by the patron and was the justification for the subsequent twelve years of unpaid service. Surviving records indicate that 635 young Africans were imported in 1833 and 1834 under this program (AGN [Montevideo], Sec. 3, Bk. 938, fols. 1–2v).

47 Nuria Sales de Bohigas, *Sobre esclavos, reclutas, y mercaderes de quintas* (Barcelona, 1974), p. 83.

48 González Arzac, *Abolición de la esclavitud*, p. 54.

49 Masini Calderón, "La esclavitud negra en la República," p. 159.

50 Alfredo E. Lattes and Raúl Poczter, *Muestra del censo de la población de la ciudad de Buenos Aires de 1855* (Buenos Aires, 1968), p. 78.

51 See Lina Beck-Bernard's description of the collapse of agriculture in Santa Fé following abolition, in *Cinco años en la Confederación*, pp. 177–78.

52 González Arzac, *Abolición de la esclavitud*, p. 54, argues this point.

53 Rout, *African Experience*, p. 188.

54 *Reseña histórica y orgánica del Ejército Argentino*, 3 vols. (Buenos Aires, 1972), 1:149–50; and M. F. Mantilla, *Páginas históricas* (Buenos Aires, 1890), pp. 365–66.

55 *Tomas de razón de despachos militares, cédulas de premio, retiros, empleos civiles y eclesiásticos, donativos, etc., 1740–1821* (Buenos Aires, 1925), p. 864; and Adolfo Saldías, *Los números de linea del Ejército Argentino*, 2 vols. (Buenos Aires, 1912), 1:201.

56 *Gaceta de Buenos Aires, 1810–21*, facs. ed., 6 vols. (Buenos Aires, 1910–13), 1:792–93.

57 Endrek, *El mestizaje en Córdoba*, p. 84.

58 Masini Calderón, "La esclavitud negra en la República," p. 155.

59 Endrek, *El mestizaje en Córdoba*, pp. 67–68.

60 See Chap. 8.

61 Ricardo Rodríguez Molas, "Negros libres rioplatenses," *Buenos Aires: Revista de Humanidades* 1 (Sept. 1961): 119; and Rodriguez Molas, "El negro," p. 49.

62 *Registro Estadístico del Estado de Buenos Aires, 1857* (Buenos Aires, 1858), 2:123; and *Registro Estadístico de Buenos Aires, 1864* (Buenos Aires, 1866), 2:182.

63 Rodríguez Molas, "Negros libres," p. 118.

64 "Tomás B. Platero," *La Broma*, Nov. 4, 1882, p. 1.

65 AGN, 10 27-7-4.

66 "Servicio doméstico," *El Mártir o Libre*, July 17, 1830, pp. 1–2.

67 "La moral doméstica," *La Tribuna*, Oct. 27, 1853, p. 2.

68 "La moral doméstica—Casa de Corrección," *La Tribuna*, Nov. 8, 1853), pp. 2–3.

69 AGN, 10 33-1-2, Bk. 46, folio 29.

70 AGN, 10 33-1-2, Bk. 46, folio 60.

71 AGN, 10 32-10-7, Bk. 18, folio 65; *Gaceta de Buenos Aires*, 4:717-19.

72 This process is best described in Ricardo Rodríguez Molas's *Historia social del gaucho* (Buenos Aires, 1968); and Orlando Carracedo's "El Régimen de castas."

73 Bohigas, *Sobre esclavos*, pp. 129–30.

74 Lanuza, *Morenada*, p. 70.

CHAPTER 5: HOW THE AFRO-ARGENTINES DISAPPEARED

1 John Brooks, ed., *The 1975 South American Handbook* (Bath, Eng., 1975), p. 32.
2 Magnus Morner, ed., *Race and Class in Latin America* (New York, 1970), pp. 32, 47–48.
3 Leslie B. Rout, *The African Experience in Spanish America* (Cambridge, 1976), pp. 205–14, 278–80; and Frederick P. Bowser, *The African Slave in Colonial Peru, 1684–1750* (Stanford, 1974), p. 334.
4 Rout, *African Experience*, p. 306; Rollie Poppino, *Brazil: The Land and the People* (New York, 1968), p. 198; Howard I. Blutstein et al., *Area Handbook for Cuba* (Washington, D.C., 1971), p. 76; and Nathan Glazer and Daniel Patrick Moynihan. *Beyond the Melting Pot* (Cambridge, Mass., 1964), p. 133.
5 Woodbine Parish, *Buenos Aires y las provincias del Río de la Plata*, trans. Justo Maeso (Buenos Aires, 1958), pp. 178–79, 605.
6 Quoted in Ricardo Rodríguez Molas, "El negro en el Río de la Plata," *Polémica* 2 (May 1970): 100.
7 Domingo Sarmiento, *Conflicto y armonía de las razas en Américas*, 2 vols. (Buenos Aires, 1900), 1:72–73, 76.
8 *Segundo censo de la República Argentina: Mayo 10 de 1895*, 3 vols. (Buenos Aires, 1898), 1:xlviii, 2:xlv, xlvii.
9 Juan José Soiza Reilly, "Gente de color," *Caras y Caretas*, Nov. 25, 1905.
10 Máximo Simpson, "Porteños de color," *Panorama*, June 1967, pp. 78–85; and Luis Grassino, "Buenos Aires de ébano," *Revista Clarín*, Dec. 5, 1971.
11 *Registro Estadístico de Buenos Aires, 1858*, 1:67.
12 Reynolds Farley, *Growth of the Black Population* (Chicago, 1970), pp. 22, 30; and Philip D. Curtin, *The Atlantic Slave Trade: A Census* (Madison, 1969), p. 73.
13 A survey of notarial registers for the 1780–1830 period suggests that the highest prices were paid for slaves between the ages of 25 and 35. Research presently being conducted by the Argentine historian Eduardo Saguier should eventually supply hard data on this point.
14 See Chap. 4, n. 46.
15 Lyman L. Johnson, "La manumisión de esclavos durante el Virreinato," *Desarrollo Económico* 16 (Oct.–Dec. 1976): 340. Similar tendencies have been noted in Mexico and Peru (Rout, *African Experience*, p. 90).
16 Henry S. Shryock, Jacob S. Siegel, et al., *The Methods and Materials of Demography*, 2 vols. (Washington, D.C., 1973), 2:469, 504.
17 Marta B. Goldberg, "La población negra y mulata de la ciudad de Buenos Aires, 1810–1840," *Desarrollo Económico* 16 (Apr.–June 1976): 90 n. 41.
18 Ibid., pp. 88 n. 37, p. 95; and figures supplied to the author by Goldberg.
19 Ibid., p. 87 n. 36, p. 95.
20 The interested reader is strongly urged to consult Goldberg's excellent article, "La población negra."

21 José Luis Lanuza, *Morenada* (Buenos Aires, 1967), p. 96.

22 See, for instance, an 1847 case in which the 20-year-old African woman Marcelina Alfaro clashed with Doña Dolores Burgois over the rights to Alfaro's daughter (AGN, 10 26–2–6). See Ana Gómez being granted a newly arrived liberta in 1831 (AGN, 10 31–9–5). See the 1830 sale of an African liberta brought in on the corsario *Triunfo Argentino* (AGN, 10 31–9–5). See the African Constantino Galiano's 1836 petition for his freedom after having served his master for six years (AGN, 10 33–3–1, Bk. 94, folio 10). See the 1835 list of libertos captured during the War with Brazil who were then serving in Argentine regiments (AGN, 10 33–2–8, Bk. 91, folio 140).

23 I examined manuscript returns and/or published totals from the 1832 census of Córdoba city (Azucena Perla M. Della Casa de Tauro, "Censo de la ciudad de Córdoba del año 1832" [thesis, Universidad Nacional de Córdoba, 1972]); the 1840 census of Córdoba province (Archivo Histórico de Córdoba, Bks. 299–301); the 1844 census of Entre Ríos province (Archivo de la Provincia de Entre Ríos, Gobierno, Ser. 7, Files 1–2); and the 1836 and 1852–53 censuses of Montevideo (AGN, Montevideo, Bks. 146–149, 465, 257–58). Persons born in Buenos Aires were minimally represented in the Córdoba and Entre Ríos censuses, but were present in significant numbers in the Montevideo census, suggesting a reciprocal stream of migration between the two port cities. This technique of studying migration, of course, says nothing concerning individuals who migrated to and from Buenos Aires and later returned to their places of origin.

24 Farley, *Growth of the Black Population*, pp. 49–51, 61–62, 106–8.

25 Ibid., p. 58; and Stephan Thernstrom, *The Other Bostonians* (Cambridge, Mass., 1973), p. 180.

26 Florestan Fernandes, *The Negro in Brazilian Society* (New York, 1969), pp. 69–70, 71.

27 Goldberg, "La población negra," pp. 80, 87.

28 All of these photos are from the magazine *Caras y Caretas:* "En honor del Cuerpo de Bomberos," Feb. 2, 1900; "Las víctimas del calor," Feb. 10, 1900; "Elección de Diputados Nacionales en la Capital," Mar. 17, 1900; Aug. 23, 1902; "El Asilo de las Mercedes," May 20, 1899; "Los premios a la virtud," June 2, 1900; "La Semana Santa," Apr. 13, 1901; "Concurso de tiros de batallones de linea," Dec. 1, 1900; "El Día de Difuntos," Nov. 19, 1901; and "El último expósito del siglo pasado y los primeros niños que nacieron en el siglo XX," Jan. 12, 1900. In order to ensure that these individuals would be considered Afro-Argentine by porteño standards, as well as by my own, I showed all these photos to Argentine friends and colleagues, who concurred that the subjects did display visible evidence of African ancestry.

29 "¿Por qué se llama 'La Broma'?," *La Broma*, Oct. 17, 1878, pp. 1–2.

30 Alexander Gillespie, *Buenos Aires y el interior* (Buenos Aires, 1921), p. 65.

31 Samuel Haigh, *Bosquejos de Buenos Aires, Chile y Perú* (Buenos Aires, 1920), p. 26.

32 Goldberg, "La población negra," p. 81.
33 Emiliano Endrek, *El mestizaje en Córdoba, siglo XVIII y principios del XIX* (Córdoba, 1966), p. 3.
34 "Para cien personas blancas hay otras tantas o más de color . . ." ("La moral doméstica," *La Tribuna*, Oct. 27, 1853, p. 2).
35 For a survey of these shortcomings, see Shryock and Siegel, *Methods and Materials of Demography*, Chap. 3.
36 Nicolás Besio Moreno, *Buenos Aires: Estudio crítico de su población, 1536–1936* (Buenos Aires, 1939), pp. 342–43.
37 Karla Robinson, a Ph.D. candidate at the University of North Carolina, has undertaken the task of tabulating the census of 1827; the figures contained in Table 5.1 are her preliminary results.
38 Besio Moreno, *Buenos Aires*, p. 350.
39 Some completed forms for the 1854 census may be found in AGN, 10 42–8–5 and 41–6–5.
40 Farley, *Growth of the Black Population*, pp. 24–25, 66.
41 Richard Wade, *Slavery in the Cities* (London, 1964), pp. 78–79; Ira Berlin, *Slaves without Masters: The Free Negro in the Antebellum South* (New York, 1974), pp. 253–59; and Leon F. Litwack, *North of Slavery: The Negro in the Free States, 1790–1860* (Chicago, 1961), pp. 168–69.
42 Francisco L. Romay, *El barrio de Monserrat* (Buenos Aires, 1971), pp. 61–63. Police instructions during the 1820s directed patrolmen to exercise special vigilance in policing this area (Alfredo Taullard, *Nuestro antiguo Buenos Aires* [Buenos Aires, 1927], p. 320).
43 Romay, *El barrio*, p. 63; and Miguel Angel Scenna, *Cuando murió Buenos Aires, 1871* (Buenos Aires, 1974), pp. 81–82, 109.
44 Shryock and Siegel, *Methods and Materials of Demography*, p. 261; and Farley, *Growth of the Black Population*, p. 66.
45 Besio Moreno, *Buenos Aires*, p. 342.
46 See the censuses headed "Relación de los esclavos aptos para armas . . . ." in AGN, 9 10–7–2, 9–5–3, 18–8–11.
47 AGN, 10 31–11–3.
48 The literature on the question of race in Latin America is extensive. Basic works to consult are Magnus Morner, *Race Mixture in the History of Latin America* (Boston, 1967); Carl Degler, *Neither Black nor White* (New York, 1971); Harry Hoetink, *The Two Variants in Caribbean Race Relations* (London, 1967); Charles R. Boxer, *Race Relations in the Portuguese Colonial Empire* (Oxford, Eng., 1963); and Rout, *African Experience*.
49 David W. Cohen and Jack P. Greene, eds., *Neither Slave nor Free: The Freedman of African Descent in the Slave Societies of the New World* (Baltimore, 1972), p. 113.
50 For a discussion of *gracias al sacar*, see Rout, *African Experience*, pp. 156–59.
51 Tulio Halperín Donghi, *Revolución y guerra* (Buenos Aires, 1972), p. 57.

52 Rout, *African Experience*, p. 171.
53 Un Ingles, *Cinco años en Buenos Aires* (Buenos Aires, 1962), p. 165.
54 J. A. Rogers, *Great Men of Color*, 2 vols. (New York, 1972), 2:187–91.
55 In the Archivo General de la Nación and the Archivo General del Ejército I encountered enlistment records for Spaniards and Italians who were described as "trigueños."
56 Elena Padilla, *Up from Puerto Rico* (New York, 1958), pp. 73–74, 75. My wife, Roye Werner, supplied the information for this and subsequent references to Puerto Rico.
57 Oscar Lewis, *La Vida* (New York, 1965), p. 619.
58 Piri Thomas, *Down These Mean Streets* (New York, 1969), p. 147.
59 Glazer and Moynihan, *Melting Pot*, p. 133. See also Thomas G. Matthews, "The Question of Color in Puerto Rico," in Robert Brent Toplin, ed., *Slavery and Race Relations in Latin America* (Westport, Conn., 1974), especially pp. 301, 310–17, 319.
60 Rout, *African Experience*, p. 222.
61 Ibid., pp. 264–65.
62 These enlistments taken from AGN, 3 59–1–1, 59–1–6, 59–2–1, 59–2–4, 59–2–7.
63 AGN, 3 59–1–1.
64 AGN, 3 59–2–7.
65 *Registro Estadístico de Buenos Aires, 1875*, p. 157.
66 See, for instance, the description of "a beautiful trigueñita with coral lips and ivory teeth" ("Unas feas," *El Proletario*, May 4, 1858, p. 3).
67 AGE, Personal File 14991.
68 AGE, Personal Files 7849, 7850.
69 Degler, *Neither Black nor White*, pp. 223–32.
70 Indianish is *achinado* or *aindiado*; dark brown is *bruno*; medium white is *entre blanco*; somewhat white is *algo blanco*; and ugly black is *negro fulo*.
71 AGN, Register 5, 1802–3, folio 398. Lyman Johnson supplied this reference and several subsequent ones.
72 AGN, Register 5, 1806–7, folio 157.
73 Bernardo Kordon, "La raza negra en el Río de la Plata," *Todo Es Historia* 3 (1969), Supplement 7, p. 17.
74 Lanuza, *Morenada*, p. 23.
75 Lina Beck-Bernard, *Cinco años en la Confederación Argentina, 1857–1862*, trans. José Luis Busaniche (Buenos Aires, 1935), pp. 180–81.
76 Goldberg, "La población negra," p. 95.
77 *Registro Estadístico del Estado de Buenos Aires, 1871*. The original death certificates from the epidemic are located in AGN, 10 32–6–7.
78 *Registro Estadístico de Buenos Aires, 1858*, 1:82.
79 *Censo general de población, edificación, comercio e industrias de la ciudad de Buenos Aires*, 2 vols. (Buenos Aires, 1889), 2:57.

CHAPTER 6: WHY THE AFRO-ARGENTINES DISAPPEARED

1 An issue of Buenos Aires's first newspaper carried a report on a shipload of slaves who overpowered the crew off the Argentine coast and then sailed the vessel back to Senegal (*Telégrafo Mercantil*, Dec. 16, 1801). News of other slave revolts in various Latin American countries include one in Cuba (*La Gaceta Mercantil*, Jan. 21, 1823, p. 3); one in Jamaica (*La Gaceta Mercantil*, Apr. 28, 1824, p. 3); one in Venezuela (*La Gaceta Mercantil*, Aug. 31, 1824, p. 2); one in Uruguay (*La Gaceta Mercantil*, June 3, 1833, p. 3); and one in Brazil (*La Gaceta Mercantil*, Feb. 19, 1835).

2 Alberto González Arzac, *Abolición de la esclavitud en el Río de la Plata* (Buenos Aires, 1974), pp. 22–24.

3 Boleslao Lewin, "La 'Conspiración de los franceses' en Buenos Aires (1795)," *Anuario del Instituto de Investigaciones Históricas* (Rosario, 1960), 4:9–58; and Ricardo Caillet-Bois, *Ensayo sobre el Río de la Plata y la revolución francesa* (Buenos Aires, 1929). A very similar incident occurred in the Brazilian city of Bahia in 1798 (Jeanne Berrance de Castro, "O negro na Guarda Nacional Brasileira," *Anais do Museu Paulista* 23 (1969): 160 n. 33).

4 Emeric E. Vidal, *Picturesque Illustrations of Buenos Ayres and Montevideo* (London, 1820), pp. 30–31.

5 Woodbine Parish, *Buenos Aires y las provincias del Río de la Plata*, trans. Justo Maeso (Buenos Aires, 1958), p. 180. Other Europeans who made similar observations were Alexander Gillespie, *Buenos Aires y el interior* (Buenos Aires, 1921), p. 73; and Lina Beck-Bernard, *Cinco años en la Confederación Argentina, 1857–1862*, trans. José Luis Busaniche (Buenos Aires, 1935), pp. 182–83.

6 Enrique Ortiz de Marco, "El negro en la formación étnica y sociocultural argentina," *Boletín del Centro Naval* (July–Sept. 1969), p. 368; Victor Gálvez, "La raza africana en Buenos Aires," *Nueva Revista de Buenos Aires* 8 (1883): 246; and José Ingenieros, *La locura en la Argentina* (Buenos Aires, 1937), pp. 30–31.

7 Quoted in José Luis Lanuza, *Morenada* (Buenos Aires, 1967), p. 237.

8 Frank Tannenbaum, *Slave and Citizen: The Negro in the Americas* (New York, 1946).

9 Leslie B. Rout, *The African Experience in Spanish America* (Cambridge, 1976), p. 314.

10 For an anthology on the debate, see Laura Foner and Eugene D. Genovese, eds., *Slavery in the New World* (New York, 1969).

11 Lanuza, *Morenada*, p. 237.

12 Eugenio Petit Muñoz et al., *La condición jurídica, social, económica, y política de los negros durante el coloniaje en la Banda Oriental*, 2 vols. (Montevideo, 1947), 1:399–400, 485; and Rout, *African Experience*, pp. 120, 197–98.

13 Bernardo Kordon, "La raza negra en el Río de la Plata," *Todo Es Historia* 3 (1969), Supplement 7, p. 19.

14 Carlos Ibarguren, *Manuelita Rosas* (Buenos Aires, 1953). Unfortunately, neither Kordon nor Ibarguren cite sources for these letters.

15 Ramón F. Vial, *Manuelita Rosas* (Buenos Aires, 1969), pp. 63–64; and *La Gaceta Mercantil*, June 22, 1843.

16 The song is printed in entirety in Luis Soler Cañas, *Negros, gauchos y compadres en el cancionero de la Federación (1830–1848)* (Buenos Aires, 1958), pp. 30–32.

17 *La Negrita*, July 21, 1833.

18 *El Avisador* (Buenos Aires), undated. The best collection of black-dialect, pro-Rosas propaganda is Soler Cañas, *Negros, gauchos y compadres*, which contains twenty pages of this material.

19 Alfredo Taullard, *Nuestro antiguo Buenos Aires* (Buenos Aires, 1927), pp. 356–57. A painting of the 1839 demonstration hangs in Buenos Aires's Museo Histórico Nacional.

20 See AGN, 10 31–11–5, for information on an 1839 grant to the Mayombé nation.

21 Luis Canepa, *El Buenos Aires de antaño* (Buenos Aires, 1936), p. 263.

22 AGN, 10 31–11–5.

23 Orlando Carracedo, "El Régimen de castas, el trabajo, y la Revolución de Mayo," in *Anuario del Instituto de Investigaciones Históricas* (Rosario, 1960), 4:178.

24 Ibarguren, *Manuelita Rosas*, p. 22.

25 AGN, 10 33–4–3, Bk. 123, folio 12.

26 AGN, 10 33–3–1, Bk. 93, folio 89.

27 Petrona Acosta de Sinclair to Enrique Sinclair, May 27, 1839, AGN, 10 24–5–3B.

28 Lanuza, *Morenada*, p. 120. For other pro-Rosas candombe lyrics, see Ricardo Rodríguez Molas, "Negros libres rioplatenses," *Buenos Aires: Revista de Humanidades* 1 (Sept. 1961): 107–8.

29 José María Ramos Mejía, *Rosas y su tiempo*, 3 vols. (Buenos Aires, 1907), 2:276–77.

30 *La Gaceta Mercantil*, June 25, 1842, p. 2.

31 Ramos Mejía, *Rosas y su tiempo*, 1:286–88; José Antonio Wilde, *Buenos Aires desde setenta años atrás* (Buenos Aires, 1903), p. 179; Vivian Trías, *Juan Manuel de Rosas* (Buenos Aires, 1969), p. 72; and Ysabel Fisk Rennie, *The Argentine Republic* (New York, 1945), p. 43.

32 "La moral doméstica," *La Tribuna*, Oct. 27, 1853, p. 2.

33 "Los cabellos de la aurora," *La Juventud*, Oct. 30, 1878, p. 1.

34 Lanuza, *Morenada*, pp. 126–27.

35 Petrona Acosta de Sinclair to Enrique Sinclair, May 27, 1838, AGN, 10 24–5–3B.

36 Ramos Mejía, *Rosas y su tiempo*, 2:276–77.

37 Wilde, *Buenos Aires*, p. 179.

38 Ramos Mejía, *Rosas y su tiempo*, 1:330.

39 Quoted in Enrique Puccia, *Breve historia del carnaval porteño* (Buenos Aires, 1974), p. 28.

40 A provocative analysis of the impact of "scientific" racism on Brazilian thought is Thomas Skidmore's *Black into White* (New York, 1974), pp. 45–77.

41 The Argentine sociologist Gino Germani sums up the Generation's "project" as follows: "the explicit and principal purpose of immigration was not simply to 'settle the desert,' to procure inhabitants for an immense territory which remained in large part uninhabited or with an extremely low density of population, but rather, and above all, *substantially to modify the composition of the population.* . . . The work of the 'national organization' could only be based on a renovation of the country's social structure, particularly its principal dynamic element, the human element. This attitude, furthermore, was reinforced by the ideas so widely held at the time concerning the role of racial factors in forming the national character. . . . It was necessary to 'Europeanize' the Argentine population, to produce a 'regeneration of the races,' according to Sarmiento's expression. Education—the other powerful means of transformation—was insurmountably limited by the psychological characteristics of the existing population: it was necessary to bring Europe *physically* to America, if what was desired was a radical transformation of men and society" (Gino Germani, *Política y sociedad en una época de transición* [Buenos Aires, 1971], pp. 240–42).

42 An English translation of the book is available: Domingo F. Sarmiento, *Life in the Argentine Republic in the Days of the Tyrants,* trans. Mary T. Mann (1868; rpt. New York, 1961).

43 Domingo F. Sarmiento, *Ambas Américas* (Buenos Aires, 1899), pp. 301–2.

44 Domingo F. Sarmiento, *Conflicto y armonía de las razas en Américas,* 2 vols. (Buenos Aires, 1900; rpt. Buenos Aires, 1953), 1:70–71. The description of Agassiz is taken from Skidmore, *Black into White,* p. 60.

45 Sarmiento, *Conflicto y armonía* (1953), 1:183, 2:405.

46 Juan Bautista Alberdi, *Bases y puntos de partida para la organización de la República Argentina* (Buenos Aires, 1952), p. 38.

47 Ibid., pp. 31, 46.

48 Ibid., p. 33.

49 Ibid., p. 38.

50 Arthur Whitaker claimed in 1965 that Ingenieros is "the most widely read author in Spanish" (quoted in Rout, *African Experience,* p. 193). He was very influential in Brazilian racial thought (Skidmore, *Black into White,* p. 53).

51 José Ingenieros, *Sociología argentina* (Madrid, 1913), pp. 41–42.

52 Ingenieros, *La locura,* p. 35.

53 Ingenieros, *Sociología argentina,* p. 211.

54 Quoted in Magnus Morner, *Race Mixture in the History of Latin America* (Boston, 1967), p. 141.

55 Ingenieros, *Sociología argentina,* pp. 228–29.

56 Quoted in Ortiz de Marco, "El negro," p. 365.

57 Sarmiento, *Conflicto y armonía,* 2:71.

58 "Los afroamericanos de North America," *Caras y Caretas,* Apr. 13, 1901.

59 "Tres mellizos de distinto color," *Caras y Caretas,* Nov. 28, 1901.

60 Juan José Soiza Reilly, "Gente de color," *Caras y Caretas*, Nov. 25, 1905.
61 Sarmiento, *Conflicto y armonía*, 1:75.
62 *Segundo censo de la República Argentina: Mayo 10 de 1895*, 3 vols. (Buenos Aires, 1898), 1: xlviii.
63 *Caras y Caretas*, May 25, 1910.
64 Juan C. Elizaga et al., *Temas de población de la Argentina: Aspectos demográficos* (Santiago, 1973), pp. 12–14 n. 5, p. 16.
65 Rollie Poppino, *Brazil: The Land and the People* (New York, 1968), pp. 190–91, 193.
66 Skidmore, *Black into White*, p. 143.
67 Sarmiento, *Conflicto y armonía*, 1:73.
68 "El Puerto Rico de Misiones," *Salimos* (Aug. 1976): 103.
69 Manuel Juan Sanguinetti, *San Telmo: Su pasado histórico* (Buenos Aires, 1965), pp. 116, 317.
70 Gálvez, "La raza africana," pp. 258–59.
71 Manuel Bilbao, *Buenos Aires* (Buenos Aires, 1902), p. 62.
72 Taullard, *Nuestro antiguo Buenos Aires*, p. 355.
73 Christopher Hayden Lutz, "Santiago de Guatemala, 1541–1773: The Socio-Demographic History of a Spanish American Colonial City" (Ph.D. diss. University of Wisconsin, Madison, 1976), pp. 421, 445.
74 Leon F. Litwack, *North of Slavery: The Negro in the Free States, 1790–1860* (Chicago, 1961), pp. 41–45; and Reynolds Farley, *Growth of the Black Population* (Chicago, 1970), p. 26 n. 48.
75 Florestan Fernandes, *The Negro in Brazilian Society* (New York, 1969), pp. 9, 59.
76 Quoted in ibid., p. 64.
77 Ibid., pp. 68–69.
78 Ibid., pp. 67–68.
79 Skidmore, *Black into White*, pp. 49–77.
80 Fernandes, *The Negro*, p. 65.

CHAPTER 7: THE BLACK LEGIONS

1 See Jack D. Foner's excellent book, *Blacks and the Military in American History* (New York, 1974), for a discussion of how North Americans have consistently ignored and denied the extent of Afro-American participation in fighting the United States' wars in order to avoid making social, political, and legal concessions to the country's black population. The post-Civil War period was the only instance in which black people experienced an improvement in their situation as a result of black men's wartime services (pp. 50–51).
2 For descriptions and analyses of this militarization, see Tulio Halperín Donghi, *Hispanoamérica después de la independencia* (Buenos Aires, 1972), Chap. 1; and Halperín Donghi, *Revolución y guerra* (Buenos Aires, 1972), pp. 210–47, 395–400.

3 *Reseña histórica y orgánica del Ejército Argentino,* 3 vols. (Buenos Aires, 1972), 1:294–300. See AGN, 10 26–2–6, for a series of sentences to military service handed down between 1842 and 1852.
4 *Reseña histórica,* 1:421–23.
5 AGN, Sucesiones 6917, Testamentaría de D. Federico Mendizábal.
6 AGN, 10 31–11–5.
7 José Torre Revello, *La sociedad colonial* (Buenos Aires, 1970), pp. 115–16; and *Reseña histórica,* 1:84–85, 97–99.
8 *Documentos para la historia argentina,* 23 vols. to date (Buenos Aires, 1913–), 12:324–25; and *Uniformes de la patria* (Buenos Aires, 1972), unnumbered pages. See also José Luis Molinari, "Los indios y negros durante las invasiones inglesas al Río de la Plata, en 1806 y 1807," *Boletín de la Academia Nacional de la Historia* 34 (1963): 663.
9 Felix Best, *Historia de las guerras argentinas,* 2 vols. (Buenos Aires, 1968), 1:218.
10 Marta B. Goldberg de Flichman and Laura Beatriz Jany. "Algunos problemas referentes a la situación del esclavo en el Río de la Plata," in *IV Congreso Internacional de Historia de América* (Buenos Aires, 1966), 6:65–66.
11 Emeric E. Vidal, *Picturesque Illustrations of Buenos Ayres and Montevideo* (London, 1820), p. 32.
12 Nuria Sales de Bohigas, *Sobre esclavos, reclutas, y mercaderes de quintas* (Barcelona, 1974), p. 78.
13 Goldberg and Jany, "Algunos problemas," p. 71.
14 Ibid., pp. 65–66.
15 For the roll calls of the Seventh Battalion, in which the notation "entregado a su amo," "handed over to his master," frequently appears, see AGN, 3 44–2–1.
16 Goldberg and Jany, "Algunos problemas," p. 68.
17 Manuel Alvarez Pereyra, *Historia del Regimiento 8 de Infantería de Linea* (La Plata, 1921), p. 22.
18 Gerónimo Espejo, *El paso de los Andes* (Buenos Aires, 1953), p. 344; and M. F. Mantilla, *Páginas históricas* (Buenos Aires, 1890), p. 368.
19 Espejo, *El paso,* pp. 400–401, 411; Alvarez Pereyra, *Regimiento 8,* p. 21; and Ramón Tristany, *Regimiento 8 de Infantería de Linea* (Buenos Aires, 1897), pp. 12–13.
20 José Luis Lanuza, *Morenada* (Buenos Aires, 1967), pp. 83–87; and AGN 10 10–2–5.
21 AGN, 3 45–4–2, 45–2–9, 46–1–10; *Reseña histórica,* 1:396; and Jacinto R. Yaben, *Biografías argentinas y sudamericanas,* 5 vols. (Buenos Aires, 1938–40), 5:293.
22 AGN, 3 5–1–3, 11–1–1; Yaben, *Biografías,* 4:727.
23 *Gaceta de Buenos Aires, 1810–21,* facs. ed., 6 vols. (Buenos Aires, 1910–13), 3:289–90, 4:717–19, 5:592, 593, 742–43, 6:93, 154: *Reseña histórica,* 1:188, 189, 298–300, 412; and Yaben, *Biografías,* 1:249, 3:708, 4:727.

24 Bohigas, *Sobre esclavos*, p. 134. The practice of slaves' substituting for their masters in the militia also occurred in Colombia. See Allan J. Kuethe, "The Status of the Free Pardo in the Disciplined Militia of New Granada," *Journal of Negro History* 56 (Apr. 1971): 105–17.

25 See the petition of Sublieutenant Anastasio Sosa, AGN, 9 26-7-4, folios 173–74. See documents concerning Lieutenant Manuel Gutiérrez, AGN, 9 12-5-3, folios 338–39.

26 *Reseña histórica*, 1:151, 153.

27 AGN, 3 59-1-1, 59-1-6, 59-2-1, 59-2-4, 59-2-7. I am indebted to Colonel Ulises Muschietti for having suggested this method of studying integration in Buenos Aires's army.

28 See, for instance, AGN, 10 26-2-6, which contains many sentences of military service.

29 AGN, 10 17-8-1.

30 Bohigas, *Sobre esclavos*, pp. 93–94.

31 Yaben, *Biografías*, 2:400.

32 *Partes oficiales y documentos relativos a la Guerra de la Independencia Argentina*, 2 vols. (Buenos Aires, 1900), 2:186–87.

33 These statistics are taken from roll calls contained in the following volumes of documents; the Battalion of Pardos and Morenos of Upper Peru, the Second Battalion of Peru, and the Eighth Battalion of Peru (AGN, 3 44-2-7); the Ninth Infantry Regiment (AGN, 3 44-2-2); the Seventh Infantry Regiment, (AGN, 3 44-2-1); and the Sixth Infantry Regiment (AGN, 3 44-1-15).

34 Alvaro Yunque, *Calfucura, la conquista de las pampas* (Buenos Aires, 1956), pp. 187–88. Florence Brooks supplied this citation.

35 This image of bones is also employed by León Pomer in his book *El soldado criollo* (Buenos Aires, 1971), p. 10.

36 "Un sargento de la independencia," *Caras y Caretas*, Feb. 25, 1899.

37 Andrés Avellaneda, "Prohibe la Junta el ingreso de esclavos," *La Opinión*, May 28, 1976, p. 8.

38 Bohigas, *Sobre esclavos*, pp. 67–68; and Carlos Monge, "Aclimatación en los Andes: Influencia biológica en las guerras de América," *Revista de la Historia de América* (1948), pp. 1–25.

39 AGN, 10 35-10-2.

40 Enrique Martínez, *Manifestación de la conducta observada por el Jefe de la División de los Andes Aucsiliar del Perú . . .* (Lima, 1823), p. 20.

41 Lanuza, *Morenada*, pp. 86–87.

42 Goldberg and Jany, "Algunos problemas," p. 73.

43 Pomer, *El soldado criollo*, pp. 44–46.

44 Martínez, *Manifestación de la conducta*, p. 24.

45 Domingo F. Sarmiento, *Conflicto y armonía de las razas en Américas*, 2 vols. (Buenos Aires, 1900), 1:76.

46 Marcos Estrada, *El cabo segundo Antonio Ruiz (a.) "Falucho"* (Buenos Aires, 1964); and Mantilla, *Páginas históricas*, pp. 349–53.

47 Mantilla, *Páginas históricas*, pp. 349-53; Espejo, *El paso*, pp. 400-401; and Lanuza, *Morenada*, pp. 168-69.

48 Quoted in José Luis Masini Calderón, "La esclavitud negra en la República Argentina—Epoca independiente," *Revista de la Junta de Estudios Históricos de Mendoza*, Ser. 2, 1 (1961): 142-43.

49 Ibid., p. 148.

50 Mantilla, *Páginas históricas*, p. 367. See also Goldberg and Jany, "Algunos problemas," pp. 72-73.

51 Yaben, *Biografías*, 5:688-89; Estrada, *Antonio Ruiz*, p. 6; and Mantilla, *Páginas históricas*, pp. 371-72.

52 José Ingenieros, *La locura en la Argentina* (Buenos Aires, 1937), p. 30 n. 3.

53 Emiliano Endrek, *El mestizaje en Córdoba, siglo XVIII y principios del XIX* (Córdoba, 1966), p. 83.

54 José María Ramos Mejía, *Rosas y su tiempo*, 3 vols. (Buenos Aires, 1907), 3: 209-10.

55 Lanuza, *Morenada*, p. 167; and Leslie B. Rout, *The African Experience in Spanish America* (Cambridge, 1976), pp. 151, 171.

56 Endrek, *El mestizaje en Córdoba*, p. 83.

57 Ibid., pp. 84-85.

58 Nelly Beatriz López, "La esclavitud en Córdoba, 1790-1853" (Thesis, Universidad Nacional de Córdoba, 1972), pp. 68-69.

59 Masini Calderón, "La esclavitud negra en la República," p. 149.

60 The units, the time periods for which the rolls were taken, and the location of the rolls, are: Corps of Indians, Pardos, and Morenos (1808), AGN, 9 26-7-6, folios 436-37; Battalion of Pardos and Morenos of Upper Peru (1813), AGN, 10 35-10-2; Seventh Battalion of Libertos (1814-15), AGN, 3 44-2-1; Second Battalion of Cazadores (1817-20), AGN 10-2-5; Fourth Battalion of Cazadores (1829), AGN, 3 45-4-2; Restorer Battalion (1834-35), AGN, 3 5-1-3; Restorer Battalion (1852), AGN, 3 56-1-2; Fourth Battalion of the National Guard (1853), AGN, 3 56-1-12.

61 Francisco L. Romay, *El barrio de Monserrat* (Buenos Aires, 1971), p. 69; AGN, 9 10-7-1, ward 14; AGN, 9 8-4-2, folios 197, 255; and Parish of Monserrat, Bk. 3 de Matrimonios, folio 120.

62 Parish of La Merced, Bk. 9 de Bautismos de Color, folio 372v; Parish of Monserrat, Bk. 2 de Matrimonios, folio 369v, 414v, and Bk. 5 de Bautismos de Españoles, folio 176v.

63 AGE, Personal File 2338.

64 AGN, 10 23-5-6, ward 20, Calle Venezuela 258; and Parish of Monserrat, Bk. 2 de Matrimonios, folio 480v.

65 For a detailed listing of the documentation by which each officer's race was verified, see George Reid Andrews, "Forgotten but Not Gone: The Afro-Argentines of Buenos Aires, 1800-1900" (Ph.D. diss., University of Wisconsin, Madison, 1978), pp. 396-410.

66 The list taken from AGN, 3 44-1-15. The black officers are Captains Juan Loy Taboada, José San Martín, Lorenzo Espinosa, Felipe Malaver, and

Dionisio Gamboa; Lieutenants Domingo Sosa and Antonio Porobio, and Sublieutenants Santiago Sosa and Casimiro Mendoza.

67 *Acuerdos del Extinguido Cabildo de Buenos Aires*, 88 vols. (Buenos Aires, 1907–34), Ser. 4, Vol. 2, Bk. 61, p. 476.

68 *Gaceta de Buenos Aires*, 4:338.

69 Yaben, *Biografías*, 5:727.

70 Ibid., 3:708.

71 Ibid., 1:468.

72 For a discussion of the *fuero*, see Lyle McAlister, *The "Fuero Militar" in New Spain, 1764–1800* (Gainesville, Fla., 1957).

73 Readers wishing to consult an expanded and more detailed version of this chapter are referred to Andrews, "Forgotten but Not Gone," Chaps. 6–7; and George Reid Andrews, "The Afro-Argentine Officers of Buenos Aires Province, 1800–1860," *Journal of Negro History* 64 (Spring 1979): 85–100.

CHAPTER 8: COMMUNITY ORGANIZATIONS: THE QUEST FOR AUTONOMY

1 Salvador, the center of a rich plantation district in Brazil, had eleven black cofradías in the early 1700s (David W. Cohen and Jack P. Greene, eds., *Neither Slave nor Free: The Freedman of African Descent in the Slave Societies of the New World* [Baltimore, 1972], p. 123). See also Frederick P. Bowser, "The African Slave in Colonial Spanish America: Reflections on Research Achievements and Priorities," *Latin American Research Review* 17 (Spring 1972), p. 82. A very useful history of an Afro-Brazilian cofradía is Julita Scarano's *Devoção e escravidão* (São Paulo, 1976). See also A. J. R. Russell-Wood, "Black and Mulatto Brotherhoods in Colonial Brazil," *Hispanic American Historical Review* 54 (Nov. 1974): 567–602.

2 AGN, 9 31–4–6, doc. 436.

3 "Relación de los esclavos aptos para tomar las armas . . .," AGN, 9 10–7–2, ward 4.

4 Manuel Juan Sanguinetti, *San Telmo: Su pasado histórico* (Buenos Aires, 1965), p. 315.

5 AGN, 9 31–8–5, doc. 1365.

6 AGN, 9 42–6–3, doc. 6.

7 AGN, 9 42–6–3, doc. 6; and AGN, 9 31–8–7, doc. 1419.

8 Néstor Ortiz Oderigo, *Aspectos de la cultura africana en el Río de la Plata* (Buenos Aires, 1974), pp. 47–51; and Eugene D. Genovese, *Roll, Jordan, Roll: The World the Slaves Made* (New York, 1972), pp. 197–98.

9 "La Hermandad del Rosario," *La Broma*, Sept. 2, 1879, p. 1.

10 AGN, 9 31–4–6, doc. 436.

11 Domingo Sarmiento, *Conflicto y armonía de las razas en Américas*, 2 vols. (Buenos Aires, 1900), 2:71–73.

12 AGN, 9 31–6–1, doc. 823.

13 AGN, 9 31–4–6, doc. 436.

14 AGN, 9 31–8–5, doc. 1365. The moral superiority of the white syndics over the black treasurers is dubious. The Spanish syndic of the Cofradía de San Benito stunned the brothers by absconding with the proceeds from the sale of two houses owned by the brotherhood (José Antonio Wilde, *Buenos Aires desde setenta años atrás* [Buenos Aires, 1903], pp. 173–74).

15 AGN, 9 42–6–3, doc. 6.

16 AGN, 9 31–4–6, doc. 436.

17 AGN, 9 31–8–5, doc. 1365.

18 For discussions of the black churches in the United States, see Ira Berlin, *Slaves without Masters: The Free Negro in the Antebellum South* (New York, 1974), pp. 296–303; and Leon F. Litwack, *North of Slavery: The Negro in the Free States, 1790–1860* (Chicago, 1961), pp. 191–96.

19 For the dissolution of the Cofradía de San Baltasar, see AGN, 10 31–11–5. For mention of the continued activities of the Cofradía del Rosario, see Victor Gálvez, "La raza africana en Buenos Aires," *Nueva Revista de Buenos Aires* 8 (1883): 259; "La Hermandad del Rosario," *La Broma,* Sept. 2, 1879, p. 1; and "Un articulista desconocido," *La Broma,* Sept. 16, 1881, p. 1.

20 AGN, 9 42–6–3, doc. 6.

21 AGN, 9 42–6–3, doc. 6.

22 Ricardo Rodríguez Molas, *La música y danza de los negros en el Buenos Aires de los siglos XVIII y XIX* (Buenos Aires, 1957), p. 10.

23 Ibid., p. 11; and AGN, 10 31–11–5.

24 AGN, 10 31–11–5.

25 Alberto González Arzac, *Abolición de la esclavitud en el Río de la Plata* (Buenos Aires, 1974), p. 51.

26 A copy of the 1823 society constitution may be seen in AGN, 10 31–9–5, doc. 1.

27 For a discussion of governmental efforts to provide a stable source of labor for Buenos Aires during the postrevolutionary period, see Orlando Carracedo, "El Régimen de castas, el trabajo, y la Revolución de Mayo," in *Anuario del Instituto de Investigaciones Históricas* (Rosario, 1960), 4:157–86. For the colonial period, see Lyman L. Johnson, "The Artisans of Buenos Aires during the Viceroyalty, 1776–1810" (Ph.D. diss., University of Connecticut, 1974), esp. pp. 135–40, 305–7.

28 AGN, 10 31–9–5; and AGN, 10 31–11–5.

29 Francisco L. Romay, *El barrio de Monserrat* (Buenos Aires, 1971), pp. 64–65; and AGN, 10 31–11–5.

30 AGN, 10 33–4–5, folio 22.

31 AGN, 10 31–11–5.

32 AGN, 10 33–3–1, Bk. 43, folios 33, 43.

33 AGN, 10 33–3–4, Bk. 101, folio 100.

34 AGN, 10 33–4–1, Bk. 117, folio 57.

35 AGN, 10 31–11–5.

36 *Gaceta Mercantil*, June 25, 1842, p. 2; and AGN, 10 31–11–5.
37 AGN, 10 33–3–1, Bk. 93, folio 66.
38 AGN, 10 33–3–1, Bk. 93, folio 43.
39 AGN, 10 31–11–5.
40 AGN, 10 31–11–5.
41 José Luis Lanuza, *Morenada* (Buenos Aires, 1967), p. 115.
42 AGN, 10 31–11–5.
43 See, for example, AGN, 10 33–3–1, Bk. 93, folio 37.
44 AGN, 10 33–1–3, Bk. 50, folio 118.
45 AGN, 10 31–11–5.
46 AGN, 10 31–11–5. Concerning the houses in the census, see AGN, 10 23–5–5, ward 20, for the Cambundá house; and AGN, 10 23–5–6, ward 28, for the Loango house.
47 Néstor Ortiz Oderigo, *Calunga, croquis del candombe* (Buenos Aires, 1969), pp. 18–19. The painting is reproduced in Lanuza, *Morenada*, between pp. 160 and 161.
48 "El Carnaval antiguo," *Caras y Caretas*, Feb. 15, 1902.
49 AGN, 10 33–2–8, Bk. 90, folio 77.
50 This information is from AGN, 10 31–11–5.
51 "Sociedad Mazambique, Buenos Aires, 4 de mayo de 1870, Reglamento," in the Library of the Museo de Motivos Populares Argentinos José Hernández, Buenos Aires. James Scobie supplied this lead.
52 AGN, 10 31–11–5.
53 AGN, 10 31–11–5.
54 AGN, 10 31–11–5.
55 "Sociedad Mazambique."
56 "La raza africana," *La Nueva Generación* 26 (1858): 1.
57 "Los bienes de nuestros abuelos," *La Broma*, Apr. 30, 1881.
58 *La Broma*, Nov. 10, 1882, p. 3.
59 AGN, 10 31–11–5.
60 Ibid.
61 Ibid.; and AGN, 10 33–3–4, Bk. 101, folio 100.
62 Monica Schuler, "Ethnic Slave Rebellions in the Caribbean and the Guianas," *Journal of Social History* 3 (Summer, 1970): 374–85; and Mary Catherine Karasch, "Slave Life in Rio de Janeiro, 1808–1850" (Ph.D. diss., University of Wisconsin, Madison, 1972), pp. 388–90.
63 AGN, 10 31–11–5.
64 Samuel L. Bailey, *Labor, Nationalism and Politics in Argentina* (New Brunswick, N.J., 1967), pp. 11–12.
65 AGN, 10 31–11–5.
66 Ibid.
67 *El Proletario*, Apr. 18, 1858, p. 1.
68 Jorge Miguel Ford, *Beneméritos de mi estirpe* (La Plata, 1899), p. 38. The collapse of La Fraternal was doubtless linked to the death of its founder in 1873.

69 Quotation from editorial, *La Juventud*, Mar. 12, 1876, pp. 1–2. See issues of *La Juventud*, Jan.-July 1876, for articles arguing this point.
70 Ford, *Beneméritos de mi estirpe*, pp. 73–74.
71 "La Protectora," *La Broma*, July 28, 1882, pp. 1–2.
72 Luis Canepa, *El Buenos Aires de antaño* (Buenos Aires, 1936), pp. 472–73.
73 "Mensaje del Presidente de la Sociedad La Protectora," *La Broma*, Aug. 24, 1879, pp. 1–2. The annual presidential reports were published each August in *La Broma*.
74 Canepa, *El Buenos Aires de antaño*, p. 473; and "La Protectora," pp. 1–2.
75 *La Broma*, Feb. 3, 1881, p. 3.
76 *La Broma*, July 28, 1882, pp. 2–3. See also Juan José Soiza Reilly, "Gente de color," *Caras y Caretas*, Nov. 25, 1905, for favorable white coverage of La Protectora.
77 Canepa, *El Buenos Aires de antaño*, p. 472.
78 Ibid.

CHAPTER 9: AFRO-ARGENTINES IN THE ARTS

1 AGN, 9 8–10–3, folios 79, 102, 174–75; and AGN, 9 8–10–5, folio 122.
2 Ricardo Rodríguez Molas, *La música y danza de los negros en el Buenos Aires de los siglos XVIII y XIX* (Buenos Aires, 1957), p. 7.
3 Ibid., pp. 11–13.
4 Ibid., p. 11.
5 AGN, 9 36–4–3, doc. 10.
6 *Acuerdos del Extinguido Cabildo de Buenos Aires*, 88 vols. (Buenos Aires, 1907–34), Ser. 3, Vol. 8, Bk. 49, pp. 627–30. The other two reports may be found in AGN, 9 36–4–3, doc. 10; and *Acuerdos*, Ser. 3, Vol. 9, Bk. 50, p. 221.
7 Rodríguez Molas, *La música y danza*, pp. 10–11.
8 AGN, 10 32–10–5, Bk. 5, folio 45; and Alberto González Arzac, *Abolición de la esclavitud en el Río de la Plata* (Buenos Aires, 1974), p. 52.
9 AGN, 10 31–11–5.
10 AGN, 9 31–4–6, doc. 436.
11 Ibid.
12 Enrique Puccia, *Breve historia del carnaval porteño* (Buenos Aires, 1974), pp. 27–28. Notices concerning the meetings and practice sessions of the comparsas may be found in any issue of the Afro-Argentine newspapers of the 1870–1900 period. For an illustration of how closely the Afro-Argentines were associated with the porteño Carnival, the reader is referred to the short story anthology *Carnaval, Carnaval* (Buenos Aires, 1968), which contains several stories featuring black characters.
13 For photographs of blackface comparsas, see Puccia, *Carnaval porteño*, p. 49; "El Carnaval," *Caras y Caretas*, Feb. 23, 1901; and Néstor Ortiz Oderigo, *Aspectos de la cultura africana en el Río de la Plata* (Buenos Aires, 1974), Photo 19.

14 An undated membership list of Los Negros hangs in the Museo de Motivos Populares Argentinos José Hernández, Buenos Aires. A group photograph of the organization's members may be found in Puccia, *Carnaval porteño*, p. 37.

15 See, for instance, *La Tribuna*, Mar. 7, Apr. 16, 1868.

16 Puccia, *Carnaval porteño*, p. 44.

17 AGN, 9 31–4–6, doc. 436.

18 Rodríguez Molas, *La música y danza*, p. 11.

19 *Acuerdos*, Ser. 3, Vol. 8, Bk. 49, pp. 628–29.

20 Un Ingles, *Cinco años en Buenos Aires, 1820–1825* (Buenos Aires, 1962), p. 86.

21 Ortiz Oderigo, *Aspectos de la cultura africana*, pp. 37–38.

22 According to the Argentine anthropologist Néstor Ortiz Oderigo, in the Kimbundu language of Angola "candombe" means "thing of the blacks" (ibid., p. 163).

23 This description is taken primarily from Néstor Ortiz Oderigo, *Calunga, croquis del candombe* (Buenos Aires, 1969), pp. 24–26. Other descriptions may be found in Ildefonso Pereda Valdés, *El negro en el Uruguay pasado y presente* (Montevideo, 1965), pp. 156–57; and Vicente Rossi, *Cosas de negros* (Buenos Aires, 1958), pp. 15–17.

24 Though for reports in the black press on noisy, public candombes see *La Juventud*, Sept. 30, 1878, p. 4; and *La Broma*, Jan. 27, 1881, p. 3.

25 Quoted in Luis Soler Cañas, "Pardos y morenos en el año 80 . . .," *Revista del Instituto de Investigaciones Históricas Juan Manuel de Rosas* 23 (1963): 289.

26 Juan José Soiza Reilly, "Gente de color," *Caras y Caretas*, Nov. 25, 1905.

27 Rodríguez Molas, *La música y danza*, p. 16.

28 Eugenio Petit Muñoz et al., *La condición jurídica, social, económica, y política de los negros durante el coloniaje en la Banda Oriental*, 2 vols. (Montevideo, 1947), 1:391–92.

29 Blas Matamoro, "Los negros han desaparecido del ámbito de Buenos Aires," *La Opinión*, July 6, 1976, p. 17; and Miguel Angel Scenna, *Cuando murió Buenos Aires, 1871* (Buenos Aires, 1974), p. 116.

30 *La Broma*, Sept. 11, 1879, p. 4. For a similar reference, see *La Broma*, Oct. 23, 1879, p. 2.

31 Artur Ramos, *Las culturas negras en el Nuevo Mundo* (Mexico City, 1943), p. 219; and Francisco García Jiménez, *El tango: Historia del medio siglo, 1880–1930* (Buenos Aires, 1965), p. 9.

32 Ortiz Oderigo, *Aspectos de la cultura africana*, pp. 70–75.

33 For a description of the phenomenon of the compadrito, see James Scobie, *Buenos Aires: Plaza to Suburb, 1870–1910* (New York, 1974), p. 229.

34 José Luis Lanuza, *Morenada* (Buenos Aires, 1967), p. 225.

35 "El Carnaval antiguo," *Caras y Caretas*, Feb. 15, 1902.

36 Rossi, *Cosas de negros*, pp. 125–28, 136, 146.

37 "El Carnaval antiguo."

38 Lanuza, *Morenada*, p. 223; and Ortiz Oderigo, *Aspectos de la cultura africana*, p. 30.

39 Puccia, *Carnaval porteño*, pp. 43–44.

40 Lanuza, *Morenada*, pp. 48–49.

41 José María Ramos Mejía, *Rosas y su tiempo*, 3 vols. (Buenos Aires, 1907), 1:330.

42 Francisco L. Romay, *El barrio de Monserrat* (Buenos Aires, 1971), pp. 69–70; Lanuza, *Morenada*, pp. 99, 100–101; Ramos Mejía, *Rosas y su tiempo*, 1:287; Néstor Ortiz Oderigo, *Rostros de bronce* (Buenos Aires, 1964), p. 30; and Fermín Chávez, *La cultura en la época de Rosas* (Buenos Aires, 1973), p. 44.

43 Chávez, *Epoca de Rosas*, p. 44; and Ortiz Oderigo, *Rostros de bronce*, p. 20. *La Broma*, May 12, 1882, p. 2, mentions Posadas's three-year course of study in Belgium.

44 Lanuza, *Morenada*, p. 100; Ramos Mejía, *Rosas y su tiempo*, 1:287; and Ortiz Oderigo, *Rostros de bronce*, pp. 32–33.

45 Jorge Miguel Ford, *Beneméritos de mi estirpe* (La Plata, 1899), pp. 92–100.

46 Soler Cañas, "Pardos y morenos," p. 288.

47 Ford, *Beneméritos de mi estirpe*, p. 44.

48 Marcelino M. Román's *Itinerario del payador* (Buenos Aires, 1957), Pt. 4, covers folk music of this type throughout the Americas.

49 José Hernández, *Martín Fierro*, trans. Walter Owen (New York, 1936), pp. 272–75.

50 Román, *Itinerario del payador*, pp. 185–86; and Ortiz Oderigo, *Aspectos de la cultura africana*, pp. 103, 114.

51 Luis Soler Cañas, "Gabino Ezeiza, verdad y leyenda," *Todo Es Historia* 1 (1967): 65–77.

52 Ricardo Rodríguez Molas, "Negros libres rioplatenses," *Buenos Aires: Revista de Humanidades* 1 (Sept. 1961): 124. For a biography of Mendizábal, see Ford, *Beneméritos de mi estirpe*, pp. 60–67.

53 For biographies of several of these figures, see Ford, *Beneméritos de mi estirpe*.

54 Ibid., p. 113.

55 *La Juventud*, Mar. 20, 1878, p. 3.

56 Rodríguez Molas, "Negros libres," p. 124.

57 "Cosas que nacen y mueren en el misterio," *La Broma*, July 30, 1881, p. 1.

58 This review originally appeared in *El Eco Artístico*; it was reprinted in Ford, *Beneméritos de mi estirpe*, pp. 94–98.

59 "Las poesías del joven Thompson," *La Juventud*, June 10, 1878, pp. 1–2.

60 Ford, *Beneméritos de mi estirpe*, p. 79.

61 Ibid.

CHAPTER 10: 1850–1900: THE IRREVERSIBLE DECLINE

1 Gino Germani, *Política y sociedad en una época de transición* (Buenos Aires, 1971), p. 244; Ezequiel Gallo and Roberto Cortés Conde, *La república con-*

servadora (Buenos Aires, 1972), p. 52; and James Scobie, *Argentina: A City and a Nation* (New York, 1971), pp. 97, 134.

2 Ricardo Rodríguez Molas, "Negros libres rioplatenses," *Buenos Aires: Revista de Humanidades* 1 (Sept. 1961): 119–20.

3 "Todas las cosas tienen su término," *La Igualdad*, June 21, 1874.

4 See the collection of *La Igualdad* in the Biblioteca Nacional, Buenos Aires.

5 See numbers 45–48, Apr. 5, 12, 19, 26, 1874, of *La Igualdad* and number 30, Oct. 3, 1873, pp. 1–2.

6 "¿Por qué se llama 'La Broma'?," *La Broma*, Oct. 3, 1878, pp. 1–2.

7 Mention of these papers can be found in Luis Soler Cañas, "Pardos y morenos en el año 80 . . .," *Revista del Instituto de Investigaciones Históricas Juan Manuel de Rosas* 23 (1963): 272–309; and issues of *La Broma* in Oct. 1878.

8 "Notas editoriales," *La Broma*, Jan. 13, 1882, p. 1, and Feb. 25, 1882, p. 3.

9 "La redacción del Tambor," *La Igualdad*, May 3, 1874, p. 3.

10 *La Juventud*, Feb. 27, 1876, May 7, 1876, p. 3, and Sept. 10, 1878, p. 2.

11 "Las clases altas de la sociedad y la de color," *El Proletario*, Apr. 24, 1858, p. 1.

12 "Bombos y bombas," *La Broma*, May 12, 1882, p. 1.

13 "La vida de la República," *La Igualdad*, May 10, 1874, p. 1.

14 "Jornada primera," *La Juventud*, Sept. 20, 1878.

15 "Las clases altas de la sociedad."

16 Soler Cañas, "Pardos y morenos," p. 287.

17 "Falsa inteligencia," *El Proletario*, May 4, 1858, p. 1.

18 For discussion of immigrant-black economic competition in Brazil and the United States, see David W. Cohen and Jack P. Greene, eds., *Neither Slave nor Free: The Freedman of African Descent in the Slave Societies of the New World* (Baltimore, 1972), pp. 263, 331; Mary Catherine Karasch, "Slave Life in Rio de Janeiro, 1808–1850" (Ph.D. diss., University of Wisconsin, Madison, 1972), pp. 412, 484–85; Richard Wade, *Slavery in the Cities* (London, 1964), p. 275; Florestan Fernandes, *The Negro in Brazilian Society* (New York, 1969), p. 5; and Leon F. Litwack, *North of Slavery: The Negro in the Free States, 1790–1860* (Chicago, 1961), pp. 162–68.

19 José Luis Lanuza, *Morenada* (Buenos Aires, 1967), p. 220; Soler Cañas, "Pardos y morenos," p. 294. Soler Cañas convincingly argues that this song was sung by a white, black-face comparsa, but it is still evidence of an apparently visible trend.

20 Alfredo Taullard, *Nuestro antiguo Buenos Aires* (Buenos Aires, 1927), p. 86; and "Los lavanderos municipales," *Caras y Caretas*, Oct. 28, 1899.

21 *Caras y Caretas*, Dec. 17, 1898, p. 5.

22 "El changador," *Caras y Caretas*, July 15, 1899.

23 Lina Beck-Bernard, *Cinco años en la Confederación Argentina, 1857–1862*, trans. José Luis Busaniche (Buenos Aires, 1935), p. 61.

24 José Antonio Wilde, *Buenos Aires desde setenta años atrás* (Buenos Aires, 1903), p. 165.

25 Manuel Alvarez Pereyra, *Historia del Regimiento 8 de Infantería de Linea* (La Plata, 1921), pp. 22–29.

26 For accounts of fierce and at times violent competition between blacks and immigrants in the United States, see Ira Berlin, *Slaves without Masters: The Free Negro in the Antebellum South* (New York, 1974), pp. 227–32; and Litwack, *North of Slavery*, pp. 162–68.

27 For a discussion of this attitude, see James Scobie, *Buenos Aires: Plaza to Suburb, 1870–1910* (New York, 1974), pp. 218–20; and Emiliano Endrek, *El mestizaje en Córdoba, siglo XVIII y principios del XIX* (Córdoba, 1966), pp. 69–74.

28 Quoted in Rodríguez Molas, "Negros libres," p. 125.

29 "El Congreso," *Caras y Caretas*, July 6, 1902.

30 *Caras y Caretas*, Oct. 25, 1902.

31 Mamerto Fidel Quinteros, *Memorias de un negro del Congreso* (Buenos Aires, 1924), pp. 153–54.

32 Ibid., p. 11.

33 Scobie, *Buenos Aires*, pp. 237–39.

34 "¿Por qué se llama 'La Broma'?," *La Broma*, Oct. 17, 1878, pp. 1–2. See the open propaganda in the pages of *La Igualdad*, for example, "El D. Avellaneda," *La Igualdad*, Dec. 7, 1873.

35 "Estamos," *La Broma*, July 20, 1879, p. 1.

36 Quinteros, *Memorias de un negro*, p. 93.

37 "En las antesalas del Congreso," *Caras y Caretas*, Aug. 25, 1900.

38 Quoted in Rodríguez Molas, "Negros libres," p. 125.

39 "La ley del embudo," *La Broma*, Aug. 19, 1881, p. 1.

40 Miguel Angel Scenna, *Cuando murió Buenos Aires, 1871* (Buenos Aires, 1974), p. 111.

41 "La opinión del estrangero," *La Igualdad*, May 3, 1874, p. 1.

42 Quinteros, *Memorias de un negro*, pp. 11–12, 41–42, 116.

43 *La Broma*, Mar. 21, 1880.

44 *La Broma*, June 4, 1880, p. 3.

45 Juan José Soiza Reilly, "Gente de color," *Caras y Caretas*, Nov. 25, 1905.

46 Scobie, *Buenos Aires*, pp. 230–31.

47 "¿Caen o se levantan?," *La Juventud*, Oct. 30, 1878, p. 1.

48 *La Juventud*, Apr. 19, 1876, p. 1.

49 "La Hermandad del Rosario," *La Broma*, Sept. 3, 1879, p. 1.

50 See, for example, the controversy over Zenón Rolón's pamphlet "A Few Words to the Brothers of My Race," first published in 1877 and reprinted in *La Juventud*, June 30, July 10, 1878. Responses included "El folleto de D. Zenón," *La Broma*, Jan. 31, 1878; and "Sobre el mismo tema," *La Broma*, Feb. 8, 1878.'

51 "El lujo es incompetente y ruinoso a la clase de color," *El Proletario*, May 9, 1858, p. 1.

52 *La Juventud*, Feb. 27, 1876, p. 1, and June 25, 1876, p. 1.

53 "La mirada retrospectiva," *La Juventud*, Aug. 10, 1878, p. 2.

54 Ibid.

55 "Preparando el porvenir," *La Broma*, Sept. 26, 1878, p. 1. For other articles promoting manual labor, see "El trabajo es la vida del hombre," *La Igualdad*, June 7, 1874, p. 1; and "Educación y trabajo," *La Broma*, Nov. 8, 15, 1877.

56 Jorge Miguel Ford, *Beneméritos de mi estirpe* (La Plata, 1899), p. 124.

57 *La Igualdad*, June 7, 1874, p. 3.

58 "Estamos," *La Broma*, July 20, 1879, p. 1.

59 "Unión, igualdad, fraternidad," *La Juventud*, July 30, 1878, p. 3.

60 "Vaya!," *La Juventud*, Oct. 10, 1878, pp. 1–2.

61 Lanuza, pp. 100–101.

62 Ford, *Beneméritos de mi estirpe*, pp. 73–74. For Sar's will, see Testamentaría de D. Eugenio Sar, AGN, Sucesiones 8310.

63 E. Franklin Frazier, *Black Bourgeoisie* (New York, 1962).

64 "¿Por qué se llama 'La Broma'?," *La Broma*, Nov. 15, 1878, p. 1. For some interesting parallels with the North American case, see Frazier, *Black Bourgeoisie*, Chaps. 8–9.

65 "*La Juventud*, May 7, 1876, p. 3.

66 "Consejos sociales," *La Juventud*, Jan. 23, 1876, p. 1.

67 "La sociedad obrera," *La Juventud*, Feb. 20, 1876, p. 1.

68 "Nuestro triunfo," *La Juventud*, Jan. 23, 1876, p. 1.

69 "El 9 de junio de 1816," *La Juventud*, July 10, 1878, p. 1.

70 "Nuestro triunfo," p. 1. Italics in original.

71 *La Juventud*, Feb. 13, 1876, p. 2. Italics in original.

72 "¿Por qué se llama 'La Broma'?", *La Broma*, Feb. 13, 1876, p. 2.

73 "Actualidad," *La Broma*, Aug. 22, 1878, p. 2.

74 "Rumores de la Protectora," *La Broma*, July 27, 1879, p. 1.

75 Among those mentioned in the black papers are the musicians Zenón Rolón and Manuel L. Posadas, who studied in Italy and Belgium, and the painters Juan Blanco de Aguirre and Justo García.

76 See "Alerta," in Horacio Mendizábal's *Primeros versos* (Buenos Aires, 1865) and "Arjentina," in Mendizábal's *Horas de meditación* (Buenos Aires, 1869). See also Ford, *Beneméritos de mi estirpe*, p. 73.

77 "El ramo de flores," *La Juventud*, Jan. 16, 1876, p. 2.

78 Soler Cañas, "Los pardos y morenos," pp. 274, 281–82.

79 Soiza Reilly, "Gente de color."

80 The most complete account of this episode may be found in Soler Cañas, "Los pardos y morenos," pp. 274–81.

81 Ibid., pp. 277–78.

82 "Club Barcala," *La Broma*, Aug. 11, 1882, p. 1.

83 "La libertad," *La Broma*, Dec. 18, 1879, p. 1. See also "Nuestros derechos," *La Broma*, Nov. 20, 1879.

84 "La ley del embudo," *La Broma*, Aug. 19, 1881, p. 1; and "La lavandera," *La Broma*, Oct. 27, 1881, p. 2.

85 Quinteros, *Memorias de un negro*, pp. 235–36.
86 *La Broma*, July 28, 1882, p. 3, and June 23, 1881, p. 3.

CHAPTER 11: BUENOS AIRES IN COMPARATIVE PERSPECTIVE:
CASTE, CLASS, AND RACE RELATIONS
IN THE AMERICAS SINCE EMANCIPATION

1 David W. Cohen and Jack P. Greene, eds., *Neither Slave nor Free: The Freedman of African Descent in the Slave Societies of the New World* (Baltimore, 1972), pp. 7–9.
2 Ibid., p. 99. The stigma that free blacks carried is also conveyed in the title of Ira Berlin's study, *Slaves without Masters: The Free Negro in the Antebellum South* (New York, 1974).
3 Berlin, *Slaves without Masters*, pp. 86–103; and Jack D. Foner, *Blacks and the Military in American History* (New York, 1974), p. 20.
4 Leslie B. Rout, *The African Experience in Spanish America* (Cambridge, 1976), pp. 181–82; Magnus Morner, *Race Mixture in the History of Latin America* (Boston, 1967), pp. 82–83; and Nuria Sales de Bohigas, *Sobre esclavos, reclutas, y mercaderes de quintas* (Barcelona, 1974), pp. 108–29 passim.
5 See Gonzalo Aguirre Beltrán, "The Integration of the Negro into the National Society of Mexico," and Carlos Rama, "The Passing of the Afro-Uruguayan from Caste Society into Class Society," both in Magnus Morner, ed., *Race and Class in Latin America* (New York, 1970). These essays are condensed from Gonzalo Aguirre Beltrán, *La población negra de México* (Mexico City, 1946) and Carlos Rama, *Los afro-uruguayos* (Montevideo, 1967).
6 See Chap. 12, at note 18, and the note itself.
7 For analyses of Brazilian race relations by an African, a Brazilian, and a North American, respectively, see Anani Dzidzienyo, *The Position of Blacks in Brazilian Society* (London, 1971); Florestan Fernandes, *The Negro in Brazilian Society* (New York, 1969); and Carl Degler, *Neither Black nor White* (New York, 1971).
8 Recent scholarship suggests this—the minority status of whites—as the basic cause for white repression of black people in the nineteenth century American South. See Berlin, *Slaves without Masters*, pp. 86–103; and Howard N. Rabinowitz, *Race Relations in the Urban South, 1865–1890* (New York, 1978), pp. 18–21, 24–27, 67–68, 329–39.
9 Degler, *Neither Black nor White*, pp. 253–61.
10 Morner, *Race and Class*, p. 141.
11 Fernandes, *Negro in Brazilian Society*, pp. 5, 10–12, 32, 52–53; and Rabinowitz, *Race Relations*, p. ix.
12 Anani Dzidzienyo, "Activity and Inactivity in the Politics of Afro-Latin America," *SECOLAS Annals*, 9 (Mar. 1978): 48–61.

CHAPTER 12: EPILOGUE: THE AFRO-ARGENTINES TODAY

1 Máximo Simpson, "Porteños de color," *Panorama*, June 1967, p. 78; and Leslie B. Rout, *The African Experience in Spanish America* (Cambridge, 1976), p. 195.

2 See Hugo Ratier's sketchy but provocative monograph, *El cabecita negra* (Buenos Aires, 1971).

3 Simpson, "Porteños de color," p. 78.

4 Marta B. Goldberg, "La población negra y mulata de la ciudad de Buenos Aires, 1810–1840," *Desarrollo Económico* 16 (Apr.-June 1976): 75–99; Andrés Avellaneda, "Prohibe la Junta el ingreso de esclavos," *La Opinión*, May 28, 1976, p. 8; Blas Matamoro, "Los negros han desaparecido del ámbito de Buenos Aires," *La Opinión*, July 6, 1976, p. 17; and "Puntos de vista: Negritud," *La Nación*, Feb. 1976, exact date unknown, editorial page.

5 "Brooke reivindicaría la muerte de Bessie Smith," *La Opinión*, Nov. 16, 1975, p. 2.

6 Néstor Ortiz Oderigo, *Calunga, croquis del candombe* (Buenos Aires, 1969), pp. 72–75.

7 M. F. Mantilla, *Páginas históricas* (Buenos Aires, 1890), p. 358.

8 José Luis Lanuza, *Morenada* (Buenos Aires, 1967), p. 7.

9 Ricardo Rodríguez Molas, "El negro en el Río de la Plata," *Polémica* 2 (May 1970): 38.

10 Vicente Rossi, *Cosas de negros* (Buenos Aires, 1958), pp. 41, 51.

11 Ibid., pp. 69–70.

12 José Luis Masini Calderón, "La esclavitud negra en la República Argentina—Epoca independiente," *Revista de la Junta de Estudios Históricos de Mendoza*, Ser. 2, 1 (1961): 156.

13 Francisco García Jiménez, *El tango: Historia de medio siglo, 1880–1930* (Buenos Aires, 1965), p. 8.

14 León Benaros, "Negros en Buenos Aires," *Todo Es Historia* 40 (Aug. 1970): 25. See also León Benaros, "Oficios de negros en el antiguo Buenos Aires," *Todo Es Historia* 34 (Feb. 1970): 31.

15 See Avellaneda, "Prohibe la Junta"; Rodríguez Molas, "El negro en el Río de la Plata," *Polémica* 2 (May 1970): 38; and Ratier, *El cabecita negra*, pp. 17–30.

16 "Carta a un legislador de los Estados Unidos," *La Opinión*, Oct. 30, 1976, p. 7.

17 Alfredo Taullard, *Nuestro antiguo Buenos Aires* (Buenos Aires, 1927), p. 355.

18 Leslie Rout also encountered this argument in Uruguay (Rout, *African Experience*, pp. 200–201). For similar observations concerning Brazil, see Carl Degler, *Neither Black nor White* (New York, 1971), p. 98; and for Venezuela, see Winthrop R. Wright, "Elitist Attitudes toward Race in Twentieth-Century Venezuela," in Robert Brent Toplin, ed., *Slavery and Race Relations in Latin America* (Westport, Conn., 1974), pp. 327–28, 331–36.

19 Torcuato Luca de Tena et al., eds., *Yo, Juan Domingo Perón* (Barcelona, 1976), pp. 86, 89–90. In the early 1950s Perón was made honorary president of Josephine Baker's International Anti-Racism Institute. Perón had invited her to Argentina several times and had supported the opening of an office of the institute in Buenos Aires. Perón recalls that at one point Baker was so moved by gratitude for his assistance that she asked to be allowed to kiss his hand. "This moved me greatly because she was a humble woman, a great artist, a fighter, and because I thought also of those prejudices that dwell in the minds of black people when they deal with whites. She was a refined and cultivated woman, somewhat overcome by age. I did not find her attractive" (ibid., p. 92).

20 Simpson, "Porteños de color," p. 85.

21 Era Bell Thompson, "Argentina: Land of the Vanishing Blacks," *Ebony*, Oct. 1973, p. 84.

22 Simpson, "Porteños de color," p. 80.

23 Ibid., p. 84. See also Luis Grassino, "Buenos Aires de ébano," *Revista Clarín*, Dec. 5, 1971.

24 Alicia Nydia Lahourcade, *La comunidad negra de Chascomús y su reliquia* (Chascomús, 1973), pp. 63–65; and Simpson, "Porteños de color," p. 83.

25 "El chisporroteo de las Hnas. Platero," *La Nación*, Sept. 29, 1976.

Bibliography

ARCHIVES

The research for this book was carried out in a number of Argentine and Uruguayan archives. Those institutions, with the abbreviations used to identify them in the footnotes, were:

Archivo General de la Nación, Buenos Aires (AGN)
Archivo General del Ejército, Buenos Aires (AGE)
Archivo General de la Nación, Montevideo (AGN, Montevideo)
Archivo Histórico de la Provincia de Córdoba
Archivo Histórico de la Provincia de Entre Ríos
Archivo de la Parroquia de Monserrat, Buenos Aires
Archivo de la Parroquia de Socorro, Buenos Aires
Archivo de la Parroquia de La Merced, Buenos Aires

The bulk of the research was done at the Archivo General de la Nación in Buenos Aires. Among the sources consulted there were judicial, military, and police records, notarial registers, censuses, official government reports and documents, and wills. Also helpful was the collection of prints and photographs housed in the Archivo Gráfico of the Archivo General de la Nación.

The military archive, the Archivo General del Ejército, houses the service records of officers who have served in Argentina's armies since independence. This material was invaluable in the preparation of Chapter 7.

The provincial archives of Córdoba and Entre Ríos, as well as the national archives in Montevideo, contain censuses which were useful for verifying the degree to which those areas were linked to Buenos Aires through migration.

The birth, death, and marriage registers stored in Buenos Aires's parish archives formed a rich source of biographical information for certain individuals, as well as for selected families who were followed through two or more generations.

Citations of documents located in these archives are fairly self-explanatory except in the case of the Archivo General de la Nación. The format for most citations from that repository consists of the initials AGN followed by four numbers, e.g., AGN, 10 31–11–5. The initial number indicates the storage room in which the document is kept, and the hyphenated numbers indicate its location on the shelves in that room.

Citations of notarial documents and wills in the AGN consist of the volume number, the year, and the location of the document within the volume, e.g., AGN, Register 4, 1894, folio 91, or AGN, Sucesiones [Estates] 8498, Testamentaría de Federico Mendizábal, 1869.

NEWSPAPERS AND PERIODICALS

Though I took information from numerous nineteenth-century periodicals (fellow researchers supplied me with many invaluable references), I concentrated on reading eleven daily and weekly newspapers and magazines from the last century. Those publications, the years in which I read intensively, and the institutions where collections may be found, are as follows:

La Broma. Biweekly. 1878–83. Biblioteca Nacional. Buenos Aires.

Caras y Caretas. Weekly. 1898–1902. AGN.

Gaceta de Buenos Aires. Daily. 1810–21. Facsimile ed. 6 vols. Buenos Aires, 1910–13.

Gaceta Mercantil. Daily. 1823–24, 1834. AGN.

La Igualdad. Weekly. 1873–74. Biblioteca Nacional.

La Juventud. Published every ten days. 1876–78. Biblioteca Nacional.

La Moda. Weekly. 1837–38. AGN.

El Negro Timoteo. Weekly. 1878–80. AGN.

El Proletario. Weekly. 1858. Biblioteca de la Universidad de La Plata.

Telégrafo Mercantil. Semiweekly. 1801–2. AGN.

La Tribuna. Daily. 1853. AGN.

SECONDARY SOURCES

Acosta Saignes, Miguel. *Vida de los esclavos negros en Venezuela.* Caracas, 1967.

Acosta Saignes, Miguel, et al. "La vivienda de los pobres." In *Estudio de Caracas.* Caracas, 1967. Vol. 2, Bk. 2, pp. 627–893.

Acuerdos del Extinguido Cabildo de Buenos Aires. 88 vols. Buenos Aires. 1907–34.

Aguirre Beltrán, Gonzalo. *La población negra de México.* Mexico City, 1946. Reprint Mexico City, 1972.

Alberdi, Juan Bautista. *Bases y puntos de partida para la organización de la República Argentina.* Buenos Aires, 1852.

Alvarez Pereyra, Manuel. *Historia del Regimiento 8 de Infantería de Linea*. La Plata, 1921.

Andrews, George Reid. "The Afro-Argentine Officers of Buenos Aires Province, 1800–1860." *Journal of Negro History* 64 (Spring 1979): 85–100.

Andrews, George Reid. "Forgotten but Not Gone: The Afro-Argentines of Buenos Aires, 1800–1900." Ph.D. dissertation, University of Wisconsin, Madison, 1978.

Andrews, George Reid. "Race versus Class Association: The Afro-Argentines of Buenos Aires, 1850–1900." *Journal of Latin American Studies* 11 (May 1979): 19–39.

Avellaneda, Andrés. "Prohibe la Junta el ingreso de esclavos." *La Opinión* (Buenos Aires), May 28, 1976, p. 8.

Bagú, Sergio. *Estructura social de la colonia*. Buenos Aires, 1952.

Bailey, Samuel L. *Labor, Nationalism and Politics in Argentina*. New Brunswick, N.J., 1967.

Beck-Bernard, Lina. *Cinco años en la Confederación Argentina, 1857–62*. Translated by José Luis Busaniche. Buenos Aires, 1935.

Benaros, León. "Negros en Buenos Aires." *Todo Es Historia* 4 (Aug. 1970): 24–25.

Benaros, Léon. "Oficios de negros en el antiguo Buenos Aires." *Todo Es Historia* 4 (Feb. 1970): 31.

Berlin, Ira. *Slaves without Masters: The Free Negro in the Antebellum South*. New York, 1974.

Besio Moreno, Nicolás. *Buenos Aires: Estudio crítico de su población, 1536–1936*. Buenos Aires, 1939.

Best, Felix. *Historia de las guerras argentinas*. 2 vols. Buenos Aires, 1968.

Biedma Straw, Juan J. *Crónica histórica del No. 2 de Infantería de Linea*. Buenos Aires, 1904.

Bilbao, Manuel. *Buenos Aires*. Buenos Aires, 1902.

Blank, Stephanie Bower. "Social Integration and Social Stability in a Colonial Spanish American City, Caracas (1595–1627)." Ph.D. dissertation, University of Wisconsin, Madison, 1971.

Bohigas, Nuria Sales de. *Sobre esclavos, reclutas, y mercaderes de quintas*. Barcelona, 1974.

Bowser, Frederick P. *The African Slave in Colonial Peru, 1684–1750*. Stanford, 1974.

Bowser, Frederick P. "The African Slave in Colonial Spanish America: Reflections on Research Achievements and Priorities." *Latin American Research Review* 7 (Spring 1972): 77–94.

Boxer, Charles R. *Race Relations in the Portuguese Colonial Empire*. Oxford, Eng., 1963.

Caillet-Bois, Ricardo Rodolfo. *Ensayo sobre el Río de la Plata y la revolución francesa*. Buenos Aires, 1929.

Canepa, Luis. *El Buenos Aires de antaño*. Buenos Aires, 1936.

Carracedo, Orlando. "El Régimen de castas, el trabajo, y la Revolución de

Mayo." In *Anuario del Instituto de Investigaciones Históricas.* Rosario, 1960. 4: 157–86.

Castro, Jeanne Berrance de. "A imprensa mulata." *O Estado de Sao Paulo* 13 (Nov. 2, 1968), Literary Supplement, p. 5.

Castro, Jeanne Berrance de. "O negro na Guarda Nacional Brasileira." *Anais do Museu Paulista* 23 (1969): 151–72.

Celton, Dora Estela. "Censo de la ciudad de Códoba de año 1840." Thesis, Universidad Nacional de Córdoba, 1971.

Censo general de población, edificación, comercio e industrias de la ciudad de Buenos Aires. 2 vols. Buenos Aires, 1889.

Chávez, Fermín. *La cultura en la época de Rosas.* Buenos Aires, 1973.

Cohen, David W., and Greene, Jack P., eds. *Neither Slave nor Free: The Freedman of African Descent in the Slave Societies of the New World.* Baltimore, 1972.

Comadrán Ruiz, Jorge. *Evolución demográfica argentina durante el período hispano, 1535–1810.* Buenos Aires, 1969.

Curtin, Philip D. *The Atlantic Slave Trade: A Census.* Madison, 1969.

Cutolo, Vicente. *Nuevo diccionario biográfico.* 4 vols. Buenos Aires, 1968.

Degler, Carl. *Neither Black nor White.* New York, 1971.

Diego, J. A. de. "Prontuario de la patota porteña." *Todo Es Historia* 101 (Oct. 1975): 28–42.

Di Tella, Torcuato S., et al. *Argentina, sociedad de masas.* Buenos Aires, 1965.

Documentos para la historia argentina. 23 vols. to date. Buenos Aires, 1913– .

Dzidzienyo, Anani. "Activity and Inactivity in the Politics of Afro-Latin America." *SECOLAS Annals* 9 (Mar. 1978): 48–61.

Dzidzienyo, Anani. *The Position of Blacks in Brazilian Society.* London, 1971.

Eblen, Jack E. "Growth of the Black Population in *Ante Bellum* America, 1820–1860." *Population Studies* 26 (1972): 273–89.

Elizaga, Juan C., et al. *Temas de la población de la Argentina: Aspectos demográficos.* Santiago, 1973. [Originally published in *Desarrollo Económico* 12 (Jan.-Mar. 1972): 7–116.]

Endrek, Emiliano. *El mestizaje en Córdoba, siglo XVIII y principios del XIX.* Córdoba, 1966.

Espejo, Gerónimo. *El paso de los Andes.* Buenos Aires, 1953.

Estrada, Marcos. *El cabo segundo Antonio Ruiz (a.) "Falucho."* Buenos Aires, 1964.

Farley, Reynolds. *Growth of the Black Population.* Chicago, 1970.

Feliu Cruz, Guillermo. *La abolición de la esclavitud en Chile.* Santiago, 1942.

Fernandes, Florestan. *The Negro in Brazilian Society.* New York, 1969.

Fernandes, Florestan. *O negro no mundo dos brancos.* São Paulo, 1972.

Fernández, Norma Cristina, et al. "Demografía restrospectiva de la ciudad de Córdoba (1823–1856)." Thesis, Universidad Nacional de Córdoba, 1976.

Foner, Jack D. *Blacks and the Military in American History.* New York, 1974.

Foner, Laura. "The Free People of Color in Louisiana and St. Domingue: A Comparative Portrait of Two Three-Caste Slave Societies." *Journal of Social History* 3 (Summer 1970): 406–30.

Foner, Laura, and Genovese, Eugene D., eds. *Slavery in the New World*. New York, 1969.

Ford, Jorge Miguel. *Beneméritos de mi estirpe*. La Plata, 1899.

Frazier, E. Franklin. *Black Bourgeoisie*. New York, 1962.

Frías, Susana R., and Méndez, Liliana E. *Censos y padrones existentes en el Archivo General de la Nación, 1776–1852*. Buenos Aires, 1974.

Gallo, Ezequiel, and Cortés Conde, Roberto. *La república conservadora*. Buenos Aires, 1972.

Gálvez, Victor (pseudonym of Vicente Quesada). "La raza africana en Buenos Aires." *Nueva Revista de Buenos Aires* 8 (1883): 246–60.

García, Juan Agustín. *La ciudad indiana*. Buenos Aires, 1900. Reprint Buenos Aires, 1955.

García Jiménez, Francisco. *El tango: Historia de medio siglo, 1880–1930*. Buenos Aires, 1965.

Garzón Maceda, C., and Dorflinger, J. W. "Esclavos y mulatos en un dominio rural del siglo XVIII en Córdoba." *Revista de la Universidad Nacional de Córdoba*, Ser. 2, 2 (1961): 625–40.

Genovese, Eugene D. *Roll, Jordan, Roll: The World the Slaves Made*. New York, 1974.

Germani, Gino. *Política y sociedad en una época de transición*. Buenos Aires, 1971.

Gillespie, Alexander. *Buenos Aires y el interior*. Buenos Aires, 1921.

Glazer, Nathan, and Moynihan, Daniel Patrick. *Beyond the Melting Pot*. Cambridge, Mass., 1964.

Goldberg, Marta B. "La población negra y mulata de la ciudad de Buenos Aires, 1810–1840." *Desarrollo Económico* 16 (Apr.-June 1976): 75–99.

Goldberg, Marta B., and Jany, Laura Beatriz. "Algunos problemas referentes a la situación del esclavo en el Río de la Plata." In *IV Congreso Internacional de Historia de América*. Buenos Aires, 1966. 6: 61–75.

González Arzac, Alberto. *Abolición de la esclavitud en el Río de la Plata*. Buenos Aires, 1974.

Graff, Gary Wendell. "Cofradías in the Kingdom of New Granada: Lay Fraternities in a Spanish-American Frontier Society, 1600–1755." Ph.D. dissertation, University of Wisconsin, Madison, 1973.

Grassino, Luis. "Buenos Aires de ébano." *Revista Clarín*, Dec. 5, 1971.

Haigh, Samuel. *Bosquejos de Buenos Aires, Chile y Perú*. Buenos Aires, 1920.

Halperín Donghi, Tulio. *Argentina de la Revolución de Independencia a la Confederación Rosista*. Buenos Aires, 1972.

Halperín Donghi, Tulio. *Politics, Economics, and Society in Argentina in the Revolutionary Period*. London, 1975.

Halperín Donghi, Tulio. *Revolución y guerra*. Buenos Aires, 1972.

Hershberg, Theodore. "Free Blacks in Antebellum Philadelphia: A Study of Ex-Slaves, Freeborn, and Socioeconomic Decline." *Journal of Social History* 5 (Winter 1971–72): 183–209.

Hoetink, Harry. *The Two Variants in Caribbean Race Relations*. London, 1967.

Hudson, W. H. *Far Away and Long Ago*. London, 1951.

Ibarguren, Carlos. *Manuelita Rosas*. Buenos Aires, 1953.

Ingenieros, José. *La locura en la Argentina*. Buenos Aires, 1937.

Ingenieros, José. *Sociología argentina*. Madrid, 1913.

Ingles, Un. *Cinco años en Buenos Aires, 1820–1825*. Buenos Aires, 1962.

Johnson, Lyman L. "The Artisans of Buenos Aires during the Viceroyalty, 1776–1810." Ph.D. dissertation, University of Connecticut, 1974.

Johnson, Lyman L. "La manumisión de esclavos durante el Virreinato." *Desarrollo Económico* 16 (Oct.-Dec., 1976): 333–48.

Johnson, Lyman L. "La manumisión en el Buenos Aires colonial: Un análisis ampliado." *Desarrollo Económico* 17 (Jan.-Mar. 1978): 637–46.

Karasch, Mary Catherine. "Slave Life in Rio de Janeiro, 1808–1850." Ph.D. dissertation, University of Wisconsin, Madison, 1972.

King, J. Anthony. *Veinticuatro años en la República Argentina*. Buenos Aires, 1921.

Kordon, Bernardo. "La raza negra en el Río de la Plata." *Todo Es Historia* 3 (1969), Supplement 7.

Kroeber, Clifton B. "Rosas and the Revision of Argentine History, 1880–1955." *Inter-American Review of Bibliography* 10 (Jan.-Mar. 1960): 3–25.

Kuethe, Allan J. "The Status of the Free Pardo in the Disciplined Militia of New Granada." *Journal of Negro History* 56 (Apr. 1971): 105–17.

Lahourcade, Alicia Nydia. *La comunidad negra de Chascomús y su reliquía*. Chascomús, 1973.

Lanuza, José Luis. *Morenada*. Buenos Aires, 1946. Reprint Buenos Aires, 1967.

Lanuza, José Luis, ed. *Cancionero del tiempo de Rosas*. Buenos Aires, 1941.

Lattes, Alfredo E., and Poczter, Raúl. *Muestra del censo de la población de la ciudad de Buenos Aires de 1855*. Buenos Aires, 1968.

Lewin, Boleslao. "La 'conspiración de los franceses' en Buenos Aires (1795)." In *Anuario del Instituto de Investigaciones Históricas*. Rosario, 1960. 4: 9–58.

Lewis, Oscar. *La Vida*. New York, 1965.

Litwack, Leon F. *North of Slavery: The Negro in the Free States, 1790–1860*. Chicago, 1961.

Lockhart, James. *Spanish Peru, 1532–1560*. Madison, 1968.

Lombardi, John V. *The Decline and Abolition of Negro Slavery in Venezuela, 1820–1854*. Westport, Conn., 1971.

López, Nelly Beatriz. "La esclavitud en Córdoba, 1790–1853." Thesis, Universidad Nacional de Córdoba, 1972.

Luca de Tena, Torcuato, et al., eds. *Yo, Juan Domingo Perón*. Barcelona, 1976.

Lutz, Christopher Hayden. "Santiago de Guatemala, 1541–1773: The Socio-Demographic History of a Spanish American Colonial City." Ph.D. dissertation, University of Wisconsin, Madison, 1976.

McAlister, Lyle. "Social Structure and Social Change in New Spain." *Hispanic American Historical Review* 93 (Aug. 1963): 349–70.

McAlister, Lyle. *The "Fuero Militar" in New Spain, 1764–1800*. Gainesville, Fla., 1957.

Mantilla, M. F. *Páginas históricas*. Buenos Aires, 1890.

Martín, Haydeé María. "El censo del año 1813 en la provincia de Buenos Aires." *América* 1 (Apr. 1976): 13–20.

Martínez, Enrique. *Manifestación de la conducta observada por el Jefe de la División de los Andes Aucsiliar del Perú . . . .* Lima, 1823.

Martínez Peláez, Severo. *La patria del criollo*. San José, 1975.

Masini Calderón, José Luis. "La esclavitud negra en la República Argentina— Epoca independiente." *Revista de la Junta de Estudios Históricos de Mendoza*, Ser. 2, 1 (1961): 135–161.

Masini Calderón, José Luis. *La esclavitud negra en Mendoza*. Mendoza, 1962.

Matamoro, Blas. "Los negros han desaparecido del ámbito de Buenos Aires." *La Opinión* (Buenos Aires), July 6, 1976, p. 17.

Meader, Ernesto J. A. *Evolución demográfica argentina desde 1810 a 1869*. Buenos Aires, 1969.

Mellafe, Rolando. *La introducción de la esclavitud negra en Chile*. Santiago, 1959.

Mendizábal, Horacio. *Horas de meditación*. Buenos Aires, 1869.

Mendizábal, Horacio. *Primeros versos*. Buenos Aires, 1865.

Mercedes Luna, Ricardo. *Los coroneles de Mitre*. Buenos Aires, 1974.

Molinari, Diego. *La trata de negros, datos para su estudio en el Río de la Plata*. Buenos Aires, 1944.

Molinari, José Luis. "Los indios y negros durante las invasiones inglesas al Río de la Plata, en 1806 y 1807." *Boletín de la Academia Nacional de la Historia* 34 (1963): 639–72.

Monge, Carlos. "Aclimatación en los Andes: Influencia biológica en las guerras de América." *Revista de la Historia de América* (1948), pp. 1–25.

Moreno, José Luis. "La estructura social y demográfica de la ciudad de Buenos Aires en el año 1778." In *Anuario del Instituto de Investigaciones Históricas*. Rosario, 1965. 8: 151–70.

Morner, Magnus. *Race Mixture in the History of Latin America*. Boston, 1967.

Morner, Magnus. "Recent Research on Negro Slavery and Abolition in Latin America." *Latin American Research Review* 13 (1978): 265–89.

Morner, Magnus, ed. *Race Mixture in the History of Latin America*. Boston, 1967.

Olgo Ochoa, Pedro. "El invento de Falucho." *Todo Es Historia* 4 (Sept. 1970): 32–39.

Ortiz de Marco, Enrique. "El negro en la formación étnica y sociocultural argentina." *Boletín del Centro Naval*, July-Sept. 1969, pp. 363–81.

Ortiz Oderigo, Néstor. *Aspectos de la cultura africana en el Río de la Plata*. Buenos Aires, 1974.

Ortiz Oderigo, Néstor. *Calunga, croquis del candombe*. Buenos Aires, 1969.

Ortiz Oderigo, Néstor. *Rostros de bronce*. Buenos Aires, 1964.

Padilla, Elena. *Up from Puerto Rico*. New York, 1958.

Parish, Woodbine. *Buenos Aires y las provincias del Río de la Plata*. Translated by Justo Maeso. Buenos Aires, 1958.

Partes oficiales y documentos relativos a la Guerra de la Independencia Argentina. 2 vols. Buenos Aires, 1900.

Pereda Valdés, Ildefonso. *El negro en el Uruguay pasado y presente.* Montevideo, 1965.

Pereda Valdés, Ildefonso. *Negros esclavos y negros libres.* Montevideo, 1941.

Pérez Colman, César B. *Paraná, 1810–1860.* Rosario, 1946.

Petit Muñoz, Eugenio, et al. *La condición jurídica, social, económica, y política de los negros durante el coloniaje en la Banda Oriental.* 2 vols. Montevideo, 1947.

Pla, Josefina. *Hermano negro: La esclavitud en el Paraguay.* Madrid, 1972.

Pomer, León. *El soldado criollo.* Buenos Aires, 1971.

Puccia, Enrique. *Breve historia del Carnaval porteño.* Buenos Aires, 1974.

Quinteros, Mamerto Fidel. *Memorias de un negro del Congreso.* Buenos Aires, 1924.

Rabinowitz, Howard N. *Race Relations in the Urban South, 1865–1890.* New York, 1978.

Ramos, Artur. *Las culturas negras en el Nuevo Mundo.* Mexico City, 1943.

Ramos Mejía, José María. *Rosas y su tiempo.* 3 vols. Buenos Aires, 1907.

Ratier, Hugo. *El cabecita negra.* Buenos Aires, 1971.

Ratzer, José. *Los marxistas argentinos del 90.* Córdoba, 1970.

Registro Estadístico de la Provincia de Buenos Aires. 34 vols. Buenos Aires, 1822–25, 1854–82.

Rennie, Ysabel Fisk. *The Argentine Republic.* New York, 1945.

Reseña histórica y orgánica del Ejército Argentino. 3 vols. Buenos Aires, 1972.

Rodríguez Molas, Ricardo. *Historia social del gaucho.* Buenos Aires, 1968.

Rodríguez Molas, Ricardo. *La música y danza de los negros en el Buenos Aires de los siglos XVIII y XIX.* Buenos Aires, 1957.

Rodríguez Molas, Ricardo. "El negro en el Río de la Plata." *Polémica* 2 (May 1970): 38–56.

Rodríguez Molas, Ricardo. "O negro na história argentina (1852–1900)." *Alfa* 4 (Sept. 1963): 189–204.

Rodríguez Molas, Ricardo. "Negros libres rioplatenses." *Buenos Aires: Revista de Humanidades* 1 (Sept. 1961): 99–126.

Rogers, J. A. *Great Men of Color.* 2 vols. New York, 1972.

Román, Marcelino M. *Itinerario del payador.* Buenos Aires, 1957.

Romay, Francisco L. *El barrio de Monserrat.* Buenos Aires, 1971.

Rosenblat, Angel. *La población indígena y el mestizaje en América.* 2 vols. Buenos Aires, 1954.

Rossi, Vicente. *Cosas de negros.* Cordoba, 1926. Reprint Buenos Aires, 1958.

Rout, Leslie B. *The African Experience in Spanish America.* Cambridge, 1976.

Russell-Wood, A. J. R. "Black and Mulatto Brotherhoods in Colonial Brazil." *Hispanic American Historical Review* 54 (Nov. 1974): 567–602.

Saldías, Adolfo. *Los numeros de linea del Ejército Argentino.* 2 vols. Buenos Aires, 1912.

Sánchez Albornoz, Nicolás. *La población de América Latina desde los tiempos pre-colombianos al año 2000.* Madrid, 1973.

Sánchez Albornoz, Nicolás, and Torrado, Susana. "Perfil y proyecciones de la demografía histórica en la Argentina." In *Anuario del Instituto de Investigaciones Históricas*. Rosario, 1965. 8: 31-56.

Sanguinetti, Manuel Juan. *San Telmo: Su pasado histórico*. Buenos Aires, 1965.

Sarmiento, Domingo. *Ambas Américas*. Buenos Aires, 1899.

Sarmiento, Domingo. *Conflict y armonía de las razas en Américas*. 2 vols. Buenos Aires, 1900. Reprint Buenos Aires, 1953.

Sarmiento, Domingo. *Life in the Argentine Republic in the Days of the Tyrants*. Translated by Mary T. Mann. 1868. Reprint New York, 1961. Original Spanish publication 1845.

Scarano, Julita. *Devoção e escravidão*. São Paulo, 1976.

Scenna, Miguel Angel. *Cuando murió Buenos Aires, 1871*. Buenos Aires, 1974.

Schuler, Monica. "Ethnic Slave Rebellions in the Caribbean and the Guianas." *Journal of Social History* 3 (Summer 1970): 374-85.

Schwartz, Stuart. "The Manumission of Slaves in Colonial Brazil: Bahia, 1684-1745." *Hispanic American Historical Review* 54 (Nov. 1974): 603-34.

Scobie, James. *Argentina: A City and a Nation*. New York, 1971.

Scobie, James. *Buenos Aires: Plaza to Suburb, 1870-1910*. New York, 1974.

Segundo censo de la República Argentina: Mayo 10 de 1895. 3 vols. Buenos Aires, 1898.

Sempat Assadourian, Carlos. *El tráfico de esclavos en Córdoba, de Angola a Potosí: Siglos XVI–XVII*. Córdoba, 1961.

Shryock, Henry S., Siegel, Jacob S., et al. *The Methods and Materials of Demography*. 2 vols. Washington, D.C., 1973.

Simpson, Máximo. "Porteños de color." *Panorama*, June 1967, 78-85.

Skidmore, Thomas. *Black into White*. New York, 1974.

Socolow, Susan Migden. "Economic Activities of the Porteño Merchants: The Viceregal Period." *Hispanic American Historical Review* 55 (Feb. 1975): 1-24.

Soiza Reilly, Juan José. "Gente de color." *Caras y Caretas*, Nov. 25, 1905.

Soler Cañas, Luis. "Gabino Ezeiza, verdad y leyenda." *Todo Es Historia* 1 (1967): 65-77.

Soler Cañas, Luis. *Negros, gauchos y compadres en el cancionero de la Federación, 1830–1848*. Buenos Aires, 1958.

Soler Cañas, Luis. "Pardos y morenos en el año 80 . . . ." *Revista del Instituto de Investigaciones Históricas Juan Manuel de Rosas* 23 (1963): 272-309.

Studer, Elena F. Scheuss de. *La trata de negros en el Río de la Plata durante el siglo XVIII*. Buenos Aires, 1958.

Szuchman, Mark D., and Sofer, Eugene F. "The State of Occupational Stratification Studies in Argentina: A Classificatory Scheme." *Latin American Research Review* 11 (1976): 159-71.

Taullard, Alfredo. *Nuestro antiguo Buenos Aires*. Buenos Aires, 1927.

Tauro, Azucena Perla M. Della Casa de. "Censo de la ciudad de Córdoba del año 1832." Thesis, Universidad Nacional de Córdoba, 1972.

Thernstrom, Stephan. *The Other Bostonians*. Cambridge, Mass., 1973.

Thompson, Era Bell. "Argentina: Land of the Vanishing Blacks." *Ebony*, Oct. 1973, 74–85.

Tiffenberg, David. *Luchas sociales en Argentina*. Buenos Aires, 1970.

Tomas de razón de despachos militares, cédulas de premio, retiros, empleos civiles y eclesiásticos, donativos, etc., 1740–1821. Buenos Aires, 1925.

Toplin, Robert Brent, ed. *Slavery and Race Relations in Latin America*. Westport, Conn., 1974.

Torre Revello, José. *La sociedad colonial*. Buenos Aires, 1970.

Torres, Felix A. "El comercio de esclavos en Córdoba, 1700–1731." Thesis, Universidad Nacional de Córdoba, 1972.

Torres, Haydeé Gorostegui de. *La organización nacional*. Buenos Aires, 1972.

Tourón, Lucía Sala de, et al. *Estructura económico-social de la colonia*. Montevideo, 1967.

Trelles, Rafael. *Indice del Archivo del Departamento General de Policía, desde el año 1812*. 2 vols. Buenos Aires, 1859 and 1860.

Trías, Vivian. *Juan Manuel de Rosas*. Buenos Aires, 1969.

Tristany, Ramón, *Regimiento 8 de Infantería de Linea*. Buenos Aires, 1897.

Uniformes de la patria. Buenos Aires, 1972.

Vial, Ramón F. *Manuelita Rosas*. Buenos Aires, 1969.

Vidal, Emeric E. *Picturesque Illustrations of Buenos Ayres and Montevideo*. London, 1820.

Wade, Richard. *Slavery in the Cities*. London, 1964.

Wilde, Jose Antonio. *Buenos Aires desde setenta años atrás*. Buenos Aires, 1903.

Yaben, Jacinto R. *Biografías argentinas y sudamericanas*. 5 vols. Buenos Aires, 1938–40.

Yunque, Alvaro. *Calfucura,la conquista de las pampas*. Buenos Aires, 1956.

Zuluaga, Rosa María. "La trata de negros en la región cuyana durante el siglo XVIII." *Revista de la Junta de Estudios Históricos de Mendoza*, Ser. 2, 1 (1970): 39–66.

Index

DESIGNED BY ED FRANK
COMPOSED BY FOX VALLEY TYPESETTING, MENASHA, WISCONSIN
MANUFACTURED BY THOMSON-SHORE, INC., DEXTER, MICHIGAN
TEXT IS SET IN CALEDONIA
DISPLAY LINES IN CENTURY SCHOOLBOOK

Library of Congress Cataloging in Publication Data
Andrews, George Reid, 1951–
The Afro-Argentines of Buenos Aires, 1800–1900.
Bibliography: p.
Includes index.
1. Blacks—Argentine Republic—Buenos Aires—
History.   2. Buenos Aires—Race relations.
I. Title.
F3001.9.B55A52   982'.11   80-5105
ISBN 0-299-08290-3